HOW TO BUILD
AFFORDABLE HOT RODS

Best Options for Your Budget

Tony Thacker

CarTech®

CarTech®, Inc.
838 Lake Street South
Forest Lake, MN 55025
Phone: 651-277-1200 or 800-551-4754
Fax: 651-277-1203
www.cartechbooks.com

© 2020 by Tony Thacker

All rights reserved. No part of this publication may be reproduced or utilized in any form or by any means, electronic or mechanical, including photocopying, recording, or by any information storage and retrieval system, without prior permission from the Publisher. All text, photographs, and artwork are the property of the Author unless otherwise noted or credited.

The information in this work is true and complete to the best of our knowledge. However, all information is presented without any guarantee on the part of the Author or Publisher, who also disclaim any liability incurred in connection with the use of the information and any implied warranties of merchantability or fitness for a particular purpose. Readers are responsible for taking suitable and appropriate safety measures when performing any of the operations or activities described in this work.

All trademarks, trade names, model names and numbers, and other product designations referred to herein are the property of their respective owners and are used solely for identification purposes. This work is a publication of CarTech, Inc., and has not been licensed, approved, sponsored, or endorsed by any other person or entity. The Publisher is not associated with any product, service, or vendor mentioned in this book, and does not endorse the products or services of any vendor mentioned in this book.

Edit by Bob Wilson
Layout by Connie DeFlorin

ISBN 978-1-61325-528-5
Item No. SA477

Library of Congress Cataloging-in-Publication Data Available

Written, edited, and designed in the U.S.A.
Printed in China
10 9 8 7 6 5 4 3 2 1

CarTech books may be purchased at a discounted rate in bulk for resale, events, corporate gifts, or educational purposes. Special editions may also be created to specification.
For details, contact Special Sales at 838 Lake Street S., Forest Lake MN 55025 or by email at sales@cartechbooks.com.

Front cover image:
Thanks to the Kennedy brothers, Jay and Joe, not only for helping enormously with the creation of this book but also for providing the perfect backdrop for the cover. (Photo Courtesy Alex Maldonado/Alex M. Design)

Title page image:
This father-and-son project built by Al and Colby Martin is a great example of what the home builder can do in a small, 1-1/2-car garage with a limited budget but a lot of ingenuity. (Photo Courtesy Colby Martin)

DISTRIBUTION BY:

Europe
PGUK
63 Hatton Garden
London EC1N 8LE, England
Phone: 020 7061 1980 • Fax: 020 7242 3725
www.pguk.co.uk

Australia
Renniks Publications Ltd.
3/37-39 Green Street
Banksmeadow, NSW 2109, Australia
Phone: 2 9695 7055 • Fax: 2 9695 7355
www.renniks.com

Canada
Login Canada
300 Saulteaux Crescent
Winnipeg, MB, R3J 3T2 Canada
Phone: 800 665 1148 • Fax: 800 665 0103
www.lb.ca

CONTENTS

Dedication 4
Acknowledgments 6
Foreword by Billy F Gibbons 7

Chapter 1: Background 9

Chapter 2: Where to Start 17
   Purchasing a Car 17
   Caveat Emptor (Buyer Beware) . 20
   Buy a Kit 22
   Time and Materials 23
   Change Orders 23
   Read Your Bill 23
   A Basket Case 23
   Start from Scratch:
      A Bare Frame 24
   Registration and Titling 25
   Bill of Sale 25
   Certificate of Origin 25
   Title 25
   Non-Op Registration 26

Chapter 3: Tools and Equipment . 30

Chapter 4: Make It Your Own 37

Chapter 5: Frame, Chassis, Steering, and Suspension 41
   Purchasing a Frame and/or
      Chassis 44
   Building a Frame 45
   Front End 47
   Mike Williams's Model A
      Frame 59
   Dick Wade's 1932 Frame 67
   James Jard's 1936 3-Window 73
   Chassis, Steering,
      and Suspension 81
   Rear-End Redo 85
   Steering 88
   Brakes 90

Chapter 6: Powertrain Choice ... 94
   Mock-Up Block and
      Transmission 94
   Ford Model A and B and the
      Russian B 95
   Ford Flathead V-8 and the French
      Block 96
   Ardun 97
   Ford Y-Block 98
   Ford 289 98
   Buick Nailhead 99
   Lightweight Buick/Oldsmobile/
      Rover 99
   Cadillac 331 Series 100
   Chevy Big-Block W-Head 100
   Chevy Small-Block 101
   Chrysler/Dodge Hemi 101
   Lincoln Flathead V-8 102
   Lincoln Flathead V-12 102
   Oldsmobile 103
   Transmission Background 104
   Adapters 105
   Adapter Plate 106
   Bellhousing, Clutch Can,
      or Scattershield 107
   Clutch Pressure Plate and Disc. 108
   Flexplate 108
   Flywheel 108
   SFI 108
   Transmission Options 109
   Rear Axles 113
   Additional Information 116

Chapter 7: Wheels and Tires 117
   Backspacing 118
   Balancing 119
   Bias-Ply versus Radial Tires ... 119
   Bolt Pattern or Circle 119
   Chrome Reverse Rims 120
   Dow 7 120
   Ford Welded Wires 121
   Ford Wide Five 121
   Kelsey-Hayes Wheel Co. and
      Motor Wheel Corporation. 121
   Milk Truck Wheels 122
   Moon Discs 122
   Mock-Ups 123
   Offset 123
   Rollers (Mock-Up Wheels) 123
   Rim Diameter and Width 124
   Scrub Radius 124
   Spindle Mounts 124
   Stagger and Stance 125
   Tire Shaving 125

Chapter 8: Body 126
   New versus Restored 128
   Top Chopping 129
   Chopping Dick Wade's 1932
      3-Window 132
   Assembling a 1934 Roadster .. 136

Chapter 9: Electrical and Wiring .. 139
   Ballast Resistor 139
   Batteries 139
   Charging System 139
   Coil 140
   Fuses 140
   Alternator versus Generator .. 140
   Distributors 141
   Distributor Cap 141
   Fuel Tank Sender 141
   Ground 141
   Horn 142
   Instruments 142
   Kill Switch 142
   Lights 142
   Points 143
   Magneto 143
   Plug Wires 143
   Starters 143
   Switches 144
   Wiring 144
   Rewiring a 1936 Ford 145

Chapter 10: Details 149

Chapter 11: Interior 157
   Seats 159
   Seat Belts 163
   Steering Wheels 163
   Instruments 165
   Pedals 166

Chapter 12: Paint 168
   Aluminum 170
   Bare Metal 170
   Primer 171
   Red Oxide 171
   The Painting Process 172

Source Guide 175

DEDICATION

This book is dedicated to all the hot rodders who over the years have inspired and helped me make a career out of this crazy business, hobby, industry, or whatever it is. Of all those men and women, two men stand out as having the most profound influence: Pete Chapouris and his oft-time partner Jim "Jake" Jacobs (a.k.a. Pete and Jake).

I first encountered the infamous dynamic duo on California's Highway 99. It was 1978, and they were blasting south in their iconic coupes from Turlock down to Merced for the NSRA Street Rod Nats West. As usual, Pete was in front, and Jake was bringing up the rear. I was hanging out the tailgate of a rented wagon and trying to photograph them at 70 mph. I got one, maybe two frames before they rocketed past. It was one of those memorable moments that is lodged on the retina.

In 1984, I was at home one Saturday with my friend Ian Gibson when Jeff Beck pulled up in his 1934 coupe and said, "We're going to Gatwick Airport to meet Pete Chapouris and the *California Kid*. Wanna come?" We jumped in Ian's Deuce roadster and tagged along.

In those times (pre-security checks), the car was unloaded from a pallet. Pete jumped in with Alan Martin, and they headed north for Birmingham and the International Custom Show. They drove straight through London and up the M1 accompanied by busloads of soccer fans throwing beer bottles at the *Kid*.

Unfortunately, the hall where the show was to be held had suffered a fire, and the attendance suffered.

When Pete went to fly home, it got worse. There were no tickets for him, his wife, Carol, Jake, or the *Kid*. That was a costly exercise, but Pete was always philosophical about it. The following year, Jake accompanied the amazingly popular *Eliminator* coupe of Billy F Gibbons on tour with ZZ Top. Jake lived at my house while he built a frame on which *Eliminator* sat as it was carried by a helicopter that flew over the crowd at the Donnington Monsters of Rock concert—crazy shenanigans before safety requirements.

By this time, Pete, Jake, and I were transatlantic friends, and they eventually persuaded me to move to the US. I lived at Jake's house and worked alongside Pete at the Specialty Equipment Market Association (they had sold Pete and Jake's to Jerry Slover). Between the two of them, they

My hero, mentor, and two-time boss, Pete Chapouris was a huge influence on myself and the entire hot rod industry. He knew how to build it right.

DEDICATION

introduced me to anyone and everyone in the hot rod scene from Boyd Coddington to Alex Xydias. During the day, Pete taught me about marketing the industry he was so passionate about; during the evenings and weekends, I sat and watched in awe as Jake whittled hot rods from lumps of scrap metal.

To this day, I'm not sure which part of the education was most beneficial, and no doubt both parts have equal importance. In 1995, Pete gathered his old buddies (Jake included) and opened PC3g, which morphed into the SO-CAL Speed Shop, which was licensed from his old friend Alex Xydias. As we launched the resurrected SO-CAL in November 1997, I came on board full-time and worked alongside Pete for the next nine years.

That decade was the most fantastic learning experience—from watching and photographing the guys in the shop to brainstorming with Pete as we planned the expansion of SO-CAL. It wasn't always easy. Money was always tighter than it looked from the outside, but Pete was resilient and worked his way into an early grave to keep the plates spinning.

From his teenage beginnings with Ed "Big Daddy" Roth working on Roth's creations and schlepping shirts, Jim "Jake" Jacobs, a.k.a. "Jitney" Jake, continues to influence generations of rod builders with his practical builds.

Pete died too young. He still had so much to give particularly with his involvement in the Alex Xydias & Pete Chapouris Center for Automotive Arts (AXC) at the Pomona Fairplex, where they recently established the Pete Chapouris Welding and Fabrication Wing with an endowment from the Petersen Foundation. There couldn't be a more fitting tribute to Pete than a welding lab. Pete always regarded himself as a welder. In fact, his emails always said "from the welding bench of Pete Chapouris." But he was so much more than a welder, and it's for that reason that I dedicate this book to memory of Pete, and to Jake, who continue to teach us the right stuff.

No image screams hot rod more than Pete and Jake blasting down Highway 99 in 1978.

Acknowledgments

Unfortunately, books don't write themselves. You can't just turn the computer on, go to sleep, and wake up with a completed book. I wish. They take an unrealistic amount of time to compile and are a collaborative exercise that requires the input and effort of many people.

In the dedication, I've thanked Pete Chapouris and Jake Jacobs for their friendship, inspiration, and support. Besides Pete and Jake, there were many others who helped pull this tome together. My good friend Mick Jenkins of MicksPaint.com has provided a home for my efforts on more than one occasion. We have great fun working together, and he has helped beyond the call of friendship. Mick's team and contractors at Mick's Paint (including Pauly Rivera, "Kiwi" Steve Davies, and Mickey Larson) have never failed to answer my endless questions or do it again while I take another photograph.

Just down the street and around the corner from Mick's is the Kennedy Boyz Bomb Factory, where Jay and Joe build the coolest, most uncompromising, traditional hot rods. To me, the Kennedys always epitomized what SO-CAL should but never could have been: a couple of guys building cool stuff in their backyard with none of the glitz. They don't bend to fashion. Heck, they barely answer the phone. They just build the kinds of cars they like, and you can get on board with that or not. They provided invaluable help when I put this book together

A huge thanks to the Kennedy brothers (Jay in the car and Joe kneeling) for all their help with this book. I couldn't have done it without them.

and built not one but several cars all at that same time and allowed me to bother them as they tried to work uninterrupted.

Thanks to Jim Busby, Ron Ceridono, Dan Clare, Chuck de Heras, Bob Florine (ARP Racing Products), Neil Fretwell (Vintage Hot Rod Association), Billy F Gibbons, Bobby Green (Old Crow Speed Shop), Max Herman (H & H Antique), Mike Herman (H and H Flatheads), Keith Harman, Troy Ladd (Hollywood Hot Rods), James and Jim Jard, Mick Jenkins (Mick's Paint), Rayce and Rick Lefever, Gary Lorenzini, Alex Maldonado (for the artwork and images), Al and Colby Martin, Dave Rocha, Specialty Equipment Market Association (SEMA), Rick Pearmain and Clive Prew (Stromberg), Steve Sbelgio (Eclipse Engineering), Jimmy Shine (Shine Speed Shop), Jason Slover (Pete & Jake's), Jonathan Suckling, Adrian Smith (Buckland Automotive), David Thacker, Greg, Ian, John, and Ray (SO-CAL Speed Shop), David Steele (American Hot Rod Foundation), Steve Strope (Pure Vision Design), Tim Sutton, Aaron Von Minden, Robert Noriega and Bobby Waldon (Walden Speed Shop), Dick Wade, Mike Williams, Suzanne Williams, and my family members (Kailay and Mia) for help with the images and manuscript.

FOREWORD by Billy F Gibbons

As a kid of the 1950s in Texas, there seemed to be only two things that were the chosen elements for escape: cars and guitars. I vividly recall standing on the front seat in a 1953 Poncho and shouting the make and model of every passing car while loud sounds were blaring from the radio. Girls immediately stepped into the mix, which became constantly entwined like a roll of unwrapped guitar strings. That was moment by moment. Playin' that guitar and rollin' the streets loud, down, and dirty; it was all there from the beginning.

It comes from a magnified inspiration; some piercing outlandish effect that sets the dice tumbling. I can hear the rumblings from a set of glasspack mufflers and an infectious racket from a Spanish electric guitar.

Let's take it back to two bros hanging out at the proverbial end of the street with a shared fervent passion toward hot rods and those irritating 'lectric guitars. These kind of cats stand as the quintessential "I wanna do that" reason for it all. Give me a wicked, lowered, black '57 Chevy and a smash-down 1927 highboy T with a pair of pinstriped 6-stringers to match. Well, that's whatcha call *impact!*

Don't be alarmed. We know. You've got to get that unsupervised driver's license—yes! There are roads to cross and sounds to make. We started peeling the onion at just 13. License in one hand, ignition keys and that git-tar in the other.

What to say to get the party

Guitar icon Billy F Gibbons poses with his "Whiskey Runner" 1934 3-window coupe somewhere out there in Area 51.

started? Well, how 'bout a slant-6 Dodge? Ugh. Yet, with a $1,500 takeaway, off it went where Jeeps fear to tread. On every corner, we'd try to kill it. Forget about it. It survived even the lead foot of all-out teenage rebellion. Despite the desire of dismissal, the damn thing could be crammed full of band gear. Well, "okay" . . . for then. Believe it or not, the insane sound of that Mopar starter can still be heard on ZZ Top's *Deguello* album on the track "Maniac Mechanic."

What's next? The customary, all-night, avenue cruisin'. This one started at San Felipe Road's naughty neighborhood (Sin Alley) at the railroad tracks fronting the infamous Deputy Drive-In. Every afternoon by 5 o'clock, the asphalt burger-and-fry lot was loaded with hot iron; cold-rolled steel; chopped, channeled, repowered, and repainted gems of all sorts rumblin' into the shade. Not to be outdone, all the big shots were constantly holding court with a grinning challenge to the next unlucky fallen angel. All them cats: Jackie Forester in his bad 'n' black, push-button Fury; Mike Nycombe's Grand Prix jimmy-blown Pontiac, alongside Chuck Seward's fluorescent orange 1934.

We're talkin' in 1963. In just about every county, town, and big city back lot, mostly on the downlow from coast to coast and border to border, a solid imprint in what ya wanna retrace here. It was all in a night's spot race. Pink slips were exchanging, egos bursting, and money was handed over just before the cops arrived. It was exciting to say the least!

Fast forward. We're not taking any detours. After a few early band

FOREWORD

excursions like The Saints and Billy G and The Blue Flames in the late 1960s, we found ourselves in the throes with The Moving Sidewalks, unloading band gear on Hollywood's Sunset Strip, when an unexpected invitation came to join The Jimi Hendrix Experience tour. Acid psychedelia. Word. All the while we maintained a solid fascination with *Hot Rod*, *Rod & Custom*, *Car Craft* . . . Well, just name 'em.

Fast forward. In 1974, it was a turning point at the Nats South in Winston-Salem. I had a chance encounter with Pete Chapouris and Jake Jacobs, who were heading up one of the premiere hot rod shops in Southern California. After a quick mean-machine powwow and with a collective imagination, what became the *Eliminator Coupe* was created. From 1976 to the unveiling of this colorful machine in 1983, the partnership work ignited the sanctified secret ranks of custom car and hot rod enthusiasts with an ever-widening spread of inspiration.

Pete & Jake's led the charge with the names, which included Don Thelen of Buffalo Motor Cars in Paramount, Kenny Youngblood with his super graphic techniques, Ron Jones and his exceptional metalworking prowess, Tom Honeycutt's artistic expressions, Bobby Walden, the Kennedy brothers, Tony Thacker, Eric Geisert, the Steves . . . Coonan and Sanford, Larry Erickson, and a league of tin benders, torch magnates, lead slingers, and paint splatterers were all rounded up for this newfound admiration of some wicked steel on four wheels. Come on! Let's bring in the silent sounders: Harry Hibler and Grey Baskerville.

Now, with this new ride featured on ZZ Top's *Eliminator* album cover, all bets were both on and off; not knowing the remarkable mark that this little red coupe would have scanning MTV screens across the globe. Wow!

So, onward we go. It's been quite a ride. That's a really good start. As luck would have it, the *Eliminator Coupe* hit the touring trail when we attempted to grind onward. Yet to come were a few choice pieces like the 1948 Pontiac Silver Streak (chopped and stretched by Dick Dean), *Kopperhed* (a chopped 1950 Ford custom), Larry Erickson's wonder car, *CadZZilla*, matched a pair of Harley-Davidson escort bikes known as *HogZZilla 1* and *HogZZilla 2* with the champion touch from Jimmy Shine at Jimmy Shine's Speed Shop in Orange County, who is making his way with a wave of fine rides hitting the streets across the boulevard around the planet!

Let's not forget . . . "Let that boy boogie-woogie."

CHAPTER 1

BACKGROUND

I discovered hot rods while on my paper route in England in the early 1960s. Somebody on my route had *Hot Rod* magazine. While I wasn't smart enough to ever find out who it was or why they subscribed, I was smart enough to sit on the curb under gray skies, surrounded by gray and brown cars, and read about red and yellow cars under blue California skies.

It was while on my paper route that I learned that the unlikely named duo of Dean Moon and Dante Deuce were bringing the *Mooneyes* dragster to England. "Dad, can we go? Can we?" As it turned out, the 1963 Brighton Speed Trials was an epiphany moment when my life was laid out in front of me like red carpet. I just didn't know it at the time. When that *Mooneyes* dragster with its bright yellow paint, front-mounted blower, and those *eyes* came to the line at Brighton, I was in heaven. The sight, the sound, and the smoke sucked me in like a drug—a habit that I have to this day, and I'm okay with it.

Eventually, I worked my way into a magazine job, and by 1985, I was the editor of the UK's *Custom Car* magazine. That same year, ZZ Top was booked to play the Monsters of Rock concert at Donington Park, England. To promote the show, Warner Brothers shipped Billy F Gibbons's *Eliminator* and hot rod builder Jim "Jake" Jacobs to England, where he built a steel platform so that the car could be flown by helicopter over the crowd. I remember spending many hours with Jake while he tried to calculate if the helicopter could even lift the car—let alone fly it—but fly it they did. There were no safety regulations back then.

The editor's chair also gave me the opportunity to build my own hot rod, and the trigger was Roy "the Deuce Factory" Fjastad's bright orange 1932

In 1985, Jim "Jake" Jacobs was sent to England to help engineer the flying of Billy F Gibbons's 1933 Eliminator Coupe *over the crowd at the Donington Monsters of Rock concert. There were no safety codes back then.*

HOW TO BUILD AFFORDABLE HOT RODS

CHAPTER 1

Roy Fjastad of The Deuce Factory was the first to develop brand-new chassis rails for the 1932 Ford. His orange 1980s-style highboy roadster inspired me to build my own version. Roy's daughter Kathy is behind the wheel. (Photo Courtesy Kathy Olson)

While I contemplated building my own roadster, I was offered this original-steel, chopped Tudor sedan. It wasn't in this restored condition, but it was a running, driving hot rod. It was a big mistake not to buy it.

then, I have spoken to numerous hot rod builders, not the least of whom is Jake, who always has a picture of what he is going to build, usually from an old magazine. A picture is worth a thousand words.

At this time, I was also offered a genuine American 1932 Ford Tudor that was already rodded with a good chop, a great stance, nice paint, and a small-block Chevy mated to a 1939 transmission. It was about $9,000 at the time, and I stupidly turned it down thinking, "I want to build my own car, not buy somebody else's." Big mistake. I would have owned a real steel 1932 Tudor sedan that was instantly on the road and always worth money because it was Henry's tin and not some piece of fiberglass. Here's the moral of the story: go for the real deal when you can.

The real steel car also had a title, as did my pair of rails, and it's very important these days to have a title because it makes registration so much simpler. Yes, cars built from the ground up can be registered, and we'll get into that, but an original title is always best.

They say that a little knowledge is a dangerous thing, and I would say that I'm a man of little knowledge. Building what I called the *Orange Whip* was a trial of determination because while the UK has a great reputation in the roundy-round motorsports world (particularly F1), it was rank amateur when it came to building hot rods. Of course, my own inexperience didn't help, but I have to say that by the end of the process I knew what I'd done right and what I'd done wrong. I should have bought the Tudor.

To begin, I'd bitten off a little more than I could chew in choosing to build such a detailed, modern-style highboy. Like a kid in a candy store, its bright orange paint hooked me. I wanted a car just like that, and as is often the case, a couple planets collided to cause a bang.

First, a company called American Street Rod Parts (ASRP) began producing a reasonably priced, faithful replica 1932 roadster body in England. Also, about that time my ex-boss, Ian Penberthy, sold me a pair of original 1932 Ford rails and a few Deuce parts. It was a good start.

What I now understand is that the impetus to finish came from having that photograph of Fjastad's roadster. I knew where I was going, and Roy showed me the way. Since

BACKGROUND

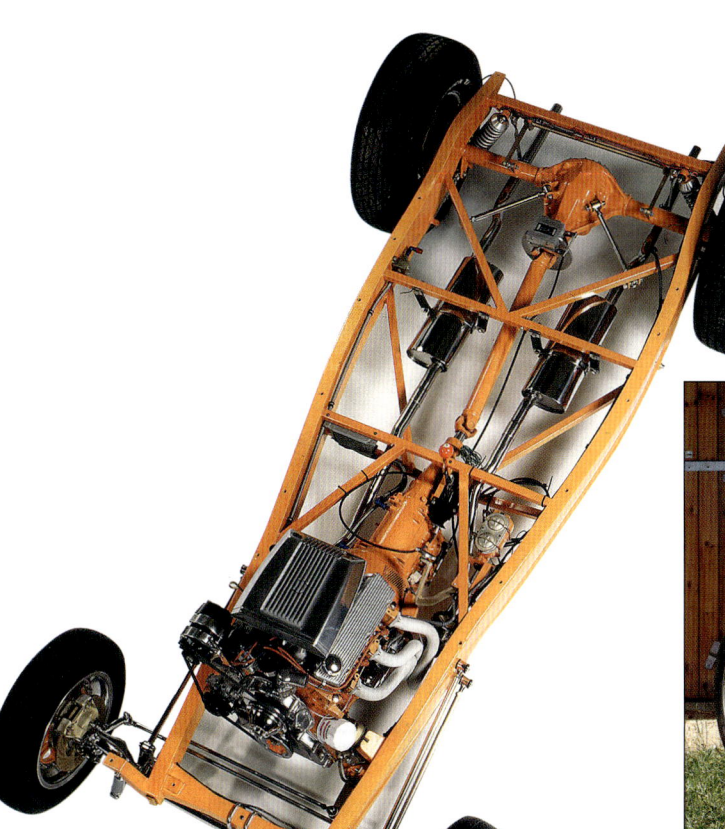

With original Deuce rails bobbed front and rear, the chassis for my Deuce roadster was well constructed by ASRP. Its Ford V-6 lacked two mandatory cylinders and should have been a Chevy V-8. It was, nevertheless, clean and tidy.

My friend Ian Gibson and I began building our Deuce roadsters around the same time and used ASRP fiberglass bodies. Ian kept it simple and finished a year ahead of me, and I think he built a better car. Eventually it went to Olle Larsson in Sweden.

rod. Had I chosen (as my friend Ian Gibson did) to build a more traditional rod, even taking into account the fiberglass body, then I could have been up and running faster, cheaper, and with many fewer headaches.

The chassis was really no big deal. ASRP did the basic fabrication of welding in square-tube crossmembers. Because of the weather in England, I chose to use a lot of stainless steel that would have been good had I known about anti-seize. Up front, there was a buggy-sprung stainless axle located on Pete & Jake's–style stainless four-bar links. The steering was a Chevy Vega, and even though I was in the UK, the car had left-hand drive. I figured that someday I'd get it to the US. Out back, I used a Mark II Jaguar live axle because they were cheap, plentiful, the correct width, and had a Chevy bolt pattern. However, the disc brakes meant that a parking brake, which is compulsory in the UK, necessitated a brake on the driveshaft that never did work worth a damn and certainly not enough to pass the test.

For power, I chose a readily available Ford Essex V-6. We were still smarting from the fuel crisis, so an economical V-6 seemed like a good idea. Besides, Fjastad's roadster had been powered by a blown Buick V-6. If a V-6 was good enough for Roy, it was good enough for me.

The ASRP fiberglass body was excellent and complete with a molded-in floor and firewall. However, I did not anticipate all the fabrication necessary to impart strength and rigidity and all the horrible fiberglass work I would have to do to make it right. Instead of living with Henry Ford's lumps and bumps and factory misalignment (as did Ian Gibson), I went down the long and tedious road to not only make sure that it all fit and had new-car door gaps but also customizing it to suit the prevailing fashion. Duh!

Thankfully, my good friend Keith Baker of Prestige Coachworks stepped up to help me with the extensive body and paint. The UK had a fender law, so I got fenders, but rather than be content with them, I punched fake louvers in the back and finished the beading around the edges.

HOW TO BUILD AFFORDABLE HOT RODS

CHAPTER 1

My Orange Whip was a typical car of the 1980s and a little confused, with its hot rod louvers and five-spoke Ferrari-style Compomotive wheels. Friend Phill Ritchie spent hours helping me make the 3-window top fit the roadster body. I'm not sure it was worth it.

I recessed Pontiac taillights into the lower rear cowl similar to Fjastad's instead of just using traditional 1939 Ford taillights. The work in making those Poncho lights fit and making brackets and bulb holders went on and on.

I purchased a three-piece Rootlieb aluminum hood. It was nicely made, but making it fit like a Boyd Coddington hood took forever because I'd shaved the cowl bead and the bead on the radiator shell for that smooth look. My biggest mistake came with the windshield and top. Instead of using Henry's tried-and-true bolt-on windshield (as Gibson did), I made a three-piece, spilt windshield with the help of Chris Glover at Brasscraft. To compound the fracture, I also made a fiberglass lift-off top because it rains a lot in the UK. After a great deal of help from Phill Ritchie, the top (when finished) took three people to lift. It seemed that I only ever put it on when it was sunny; if I left home without it, it rained. I ended up making a simple collapsible, fold-up top that could be easily stowed in the trunk.

All of this is to say that I overthought it and spent far too much. It was a hot rod; by definition, it should have been simple. Instead, I made it way too complicated for an amateur. So, here's my advice: keep it simple, especially if you are new to this.

Despite all my mistakes and unnecessary work, I had a lot of fun in that car. It wasn't super reliable, but I drove it all over England and took it to France for the 24 Hours of Le Mans where the French wondered, "Wot is it?"

Done with the UK's weather, I moved to Los Angeles, where I rented a room from my friend Jake. It was a revelation, and I learned so much about building hot rods. I'd stand for hours and watch him grind and file, shape and form scrap metal into hot rod art. Meanwhile, I shipped the *Whip* to the US, where it became a frat bike with everybody using and

Topless on my way to Le Mans for the 24-hour race, the roadster was great fun. However, it was just too complicated to be reliable, and therefore it was not as much fun as it should have been.

BACKGROUND

Bandanaed and beanied against the sun, Pete Chapouris and SO-CAL founder Alex Xydias hammer the then-new SO-CAL roadster across Colorado en route to the first-ever Rod & Custom *Americruise. As you would expect, the roadster was flawless.*

A very early version of the Thacker and Shine (T&S) roadster is shown making a run at El Mirage. Buying a running, driving rod that you can put your own stamp on is, in my opinion, a good way to go. Shine drove, but I usually got to drive it home down old Route 66.

abusing it. Unfortunately, it proved to be too unreliable on the freeway; ultimately, it left home without me and I never missed it.

After a good career at SEMA, I received another call from my friend and mentor Pete Chapouris. Pete was struggling with his new business PC3g and needed some public relations and marketing help to resurrect Alex Xydias's So-Cal Speed Shop. I was all over it. These were my kind of guys building my kind of hot rods, and I really felt that we could do something special because people seemed tired of the smooth look—read expensive—and desired something more traditional that Pete tagged "New Traditionalist."

In November 1997, we launched the new, uppercase SO-CAL Speed Shop, to differentiate it from the old, lowercase So-Cal Speed Shop that had closed in 1963, and it worked. It was the right stuff at the right time. There's no doubt that Pete and his team (comprised of his old partner Jim "Jake" Jacobs, Pete "P-Wood" Eastwood, and others) knew how to build traditional hot rods that you could jump in, drive clear across the country, and get out like you'd just gone to the grocery store.

Everything was simple and straightforward. Basic tech with no fancy parts machined on a lathe that you couldn't buy in a NAPA store in Iowa. Everything was just where it needed to be. Jake developed the step-boxed frame that pushed the boxing plates inside the frame rails to give the strength of an un-ground weld as well as increased space for fuel and brake lines. It was a revolution. Pete, meanwhile, pushed the adjustable Glide seat under the rear cowl to provide extra leg room and increased comfort. Outside the company, Paul Carroll of Fake Brakes engineered a way to slide a disc brake assembly inside a fake Buick drum. It completed the package: a traditional-looking hot rod (warts 'n' all) with the drivability and convenience of a modern-ish car.

The early history of SO-CAL was

HOW TO BUILD AFFORDABLE HOT RODS

Driving the T&S roadster to Bonneville was all part of the fun, but the work needed to get it race ready, such as installing the blower, once we arrived got in the way of the goal. We eventually gave it up. It was fun though.

steeped in land speed racing. Alex cannily saw that a win on Sunday could mean a sale on Monday. He therefore raced consistently at the lakes, Bonneville, and the drags to promote his speed shop. It worked then, so why not now? Somehow, I heard that a friend, "Kiwi" Steve Davies, was selling his lakes roadster: a fiberglass A-Body atop an original Deuce frame. Steve's modus operandi was to drive the car from Los Angeles, race it at speeds around 165 mph at Muroc or El Mirage, and drive home. Meanwhile, he'd let family and friends enjoy the driving experience.

The car had good bones, appeared to fit my needs, and the price was right. It was $16,000 if I remember correctly. I talked to Chapouris about it, and he was enthusiastic, so I approached my coworker Jimmy Shine to see if he would partner with me on the car—me as the wallet and him as the wrench and driver. Shine was down for it, so I forked over my hard-earned money.

At this point, I should say that buying a running, driving car like this is a very good option, especially if you're an inexperienced builder and just want to get a rod on the road.

McLaren F1 designer Peter Stevens, an avid hot rodder, helped pre-shape cardboard at Colin Jones's Dove Company and enabled us to maximize our time in the MIRA wind tunnel. Theoretically, we gained almost 50 hp. We hoped that would be enough to get a record.

BACKGROUND

Peter Stevens, Custom Car editor Kev Elliott, and I took turns wheeling the heavyweight Thacker and Shine roadster up the Duke of Richmond's Goodwood driveway. It might not have been fast, but it was loud and fun.

The major work is done, and all you have to do is make it your own. And, because of our aging population, there are many bargains to be found.

Shine and I went to El Mirage in November for the final meet of 2001. We loved the car and took possession of it a few weeks later. To begin with, I drove the car on the street to and from work just to get the feel for it, see how I liked it, and see if there was anything we needed to do. As it happened, it didn't need much and I loved it. It was an easy, simple, affordable hot rod.

Our first foray to Bonneville was in 2002, and I think we ran about 170 mph. It was obvious that the car had potential. In 2003, we became involved with David Freiburger, then editor of *Hot Rod* magazine. David hooked us up with Bill Mitchell at World Products, who supplied a carbureted 427-ci small-block. We drove the car to Bonneville, and I went 177.965 mph, which is not bad with a Turbo 350 transmission. Soon after, Shine bumped the terminal speed to 181.386 mph, and with it came the realization that maybe this could be a 200-mph car... you can always hope. The record in our B/Street Roadster class was only 203 mph.

It's a far cry from my original $16,000 purchase and was no longer streetable, but what fun we had with this car and what a learning experience. Soon after its record run, the car was sold to Steve Van Blarcom, who continued to push it to 225 mph.

HOW TO BUILD AFFORDABLE HOT RODS

CHAPTER 1

After a few years of struggle, thanks to a blown small-block from World Products, we managed 201 mph. I remember calling my wife to tell her we ran over 200. "Did you get a record?" she asked. "No," I replied. "Then you ain't done yet are you?" she responded as she put the phone down.

She was right. We weren't done. Fortuitously, my hot-rodding friend Peter Stevens, designer of the McLaren F1, was there and declared, "That Pro Stock scoop is no good. You'd be better off turning it around—or better still, throwing it away." I suggested this to Shine, who was having none of it. He responded, "It looks cool."

"Yeah, but do you want to look cool or go fast?" I asked.

"Both," replied Shine.

"Well, I want to go fast and get that record."

For that season, Shine installed a lot of SO-CAL products that weren't originally on the car: the front axle, complete with SO-CAL New Traditionalist batwings, radius rods, shocks, headlights, etc. We even developed a bolt-in roll cage that was SCTA-legal. Using these products on our race car enabled SO-CAL to market this phrase: "Traditional hot rod parts tested at 200 mph." There were not many other shops that could legitimately use that tagline.

My problem was that I had a family, and money was tight. I couldn't really afford to buy horsepower, but what Peter Stevens showed me was that I could obtain performance for next to nothing if I just made the Model A more aerodynamic—within the rules, of course.

I still occasionally drove the car on the street, and it was great to pull into a gas station and have somebody ask, "How fast?" To which, I would reply with a straight face, "200 mph." Well, you know they thought you were a jerk because there was no way that POS would go 200. But, of course, I knew differently, and there was more to come.

At the time, there really wasn't a wind tunnel in the US that was open to the public, so I finagled a way to get my car to the UK, where Peter helped me improve the aero using the Motor Industry Research Association (MIRA) tunnel. We spent a few days at Colin Jones's Dove Company doing origami and folding bits of cardboard to prepare for the tunnel. Back then, tunnel time was about $15 a minute, which proves that there is no such thing as free speed.

I had enough sponsorship and cardboard for four hours of testing, and what we learned was fascinating. Certainly, removing the scoop improved the airflow, as did a convex (rather than concave) tonneau cover. Inner front wheel discs helped, as did increasing the height of the windshield and decreasing the size of the headlights. When our time was up, we had theoretically gained almost 50 free hp with a few bits of cardboard. That is to say that when we started, 551 hp was required to push the car through the air at 200 mph. With our modifications, only 504 hp should be required.

I was so elated that I took the roadster down to the Goodwood Festival of Speed where Peter, Kev Elliott (editor of *Custom Car* at the time), and I took turns running it up the Duke of Richmond's famous driveway. Weighing it at almost 5,000 pounds, the car was not fast, but it was fun.

Jimmy and I had unfinished business at Bonneville. We were ready (kind of), and we felt that 2006 was going to be our year. Thanks again to Bill Mitchell, we had a blown World Products 302-ci engine dyno tuned by our friend Jon Beck at 841 hp. On the first run, Shine holed a piston and my heart sank. Luckily, our friend Robin "Silky" Silk had grabbed the one spare as he left the shop. They popped it in, and Shine ran 208 mph. On the backup run, he went 204 for a new D/Blown Street Roadster record of 206.454 mph. Finally, after six years, Shine became a member of the 200 MPH Club, and we had that coveted $14 red hat.

We only had a tenuous hold on that record, and knowing I couldn't afford to make the car any faster, it was sold to our good friend Steve Van Blarcom, who eventually got it to 225 and change. It's now owned by Wayne Carini of TV's *Chasing Classic Cars*.

Those years were fantastic fun and full of emotion as we tried and tried for that record. But they were also great learning years where I discovered what it really took to build and race a hot rod and go for a record at 200 mph. I have to say, I'm hooked on Bonneville, and since 2015, I've worked with Ron Hope's Rat Trap Racing. Besides the awesome Rat Trap AA/Fuel Altered, Ron and son Brian race modified roadsters. Brian's daughter Victoria set a record at 216.522 in 2012, and Brian set a record in B/BGMR at 227.522. Ten minutes later, Ron set the BGMR at 257.729 mph. I'm also involved with Geoff Stilwell's 7707 land speed racer that set the A/BFRMR record at 258.679 mph in 2018.

All of this keeps me very active in the hot rod hobby, albeit in the land-speed-racing end of it, but I'm still a hot rodder at heart and I love it all.

CHAPTER 2

WHERE TO START

Chapter 1 provides several hints as to my somewhat-educated recommendations on where to start with a budget hot rod project build. I've tried it both ways: starting from scratch with some plans, a photograph, or even just a vague idea of what the finished result should look like; and buying a project that is complete and may be up and running that you can drive home. You might even consider something in between: a partially complete car that needs some but not a whole lot of work.

You must be honest with yourself and answer these questions honestly:
1. Can I see this project through?
2. Do I have the funds to finish it?
3. Do I have a place to work and the necessary tools?

If your answer is no for all three, you might want to reconsider your choice of hobby. That said, if we all did what was right (me included), a lot of things wouldn't get accomplished and a lot of rods wouldn't get built. I didn't have a place to build my roadster. Looking back, I don't think I had the money either. However, I didn't waver on the get 'er done question. What I'm saying is that even if you answer no to all three questions, that doesn't mean you can't get a car built. It just means that it may not be as easy as you thought.

Let's assume that the mere act of reading this book puts you below the expert level. You might have some skills, but you're not a proficient, experienced car builder. Maybe the answer for you is to just buy a car.

Purchasing a Car

If this is your first go-round, I strongly suggest that you buy a complete, running car. Purchasing a car that is up and driving achieves a lot. You can be on the road in an instant, driving and having fun.

My best experience of rod ownership was when I purchased what

In the late 1990s, "Kiwi" Steve Davies built this small-block Chevy-powered A V-8 that he drove to the lakes and raced at around 165 mph. I bought it in 2001 and did the same. It was my best purchase ever.

CHAPTER 2

It's funky without a doubt and not to everybody's taste, but I like David Edward's little roadster. It was found on eBay and built in a Washington shipyard with some ship-gauge steel, 1934 fenders and wheels, a Deuce truck grille, and plenty of ingenuity.

became the Thacker & Shine (T&S) roadster from friend "Kiwi" Steve Davies. Steve built the car to drive to the lakes, race, and drive home. Steve put at least eight people in it, and I think Jimmy and I let almost as many drive it. It was a very simple, reliable car with a small-block Chevy, a Turbo 350, and a 9-inch.

Until it got too radical, I drove it to work most days and took it on all sorts of runs. Even though the roll cage was welded in, I installed a little jump seat for my daughter, and we had so much fun, and all for less than $20,000.

These days, there are so many avenues online for making a purchase: Bringatrailer, Craigslist, eBay, Hemmings, racingjunk, etc., are all excellent sources. Don't be afraid to look out of the box. My good friend David Edwards was looking in "Other Vehicles and Trailers" on eBay when he found a funky little sports roadster that had some Pacific Northwest racing history. The body was hand-beaten out of steel by some guys in a shipyard in Washington state and road raced.

Barn finds are the buzz as of late, and just when you thought they'd all have been found, another will surface. For example, Troy Ladd of Hollywood Hot Rods recently received a call from a friend who told him of a garage full of cars the family needed to sell. Out of that garage came a stock Model A Sport Coupe and a cherry 1960s-style 1932 3-window coupe. The sale of the other cars more or less paid for the coupe.

Meanwhile, I had seen the red, drag-style 1940 coupe shown for sale at a number of Southern California swap meets for a few years, and nobody seemed interested despite its stance and provenance. It finally went to England and is now in the hands of Giles Hanauer.

Also across the pond is Dean Lowe's roadster pickup that appeared on the cover of the January 1962 issue of *Hot Rod* magazine. It was a

Shug Hanchard, holder of multiple land speed records, builds and sells basic hot rods such as this Chevy-powered A small-block V-8 that can be purchased for a very reasonable price.

A good place to start is this original Deuce roadster spotted at the Kennedy brothers' shop in Pomona, California, for $35,000 or best offer.

Troy Ladd of Hollywood Hot Rods was lucky enough to get turned on to this barn-find 1932 3-window. The Dewar Coupe was built in 1963, put away, and not touched again until 2018.

favorite of British rodder Stephen Hill, who traveled to the US to buy an old hot rod. He saw a few cars but didn't find what he was looking for until he found Dean's truck.

The truck had been torn apart, and (as so often happens) he got no further. All the original parts from the quick-change to the Panhard bar were there, and the original Frank Kurtis–engineered frame was leaning up against the fence. Stephen bought the whole caboodle and shipped it back to England, where he regularly drives and races it.

Perhaps one of the most famous rods to be "discovered" was Tom Cobbs's blown Model A roadster that famously lost a drag race in 1949 at Goleta Airport against Fran Hernandez in his Edelbrock-equipped 1932 3-window that was running a splash of nitro. Cobb's rod was put away around 1978 and forgotten until the late Ralph Whitworth went in search of parts. The young man he was dealing with said, "Would you like to see my grandpa's rat rod?" It turned out to be Cobb's roadster.

They're out there, and they will continue to be out there.

This 1940 Ford coupe, a fugitive of the drag strip with a scoop and pie-crust slicks, had been kicking around the Los Angeles region for a number of years with no takers until Giles Hanauer took it to England and got it running again.

HOW TO BUILD AFFORDABLE HOT RODS

CHAPTER 2

Buzz and Dean Lowe's 1929 roadster pickup graced the January 1962 cover of Hot Rod *magazine and did double duty as a street rod and a drag car. It was discovered in parts by British rodder Stephen Hill, who regularly races it at Pendine.*

Caveat Emptor (Buyer Beware)

Recently, a friend asked me to go and look at a Model T speedster he was thinking of buying. It was a nice car and worth the $5,000 asking price. While my friend was talking to the seller, I thumbed through the scrapbook that was with the car. I kept looking at it and thinking, "It's not the same car."

Finally, I said to my friend, "This doesn't look like the same car."

Bold as brass, the seller said, "Oh, it is. I just made two cars out of the one."

"What do you mean?" I asked.

He replied, "Well, I took that car and made two out of it. This one has the frame, engine, and radiator, so it's essentially the same car."

I wasn't sure about that, but my friend was happy. He liked the car, liked the price, and bought it.

One thing to be aware of when buying old rods is that the bodies can be full of body filler. Remember, these cars are almost 100 years old. Many were raced hard and put away wet. They may have had their bodies channeled over the frame with the floor just torched out. Many, if not most, have been restored at some time in their lives, and often those restorations were less professional than we would hope for. Put a magnet on the quarter panel, door, or cowl of any of those old cars, and 9 times out of 10, it will fall right to the floor.

Everything is repairable, and today there are patch panels for early Fords from companies such as

A good friend of mine went to purchase this Model T speedster, and the seller was quite bold about the fact that he took one speedster and built two out of it. He wasn't trying to sell it as something it wasn't, but it was an odd admission all the same.

A large number of early Ford patch panels and even complete bodies are available from a number of companies, such as Brookville and United Pacific, which make panels and complete bodies for vehicles, such as this 5-window coupe.

Brookville, United Pacific, etc. You can also buy complete bodies for some models, including Model As, many of the 1932 models, 1934s, and even a reproduction 1940 coupe from RealDealSteel.com.

Be aware that repairing an original car can sometimes be more expensive than buying a new body. A good body shop can easily charge $100 an hour, and $25,000 (the price of a Brookville 3-window body) is only 250 hours of labor. Unless you have a fast body shop, you could easily spend more on labor than the cost of a new body.

Why does the condition of the car you buy matter? Because you have to ask yourself if you are capable of fixing it. If not, are you prepared to pay for fixing it? Thankfully, we're less concerned with budget hot rods being perfect. With that being said, they need to look right.

Pete Chapouris, founder of Pete and Jake's Hot Rod Parts and resurrector of the SO-CAL Speed Shop, always stated that while hot rodding is about personal expression, there are rules that must be followed if the car is to look right.

We had Kelly Brown's 1927 T in the shop, but somehow it didn't quite look right. Pete walked me around the car and pointed out all the things that were off. It was everything from the wheel and tire size and the stance to the panel fit and the blister in the hood. Pete's critique was an eye opener. I knew the car was not quite right, but I couldn't articulate it. Pete had the eye and, more importantly, knew what was wrong and how to fix it.

Eventually, that car went to Roy Brizio who made it the winner of the 2013 America's Most Beautiful Roadster Award for owner John Mumford.

It doesn't look so bad here, but I remember Pete Chapouris walking me around Kelly Brown's 1927 roadster and explaining what was not quite right. Roy Brizio fixed it up for John Mumford and won the America's Most Beautiful Roadster Award in 2013.

Meanwhile, my good friend Richard Sherman purchased a steel 1927 T roadster body with the intention of emulating the Chapouris car only to realize just how hard that would be (see sidebar on page 26).

Another thing to be aware of is the old switcharoo trick. It happened to a friend who agreed to buy a car at an event. The seller suggested that

By the time Roy Brizio and his team worked its magic and shoehorned an Ardun V-8 in place of the banger, John Mumford's 1927 was good enough to win the 2013 America's Most Beautiful Roadster Award.

HOW TO BUILD AFFORDABLE HOT RODS

CHAPTER 2

my friend pick it up from his house in a couple of weeks. My friend got the car home and discovered that the four-bolt block had been replaced with a run-of-the-mill two-bolt block.

When you go to buy a car that you can't drive or take away there and then, use your phone's camera or make sure you have a camera with you to document everything, particularly the engine number and any identifying details.

When buying a rod, check the tires to see if they are worn irregularly because that could indicate that the suspension is out of alignment. It might be a simple fix that you can handle easily, but not if you're not proficient.

Finally, remember that valid registrations are worth as much as the car, and don't go home without it. If the seller says, "I'll mail it," be prepared to walk because the pink slip may never arrive, and you don't know what problems it might cause you in terms of registration, back taxes, etc. (see sidebar on page 26).

Buy a Kit

One alternative to buying a complete car is to buy a kit. Note that we are only talking steel bodies here, not fiberglass. Companies, such as Brookville, offer kits in various stages of build. They offer a 1932 3-window kit complete with or without fenders, hood, grille, etc.

Bobby Walden produced this chopped and slightly raked coupe when he took a brand-new Brookville body and sliced 3 inches out of the top. That's not cheap, but it saved the wannabe builder a lot of time and trouble.

Steve's Auto Restorations/Real Steel in Portland, Oregon, produces steel versions of 1933–1934 roadster and coupes, along with fenders and replacement panels.

Kits like this A V-8 with a Brookville Model A roadster body atop a SO-CAL Deuce chassis are quite common and a good place to start. However, while some heavy lifting is done, there is a still quite a lot of work to do. You could probably do it all at home with hand tools.

Steve's Auto Restorations offers a fairly accurate 1934 roadster body for less than $17,000 that is dimensionally correct but has a smooth cowl and dash, and the firewall is not quite stock. Steve's also offers a 1934 roadster pickup body that is similar to the roadster for less than $12,500. Besides the bodies, Steve's also offers body and chassis packages for both bodystyles with a wide range of options.

Many hot rod shops can assemble a rolling project that you can take home and complete. For example, DearbornDeuce32.com apparently collaborates with chassis builders to assemble a body and chassis package using its Deuce-like body that has a fully disappearing top assembly. That said, be careful when ordering to be certain that you get what you want.

One of the common pitfalls of having a shop build your car or part of your car is that the customer tends to say, "Oh, just do that," without thinking of the financial consequence for either party. They either think the shop will eat the cost, or they think it's inconsequential and therefore carries no financial burden, which is ridiculous.

What can also happen when a customer makes running changes that were not on the original quote is that the shop just adds it to the invoice. After all, the customer asked for it to be done, and then the customer is shocked by the bill. Both parties are equally at fault because the shop often forgets to update the work order—paperwork is not always one of our industry's strong points—and the customer can also forget (or more likely not understand) that there's a cost involved in changing the dash from a regular panel to an Auburn panel, for example. Believe me, it happens often, and it's not a comfortable situation.

If you're not entirely handy in the shop, a kit project might be the way to go. However, beware of the registration issues involved (see page 25).

Time and Materials

Most hot rods shops won't even give you a quote for a project and say, "It's time and materials," which means that they bill you hourly for the labor plus the cost of parts and materials. You can see that this can add up staggeringly quickly.

For example, if a shop charges $100 an hour, that's $800 a day (or $4,000 for a 40-hour week) plus materials. It adds up quickly, so plan accordingly if you have a car worked on in a shop.

Change Orders

In the world of concept car building, they use the term "change orders" to signify when a project has deviated from the original plan and quote. That's when the customer has said, "I think I'll have twin turbos." That's a change order, and while most rod shops don't generate a formal change order, I think it's a wise procedure to follow. That way, when the customer sees the bill, the shop owner can say, "Well, you changed the spec on this day, and this is what that change will cost you." It's good for both parties.

Read Your Bill

This doesn't happen often, but I've seen shops that pad the invoice. In one extreme case, I know of a shop that double-billed a customer just to see if he was paying attention. Had he paid without questioning it, the shop knew that he wasn't paying attention. As it happened, the customer was canny enough to scrutinize his invoices, and the so-called error was caught.

A Basket Case

For some people, buying a pile of parts is the way to go. I've done it and have to say it's not for me. I'm cheap and think that by getting in for a low-ball price I can save money. However, what I've invariably

Mike Herman of H & H Flatheads had this nice 1931 Model A coupe for sale. It was fairly complete except for the rear fenders and the hood, but the glass, interior, and wood were shot.

found is that the pile is incomplete, hard-to-find parts are missing, and it sometimes just doesn't fit together.

That said, a basket case could work out to be a great jumping-off point for some people. Take a look at the 1930 Model A coupe that was for sale by Mike Herman at H & H Flatheads for around $5,000. If you're looking to build a no-frills budget rod, then something like this could be the perfect starting place. It could also be the perfect storm when you look at what it will take to complete something like this because when all is said and done, you might use only the body and frame. This is only a place to start.

Start from Scratch: A Bare Frame

Unless you're experienced, starting from a bare frame might be the most difficult approach to building your dream ride. It looks simple and cheap: get a frame and a body and off you go. There's a lot more to it than that. It's making decision after decision, and the first- or even second- or third-time builder is bound to make mistakes. It's inevitable.

If you're new at this, I suggest that you buy a complete chassis or, better still, a rolling chassis that will at least

Top: Building a car from a bare frame, such as this A V-8 from Walden Speed Shop, is a daunting prospect if you're a first-time builder. Just think of all the decisions to be made.

Bottom: A rolling chassis, such as this example for a 1932 Ford, will take you another step closer to completion, and a lot of decisions have already been made for you.

get you well underway with many of the primary decisions already made. It will probably save you money in the long run.

Registration and Titling

Getting your rod registered should not be too much of a problem as long as you have a bill of sale and a title for the original car. If you have neither, then you have some work ahead of you. The state or country where you reside will determine how much work that is because each state and country has different regulations.

First, get on the internet and determine exactly what your state or country requires. Once you have done some research, talk to a few friends who have gone through the process. Finally, when you think you have learned as much as you can, go to your local DMV and see what it says. If you're lucky, you might have access to a private DMV service, where they can handle the registration for a fee.

Most people think of the Specialty Equipment Market Association (SEMA) as only the annual SEMA Show in Las Vegas. SEMA also works to help protect our hobby by fighting unfair automotive laws and regulations and formed the SEMA Action Network (SAN) to help shape the course of vehicle-related proposals before they become law. Visit SEMA-SAN.com. Without cost or commitment, you can stay informed and access the tools to influence bills in your jurisdiction.

You can visit semasan.com/resources/titling-registration to learn how your particular state defines a hot rod and its particular registration requirements. In some states, such as California, it gets a little complicated. However, some states, such as Alabama, appear to have very simple definitions.

Because each state has its own definitions and registration guidelines, there is no point to go into it here. Suffice to say that we strongly suggest you visit semasan.com and see for yourself the requirements of your particular state.

SEMA has also developed the Model Street Rod/Custom Vehicle Bill to create titling and registration classifications for street rods and custom vehicles, including kit cars and replicas. Under the SEMA model, eligible vehicles are titled as the production year that they most closely resemble, required to meet the equipment standards for that model year, and exempt from periodic vehicle inspections and emissions inspections.

So far, the bill has been enacted in the following 22 states: Arkansas, California, Colorado, Florida, Hawaii, Idaho, Illinois, Iowa, Maine, Massachusetts, Missouri, Montana, Nevada, North Carolina, Oregon, Pennsylvania, Rhode Island, Tennessee, Texas, Utah, Virginia, Washington, and Wyoming.

Bill of Sale

A bill of sale is a simple, written agreement between the seller and the buyer that states that the seller is selling a vehicle, the details of the sale, and that the buyer agrees to purchase it. It can be a simple handwritten agreement as long as it contains the pertinent details. However, if you want something more legal-looking, you can search the internet for free samples. I found a site called formstemplates.com that gives you a free vehicle bill of sale template for all 50 states.

Certificate of Origin

A vehicle's certificate of origin (COO), also known as a manufacturer's statement of origin (MSO), is a document from the vehicle's manufacturer that typically includes the vehicle identification number (VIN), make, model, and description of the vehicle. It also includes the name of the dealer that took delivery of the car or (in some cases) the purchaser. Usually, the vehicle dealer provides it to the state department of motor vehicles when the car is sold. This document is a legal requirement in several states for the registration of a new vehicle. These states keep the certificate of origin and subsequently issue a title to the vehicle to the new owner.

In most cases, a COO will not apply to a hot rod, but you might come across a car that has no other paperwork than a COO. This may be the case if you purchased a kit rod from a company such as Factory Five Racing Inc. or if you purchased a kit rod or partially assembled kit from someone who purchased it from Factory Five. You will have to research the regulations for your particular state regarding titling and registration.

Title

A certificate of title, or pink slip as it is generally known (pre-1988 California titles were pink), is a state- or municipal-issued document that states the owner of a vehicle. Each state has its own rules regarding a certificate of title, so do some research before you dive into this morass.

Much like a COO, a certificate of title contains pertinent information about the vehicle, including the VIN or frame number, license number, body type, class, and sometimes the odometer reading and the owner's name and address. We advise you to buy a car with a title.

Non-Op Registration

There's a cost attached (isn't there always?), but the DMV offers a non-operational car registration for vehicles that are not used or parked on the driveway, such as cars being worked upon. There's a planned fee for this, and owners are required to check the *non-op* box on the registration renewal form before the expiration of the vehicle's current registration before it is taken off the road.

You might think this is a waste of time and money, but in my experience, having an up-to-date non-op registration is a lot better than having no registration when you sell a car. If you've let the paperwork lapse, you may find that back taxes are due before the new owner can cleanly register the vehicle. As mentioned elsewhere, private DMV services can be used to great effect to clear up any complications.

Built with a lot of help from his father, Al Martin, Colby Martin's 1931 Model A on Deuce rails is powered by a 348 from a 1958 Impala. It's a fitting ambassador for SEMA.

How to Avoid Expensive Mistakes

I wrote this article on February 11, 2002. It's as relevant today as it was then. Thankfully, Bill kept the article.

Note: The following is a true story. The names have been changed to protect the author. However, Bill's story is by no means unique, and no doubt thousands of enthusiasts can relate.

I have a friend; let's call him Bill. Bill was born in the 1940s, grew up in the 1950s, and has been a gearhead all his life. Like many of us, he parlayed his love of automobiles into a job, and over the years worked his way up to an executive position. Along the way, he had a string of hot rods and cool cars, all with perhaps a tad more horsepower than was absolutely necessary. But that's the definition of a hot rod, right?

Like all of us, Bill got the hots for a particular car. In this case, it was a 1927 T track

This timeless 1926 roadster built by Pete Chapouris for his father around 1978 inspired Bill. It featured a 2x3-inch box-tube frame and a Ford V-6 engine. It was deceptively simple, reliable, and looked good with any wheel and tire combination.

WHERE TO START

Bill's find in his quest for the perfect 1927 roadster was this fairly rusty body he found at the swap meet for $2,700 that included a set of Kelsey-Hayes wires. Unfortunately, for Bill, it was more than he could chew.

Blasting revealed a body in fairly good condition with some minor patching. However, 1926–1927 Ts are deceptively complicated to build and rarely look right. Bill ultimately made the tough but correct decision to cut his losses and move on.

roadster. A track roadster is one of those cars that looks easy to build, but it is, in fact, very tricky to build. They fool you with their simple looks, but underneath they're very hard to get right. They're short on space both in the cockpit and under the hood, and they're very difficult to proportion correctly. I have another acquaintance who has 150 large ones in a 1927 that needs another to correct and finish. Most just don't cut it. However, Bill's dream car was the British racing green roadster built by Pete Chapouris of SO-CAL Speed Shop for his father back in the mid-1970s. *Sirod* (it was Doris, Pete's mother's name, spelled backward), as it was known, was one of the few that was right on the money and is regarded as one of best-looking track roadsters ever built.

Armed with reference photographs of his dream (which all car builders should have), Bill approached a high-profile shop that he knew had the capability of realizing his dream. Bill laid out his photos, spec'd out his powertrain, which was a bit over the top given the confines of the 1927's engine bay, and asked for a quote.

Unfortunately, the quote was way higher than Bill had anticipated. Frankly, he was speechless. He went home to think about it, but his mind was made up. He wasn't going to spend that kind of money.

He noodled the project around in his head and decided that he could "build" the car himself by subcontracting the work out to local shops. He bought an original steel body (it was a bit rusty and some parts were missing) and sent it out for restoration while he collected parts and had a frame built. When he had a good pile of parts, he heaped them all together into the shape of a car, took some photographs, and sent them to me.

Unfortunately, it didn't look quite right. Track roadsters are very, very difficult to get right, and this one wasn't. I think Bill must have known that because the next thing I know, he bought a cherry, original 1934 3-window coupe. It was a rust-free California car, and in the vernacular all it needed was "Pete and Jaking." By that I mean the retention of the stock chassis, the addition of a complete Pete and Jake's bolt-in suspension system, and a transmission adapter for a small-block. Then, you'd have a nice little driver.

However, that wasn't the direction Bill took. Being a horsepower junkie, he opted for some big-ass Ford motor and an aftermarket chassis. There's nothing wrong with big-ass Ford motors. That's what hot rods are all about, but in this case, it didn't help the situation. Meanwhile, because the car was in such good shape, Bill had no intention of giving it Lexus-like gaps, and he had some friends who wanted to help, so the

HOW TO BUILD AFFORDABLE HOT RODS

How to Avoid Expensive Mistakes *continued*

Bill fared little better with his next project based on this cherry 1933 3-window. Instead of building it up in bare metal, he bought a new frame, dropped in a big engine, and had the body painted. Only then did he realize that the firewall needed to be cut.

body went out for paint. In our world, the last thing you do before final assembly is paint the body, so having it painted at this stage (the beginning of the project) was a complete mistake—and an expensive mistake as it turned out.

Eventually, the chassis arrived, the motor and transmission were installed, and the painted body was lowered into place. Guess what? The motor was set too far back, and the only way to fit the body was to hack out the aftermarket firewall, which already had a setback. Not being that crafty, Bill hacked it out until he could lower the body onto the frame. Suddenly, that cherry body was starting to look a little worse for wear. Figuring he could make it right (or at least have somebody else make it right), Bill pushed on and decided to install the gas tank, rear fenders, rear apron, and bumpers.

Well, guess what? The aftermarket chassis was half an inch narrower in the rear than the stocker, and nothing would bolt up as it was supposed to. And there the second project came to a halt, and it was pushed into a corner alongside the pile of parts that vaguely resembled a 1927 track roadster.

The message here is that while all aftermarket parts for early Ford hot rods are fashioned after Henry's original, few are an exact copy, and almost none of the aftermarket manufacturers talk to each other (for fear of being ripped off), so parts from one company are not necessarily engineered to work with parts from another. The exceptions are perhaps Pete and Jake's, Super Bell, and SO-CAL, whose products were (for the most part) developed to work together.

That said, all hot rods should be assembled in the rough before anything is plumbed, painted, or plated. Engine placement for cooling and clearance is critical. Driveshaft alignment is critical for a vibration-free ride. Body alignment for ultimate fit and finish is critical. You can't build a car out of order and hope that it will all just fall together. It doesn't happen that way even in professional and experienced shops. That's because the very essence of a hot rod involves some amount of experimentation; everybody wants their car to be a little different. Bill likes high-horsepower engines, and they don't usually fit as easily as your basic but perhaps hackneyed small-block Chevy.

Bill now decided that a traditional A V-8 (a 1932 frame and a 1928–1929 roadster body) was the way to go for the third attempt. For some reason, and I can't explain this, he went back to the aftermarket chassis builder who supplied him with the 1934 frame that wasn't quite right. Again, he chose some goofy engine that was a squeeze in the tight confines of a Model A hood.

A V-8s (like track roadsters) are deceptive. They both look simple, so people think they're simple (perhaps read cheap) to build. They're not. Knowing this but not knowing exactly why, I asked Pete Chapouris, president of SO-CAL Speed Shop to explain.

"To begin with, you have to make a chassis choice," said Pete. "You can either opt for a stock chassis and live with the different plan views of the Model A body versus the 1932 frame which, of course, is what they did back in the 1940s. Or you can contour the frame to fit the body. The choice is yours, but nevertheless, it's a choice you have to make.

"The A body is also flat on the bottom, whereas the Deuce body was contoured to fit the frame. Hence, some work is necessary to fit the A body to the 1932 frame. You have to decide how to shim the gap between frame and body, and how to cut out the rear floor to clear the 1932 kick-up. Also, as the A body is narrower than the 1932 in the rear, you must decide whether to narrow the frame or pull the body out over the rails. Decision, decisions. It's all decisions.

"At the front, things get even more tricky," continued Pete. "The big problem with an A V-8 is with the grille position and hood line. If you're using a Deuce grille shell, it has to be positioned just right (as does any shell) for the correct stance so that the hood line neither runs up nor downhill. It's very difficult to get right and can't be done without the chassis set up at the exact ride height and stance and without the body being bolted down in position. Only then can you tape it all out (using masking tape) and see how it's going to look. Then, you can cut your grille shell and take a measurement for a radiator."

That's where Bill went wrong once again. Instead of following my advice, he went ahead and ordered a radiator. When it was installed with the shell, the hood line ran uphill. Time to start over in the rad and hood department.

"People think A V-8s are a cheap way to go because the Brookville steel Model A roadster body is cheaper and faster to get than a 1932 body. That's correct, but everything else is more expensive," said Chapouris. "If you contour the frame, it gets expensive. You have to do some kind of work to the floor, and the whole grille shell, radiator, and hood alignment is a problem. Where are you going to get a hood? Nobody makes a hood for an A V-8 because they are different, so you have to have one fabricated, and that costs money. A V-8s are deceptively expensive unless you're building a rat rod, which is a whole different style where fit and finish matter less."

Bill is finally getting close to finishing his A V-8 but not after more than a few struggles and some expensive mistakes. At one point, I suggested he'd have been better off going with what he felt was an expensive quote for the 1927 track roadster. He'd be on the road by now. This learning curve has been a four-year odyssey, and he would have saved a ton of money. He had to agree that I was right. What seemed expensive up front was actually cheaper in the long run.

So, what did Bill learn? It ain't easy to build a hot rod.

Being different is not what it's all about; the right look is what it's all about. The simpler they look, the harder they are to build and make look right. Keep it simple. Complicated often (but not always) equals costly. You need to have a point of reference, such as a picture of the car you like.

Have a plan and stick to it.

Don't change direction mid-project. That does get expensive.

Don't be swayed by so-called experts. Build your car, not theirs.

Don't throw anything away. You never know when you'll need it.

Build the car, especially if you're an amateur, in bare metal and get it up and running before you paint or chrome anything. When you know it all works in harmony, tear it apart, finish everything, and assemble.

Measure everything twice and cut once.

Don't run with scissors.

Listen to your mother . . . ■

Finally, Bill got his A V-8 hot rod on the road. Despite three false starts, we have to say it looks pretty good.

CHAPTER 3

TOOLS AND EQUIPMENT

To build a rod at home, you're going to need an arsenal of tools and equipment—everything from a set of wrenches to a welder and a whole lot in between. Thankfully, between the internet, swap meets, and companies such as Harbor Freight, there is a vast range of equipment and prices.

You may also find that you'll need some special tools, such as hub pullers. However, some of those specialty items can be rented. It's always good to own your own tools, but you have to ask yourself how often you will use them and if you will receive a good return on the investment. Some companies, such as Baileigh Industrial, have a used and demo section on their websites where you can save some money. We are very lucky in the US that tools and equipment are readily available and fairly reasonably priced. And remember that tools are like wives—best not lent out.

Angle Grinder

An angle grinder can be the rod builder's best friend, and my toolbox contains a Hitachi G10SR that has proved to be reliable and invaluable, but there are plenty of other brands.

Axle Stands

You will need at least four but preferably six or eight axle stands. You'll need one for each corner of the frame, and probably two or four more for mocking up.

Brake Line Bender

You will probably bend your own brake lines because it's not that difficult. However, if you are buying an off-the shelf frame or chassis, then you can possibly order brake lines to go. Brookville has unpolished stainless line kits for just under $500, but they also sell all the necessary components, as do several other companies. Of course, you'll need to know which front and rear brakes you are using before you buy the kit. Tools, such as the one shown, as well as complete line-bending kits, are available for less than $10 to almost $200 from a wide range of suppliers.

HOW TO BUILD AFFORDABLE HOT RODS

TOOLS AND EQUIPMENT

Camera

Most people have a camera on their phone, and while you might not think it a piece of necessary equipment, it is because photos become a handy reference. Say you're at an event, and you see the way someone has done something that you want to replicate. A quick photo gives you reference for when it's time to make a part.

Chemicals and Rags

You'll be surprised by how many chemicals you will need in the assembly of your project. Everything from the ubiquitous all-purpose brake cleaner to grease and penetrating oil for removing those rusty bolts. I tend to stick with Lucas Oil products because they have a good range and

work for my needs. You'll also need plenty of shop rags, paper towels, and handy wipes.

Clamps and Magnetic Holders

Clamps of all shapes and sizes are necessary for mocking up the chassis and body. Clamps are particularly important if you're working alone. Magnetic holders are great for this, and they're available from companies such as Adjust-O and Welding-Supply.com.

Air Compressor

A compressor might be too much equipment for you, but you can buy them almost anywhere, and the 30-gallon electric-powered portable Kobalt shown was for sale at Lowes for $449. It can be used for many tasks from small paint jobs to heavy-duty nailing. Some are two-stage units that can be run on 120 volts (household) or 240 volts (professional). Of course, you'll need air-powered tools; they can really speed up the work when it comes to cutting, grinding, and sandblasting.

Drifts

Nothing ever goes easy, so you are going to need a selection of aluminum, brass, and steel drifts to encourage certain recalcitrant parts.

Engine Hoist and Stand

An engine hoist is a must-have item because you'll remove and install the engine a few times. Traditional hot rods tend to be powered by traditional engines that were traditionally heavy. If you intend to rebuild your own engine, an engine stand can be helpful.

HOW TO BUILD AFFORDABLE HOT RODS

Green Book

The *Green Book* is known as the Bible in Ford circles. It lists thousands of parts and specifications for early Ford passenger cars 1928–1948 and trucks 1928–1947. It's not essential, but it's definitely handy because it provides all the factory technical specifications.

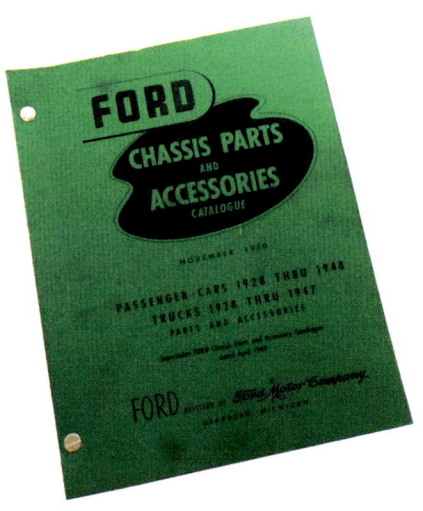

Floor Jack

You're going to need one or two floor jacks because as you set up the chassis, you might be maneuvering more than one component into position. There is a wide selection of lightweight aluminum jacks on the market, and you might want to consider one of the low-profile jacks just in case you are building a low car. For example, Arcan has a steel jack with a 2.75-inch minimum saddle height, which is the lowest I could find.

Hammers and Punches

You can't have enough hammers. At least, not enough big hammers. You'll need large and small ball-peen hammers for minor adjustments and brass, plastic, and rubber mallets for whack jobs. You'll need punches, and preferably a spring-loaded punch that can be used one-handed. You might even need some body-shaping hammers and dollies.

Files

With all kinds of power sanders available, the need for hand files is less necessary than it was previously. Nevertheless, I always find that I need some for a quick adjustment or for light finishing.

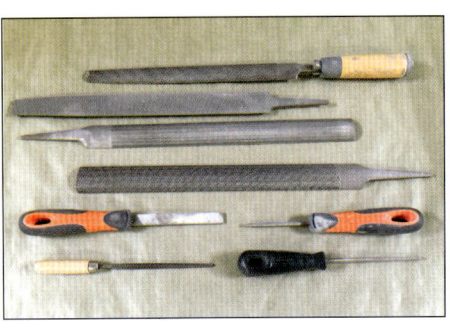

Jigsaw

You probably won't use it often unless you have a lot of wood in your car, but a jigsaw is handy when working on the floorboards and cutting holes for the transmission and pedals.

Lighting

Auxiliary lighting, such as this magnetic unit from Snap-on (below), is handy because you can place it at any angle to illuminate the work area.

Measuring Equipment

You will need a 25-foot tape measure to measure the diagonals of your chassis when ascertaining its squareness. A steel or aluminum yard stick (3 feet long), a level, and a metal square will come in handy, as will smaller versions for the places where the big versions don't fit. Another necessary tool for chassis setup is a magnetic angle-finder/protractor, such as those from Empire or Snap-on.

Drill Press

A drill press is a must because it enables you to drill things square and precisely. A hand drill can do the job but not always as accurately. You can buy a new drill press for as little as $100, but obviously you get what you pay for in terms of quality. At home I use a little bench-top Shopmaster by Delta that was less than $100. It's a 10-inch 10-speed with a 1/2-inch chuck and is about as small as you'd want to go.

McMaster-Carr Catalog

For many hot rodders, the McMaster-Carr catalog is the Bible. With almost 4,000 pages, the catalog contains hardware, tools, raw materials, and maintenance equipment and supplies that you can't easily find in a store. The catalog is usually only available to established customers, but I found used copies for sale on eBay.

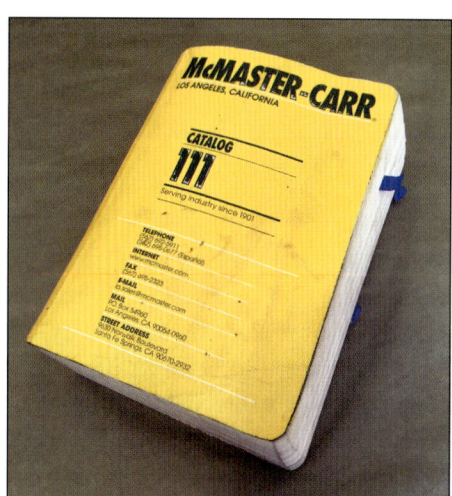

Machine Tools

Not everyone has the space or budget for machine tools, such as a disc grinder, belt sander, grinder, or band saw, but they are invaluable if you have the space and the budget. Baileigh Industrial has a combination belt and disc grinder DBG-106 for about $1,300 that will certainly save on space. A bench grinder can

CHAPTER 3

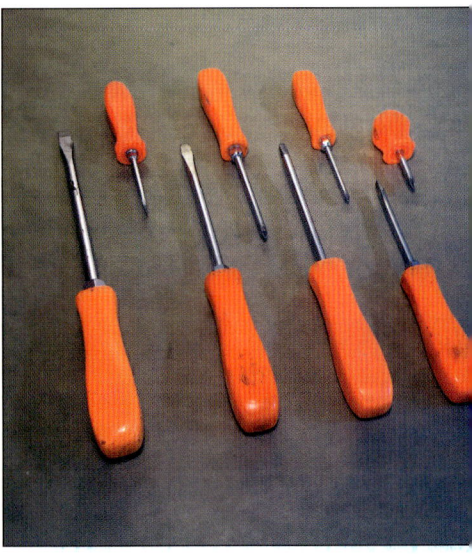

be used for cleaning, polishing, and sharpening with different wheels. Don't forget to get a bucket of water for quenching.

Power Drills and Drill/Drive Bits

I like to have both corded and cordless drills in my toolbox because you never know which one is going to be the most useful. There are plenty of brands to choose from and prices vary, but get a corded drill with at least a 1/2-inch chuck and variable speeds. Hammer drills are handy, as are the reversible type. You're also going to need a selection of drill bits, and I recommend you buy the best you can afford.

Sandblaster

A small gravity-fed, handheld sandblaster, such as this one from Central Pneumatic/Harbor Freight (below), is invaluable for cleaning small parts. You will need a compressor to power it.

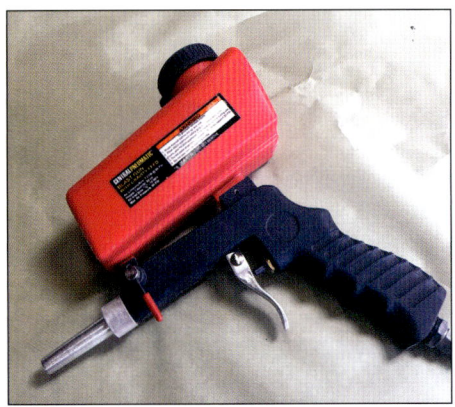

Screwdrivers and Impact Driver

A good selection of screwdrivers is a must, and something else for your toolbox is an impact driver. You can either go the standalone route, or you can step up for something like the DeWalt cordless impact driver kit. Reasonably priced versions are available from Ryobi or Ridgid.

Shop-Vac, Dustpan, and Brush

I'm forever sweeping and vacuuming as I go, and I've had great luck over the years with the Ridgid Wet Dry brand. However, I recently replaced a large 16-gallon unit (5 peak hp) with a smaller 9-gallon unit (4.25 peak hp), and I have to say, size does matter. I should have gone for the 5 peak hp.

Special Tools

If you have never worked on the vehicle that you are rodding, it is well worth researching special tools

34   HOW TO BUILD AFFORDABLE HOT RODS

TOOLS AND EQUIPMENT

for that model. You might be amazed at what you might find that you will need. I looked up special tools for early Ford on MacsAutoParts.com, and a list of 148 items popped up. Obviously, you won't need them all, but I recommended you do some advance research before you start. That way, you can order the tools in advance and not get stuck partway through a job because you didn't plan. Maybe it would be a clutch disc alignment tool or a Stromberg jet wrench.

Template/Pattern–Making Tools

You're going to need cardboard for creating templates. You can buy cardboard from companies such as Kilmer, Wagner & Wise. A bundle of 51 26x38-inch sheets that are 0.042-inch thick costs $73.20. You'll also need scissors, a pencil, and a permanent marker. You might want to get some plastic drafting supplies, such as triangles. Adjustable triangles

are available, and they can be very handy when designing brackets.

Tie-Downs

They are not absolutely necessary, but tie-downs can be handy (especially when you are working alone) to hold an engine or to secure a front or rear end when trying to figure out the suspension.

Vise

More than any other piece of equipment, a vise is invaluable. It can be either standalone (enabling you to work in the round) or bolted to a steel bench. A good one from Baileigh Industrial costs around $200. Don't forget a pair of aluminum or brass soft jaws to protect whatever you're working on.

Vise-Grips, Crescent Wrenches, and Pipe Wrenches

Vise-Grips are invaluable extra-hand tools if you are working alone. Likewise, my toolbox contains several different sizes of crescent wrenches. I also recommend having a couple of pipe wrenches or Channellocks.

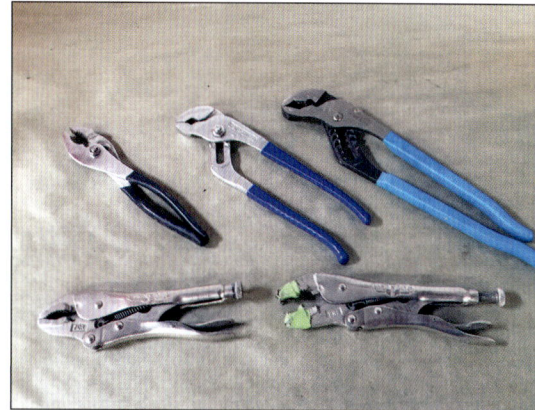

Welder

For general-purpose welding, I like this Miller Dynasty 200 tungsten inert gas (TIG) welder (below). It can be used to make precise welds when joining mild steel, aluminum,

HOW TO BUILD AFFORDABLE HOT RODS

or stainless steel. TIG welding is a two-handed process (one hand holds the torch while the other feeds filler metal), and it commonly involves a foot pedal or fingertip remote to control the arc voltage while welding. Like MIG welding, a shielding gas (typically argon) is required.

Wire Strippers

Known in the trade as grip-and-strip wire strippers, this handy tool will help you strip 10-22 AWG with, as they say, one-third less hand pressure. This one is from Ideal and costs about $40.

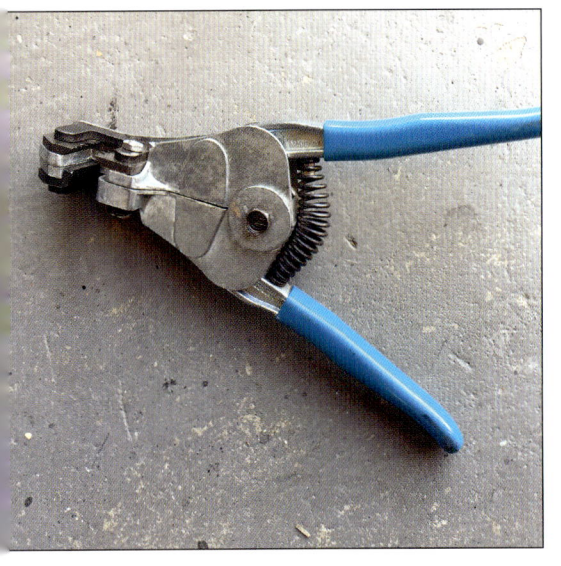

Wiring Tools

A pair of side cutters will suffice for any little wiring job, but if your intention is to tackle a lot of wiring, get yourself a crimper and perhaps even a wire terminal kit. They are available from companies like Del City. You're also going to need a heat gun for shrink wrap, a soldering iron and solder, regular and long-nose pliers, electrical-size screw drivers, and a good selection of the correct-size wire.

Workbench

A metal workbench might appear to be a luxury, but you're going to need a bench of some kind, so a sturdy metal bench that you can clamp your welder ground to is far better than a rickety wooden bench. Metal benches are available from a number of suppliers. However, you can make your own, and don't forget to put a bar on the side for hanging your clamps.

Wrenches (Spanners)

There are a lot of options for wrenches. Everyone has his or her own brand preference, and you will need a good selection of both open-ended and ring spanners. You will also need a good socket set—maybe a large 1/2-inch drive and a small 3/8- or even 1/4-inch drive. Don't forget a couple of large and small adjustable wrenches.

CHAPTER 4

MAKE IT YOUR OWN

It takes a strong person to buy a well-known rod, drive it, and live with people who say, "Oh that's so-and-so's car." For example, collector Bruce Meyer owns numerous famous hot rods, including the Doane Spencer roadster and the Bob McGee roadster. Bruce has owned those cars for more than 20 years, could own them for another 20, and yet they always will be known by the names of their original owners or builders, never as the Bruce Meyer roadster.

Bruce doesn't mind. He said, "Some hot rods were seminal in their design and build and should never be changed. Other cars, however, even though they might have been loved and admired in their day, can in my opinion be changed and personalized by their current owners.

"A good example is the Barry Lobeck roadster that Steve Coonan, publisher of *The Rodder's Journal*, owned. That was a well-loved car, but for me to own it, I needed to change it and make it my own, hence the rebuild by Pete Chapouris and the distinctive, scalloped checkerboard paint scheme. That said, I'm just the custodian of these cars for now."

Another example of making it

Preservationist Bruce Meyer purchased and restored the famous Doane Spencer Deuce Roadster, but it will always be known as the Doane Spencer Roadster no matter who is the custodian.

Despite being built by legendary builder Barry Lobeck and owned for some time by Steve Coonan, publisher of **The Rodder's Journal,** *this roadster will always be known as Bruce Meyer's Checkered Past Roadster.*

HOW TO BUILD AFFORDABLE HOT RODS

CHAPTER 4

A very young Tommy Sparks (right) stands with his Model A roadster pickup at El Mirage just after World War II. The hot rod was typical of the times with an Eddie Meyer-equipped flathead behind the Deuce grille. (Photo Courtesy David Steele)

your own is the Tommy Sparks 1929 roadster pickup that he bought in the 1940s. He reassembled the survivor in the 1980s and used a flathead V-8 that he built in 1947.

"It was ported and relieved with a standard bore and stroke," Bruce said. "I just left it that way and then used the set of Meyer heads and the Meyer intake I'd kept from my other roadster that I sold in the late 1940s."

Tommy's roadster pickup (RPU) succumbed to the trends of the time and got gussied up in the resto-rod style that was prevalent in the 1980s. According to the current custodian, David Steele, executive director of the American Hot Rod Foundation, "It was a fenderless highboy roadster, but Tommy added an eclectic choice of accessories like the radiator stone guard, wind wings, and an interesting set of knockoff wire wheels that were actually rare Aston Martin wires."

Looking back, it was a little confused, but remember that was the style of the time for some rodders. However, it retained that Meyer-equipped flattie.

Years later, when Tommy and David had become great friends, the pair attended a Throttler's Picnic. David remembers that Tommy was excited to see all the young rodders there with their traditional rods and commented about all the things he would have to change on the RPU if he wanted to take it back to how it was when he had built it as a kid.

Tommy revamped the RPU in typical 1980s style—sort of. It was a highboy when most resto-rods were full fendered. It had atypical knock-off wires from an Aston Martin and accessories that included a full-size stone guard and wind wings.

Before he passed away, Tommy sold the RPU to David Steele, executive director of the American Hot Rod Foundation. It came with a list of things Tommy wanted to do to return the truck to the way it was when he first built it.

"I didn't think he would care enough to adjust his old roadster to fall in line with the traditional movement, but he did," said David. "He outlined what he would do. I am so thankful that he did this because we had already done our deal for me to buy the car, and here he was giving me this gift of permission to make the changes I knew I would want too, such as removing the doodads and replacing the wires with the 1940 Ford steelies that he had already set aside.

"I like to think the Tommy Sparks RPU is exactly the way Tommy would have redone it if he had the chance. After all, I've never felt like this is my roadster. I'm just the current caretaker. It's the Tommy Sparks roadster pickup and always will be."

Perpetuating the provenance of an historic rod can spell money in the bank. For example, the *Kookie Kar* T-bucket, Norm Grabowski's car that was immortalized on the TV show *77 Sunset Strip,* was owned for many years by Jim "Street" Skonzakas. Jim decided to make the *Kookie Kar* his own and altered it almost beyond recognition, and that was his prerogative. It was his car. But it's also *our* car, and thankfully current custodians Ross and Beth Meyers had Roy Brizio return it to its former glory. According to *Hot Rod* magazine, the *Kookie Kar* sold for $484,000 including buyer's premium.

Preserving a rod's provenance can be financially beneficial, but what if the history and provenance is fake? "How can that be?" you ask. It's actually kind of easy. You go to an old magazine, find a rod that you like, and do some research to see if it still exists. If you can't find it, then what's to stop some unscrupulous person from merely recreating it?

The late Norm Grabowski redefined the hot rod when he built what became known as the Kookie Kar *that grabbed many kids' hearts when it appeared on in the hit TV show* 77 Sunset Strip. *This is the original car that was restored for Ross and Beth Meyers by Roy Brizio.*

Knowing that this version of Ak Miller's El Caballo, *seen here at Rod Millen's Leadfoot Festival, was sitting in the Wally Parks Motorsports Museum, I was surprised to see another version at the Monterey Historics. (Courtesy Greg Stokes, GMS Hot Rods)*

This 3-window first gained attention in 1961 when 22-year-old builder Walt Banker debuted his $75 purchase at the 1961 Winternationals show. It was voted one of the 75 Most Significant 1932 Fords.

Fast-forward 20 years, and Walt Banker's coupe is now owned by Gary Lorenzini. It became the first car flamed by builder Boyd Coddington.

Gary eventually swapped out Boyd wheels for a set of Halibrands, including spindle mounts for the front, and he had Mick's Paint of Pomona, California, strip the flame paint and give it a coat of red primer for a tougher, more contemporary look.

take on history to that car and has promoted it as something far more historic and important than the car Jay built.

I was at the Monterey Historics a few years ago and saw the old Ak Miller *El Caballo* 1927 T roadster. At first, I didn't think too much about it. However, I knew that another version of that car was sitting in the NHRA Motorsports Museum. I wasn't even sure that the car in the museum was the original, and yet here was another one.

"Our most frequent call is from people looking for images of old hot rods to either research or restore a car," David Steele said. "I'm sure a percentage of those calls are from somebody trying to recreate a car."

I'm certain that is true, but as time goes by, I wonder if it matters. So many cars have been changed, enhanced, updated, or completely recreated over the years. Do we really know right from wrong, and will it really matter in 10 to 20 years? I remember when we were working on the 75 Most Significant 1932 Fords and no one could find the Banker Brothers 3-window. Everybody in the L.A. hot rod scene was asked if they knew where the car was, and no one could remember what happened to it. Then suddenly, as it was about to be given up as lost, someone remembered that it had been re-rodded for Gary Lorenzini by Hot Rods by Boyd.

The coupe has since been re-done yet again by Gary and his son Scott and was painted red oxide primer by Mick's Paint. This is the question: Was it more famous as the Baker Brothers car or the flamed version built by Boyd? Well, it doesn't really matter. It's Gary's car and he made it his own. That's what hot rodding is about.

Jay Deane of Nostalgia Ranch experienced something similar when he built an A V-8 roadster out of parts he had laying around. It turned out to be a nice roadster that he eventually sold. The buyer applied his own

CHAPTER 5

FRAME, CHASSIS, STEERING, AND SUSPENSION

The hot rod aftermarket offers a wide range of frames in numerous configurations—so many that it makes almost no sense to attempt to build your own. However, here we will look at store-bought, home-built, and modified frames, and the pros and cons of each.

The great thing about building any budget rod is that it should be simple, so no trick independent front or rear suspension, fancy LS engine with electronic fuel injection (EFI), or fancy body modifications beyond a roof chop. Don't get me wrong. It can be cleverly detailed if you have the time, patience, skill, and/or budget to do that, but it doesn't need to be complicated because traditional rods are simple, since they're based on simple early Fords.

A Ford Model T chassis is basically a pair of stamped steel, 3-inch U-section parallel side rails held apart with riveted front and rear stamped crossmembers that also act as spring hangers. In the middle, there is another stamped steel crossmember that supports the tail of the transmission. According to the books, the Model T had a 100-inch wheelbase, but according to a tape measure, it's closer to 99.25 inches. The rails were 0.125 wall thickness. However, the gauge did change over the years.

The 1928–1931 Ford Model A with its wheelbase stretched to 103.5 inches was slightly beefier than the T with its slightly splayed U-section 4-inch-deep rails. It was little better than the T it replaced. However, for 1932, Ford extended the wheelbase to 106 inches, increased the side rail depth to 6 inches, and stamped the reinforcing beauty line in the side. Ford also added a pair of forward-facing legs to the transmission crossmember to form a K-member.

Incidentally, all early Ford crossmembers were pressed carbon steel of 7/64-inch thickness. Nevertheless, the frame continued to flex, which caused body cracking until reinforcement plates became available in May 1932.

The condition persisted until the following year when the 1933 Model 40 was introduced. The wheelbase was stretched to 112 inches, and

Nothing is simpler than a Model T frame that consists of little more than two lengths of 3-inch channel with a pair of crossmembers tying the rails together. Some later 1927 frames are thicker gauge, and they're the ones to go for.

HOW TO BUILD AFFORDABLE HOT RODS

CHAPTER 5

A stock Model A frame is shown at the Kennedy brothers' shop about to be heavily modified by Matt Bryant and Jay Kennedy for Mike Williams's tribute to the pickup trucks of Stan "Pete" Faruga and Dean Lowe. It even has its original running board brackets—for now.

Here's an original 1932 Ford Deuce frame, complete with stock front and rear crossmembers. Note the original central transmission mount (known as a K-member) is missing its left leg and has more than a few non-factory holes.

Some stock 1932 frames had factory strengthening plates, such as this one over the rear kick-up. This frame came together at Kev's Rod & Custom in La Habra, California.

The 1932 Ford frame had this central, riveted K-member. It was better than its predecessor in the Model A, but it was far from perfect. Running production improvements had to be made at the factory in an effort to impart some strength.

FRAME, CHASSIS, STEERING, AND SUSPENSION

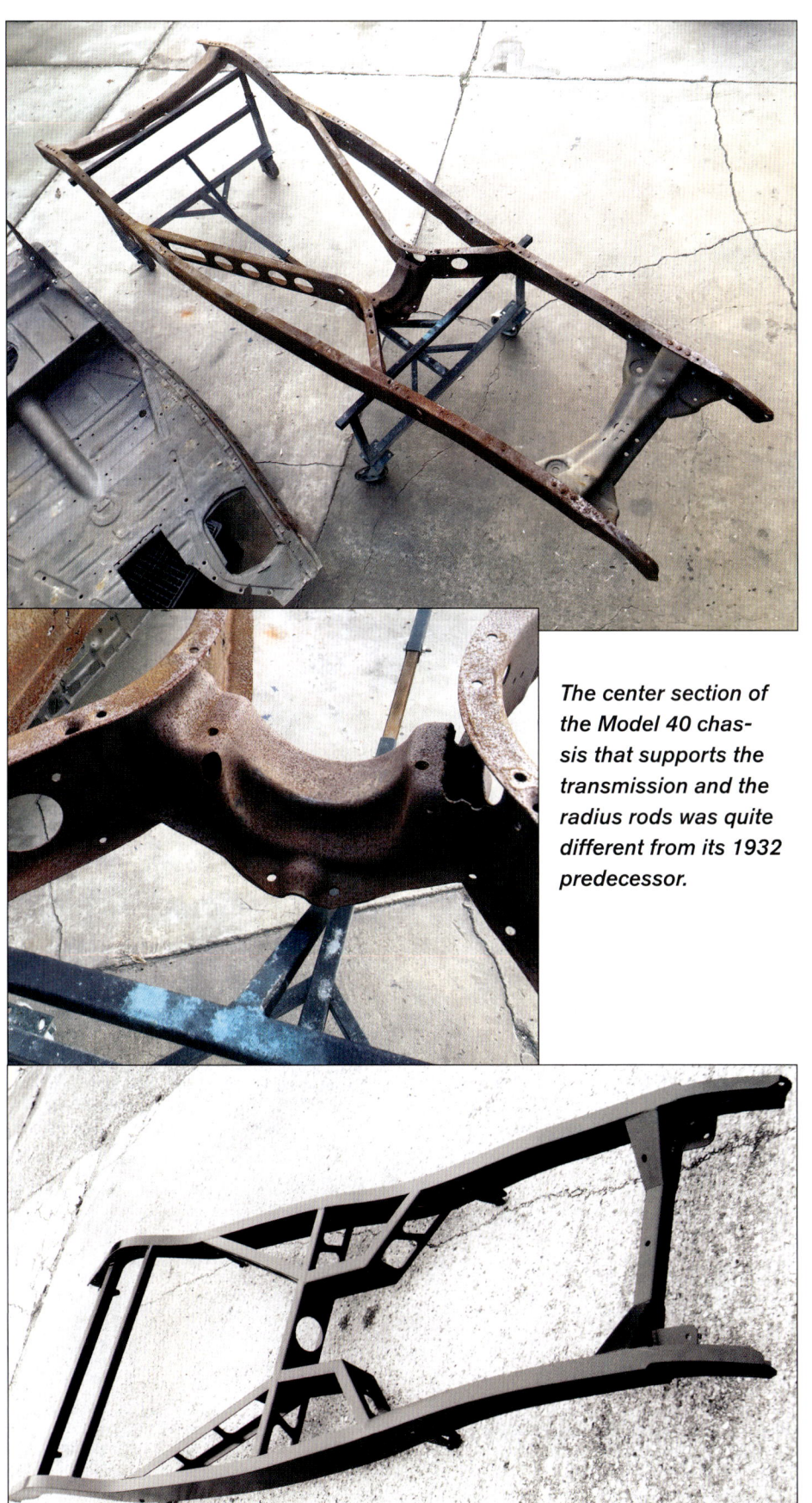

The 1934 Model 40 Ford's 112-inch wheelbase had a much more robust X-member in place of the Deuce's K-member. The frame was made of 0.1-inch pressed carbon steel.

The center section of the Model 40 chassis that supports the transmission and the radius rods was quite different from its 1932 predecessor.

This is a frame with nothing but crossmembers. In this case, it's an aftermarket 1933–1934 frame fabricated from welded sheet metal. Note the central X-member that mimics the factory X-member with cutouts for the exhaust.

finally the X-member was adopted. All frame members were now 0.1-inch pressed carbon steel, which made for a stronger frame, but remember that those cars barely had 75 hp.

If you want to build a hot rod with much more power, the chassis needs to resemble an early Ford for authenticity, but it needs to be much stronger. You can make an original frame stronger, but it might be easier to buy a reproduction frame or chassis. It all depends on your capabilities and wallet.

Something to remember about the 1932–1934 frames is that the rear spring was curved, and that needs to be considered when using those early components in a hot rod chassis.

But wait, what's the difference between a frame and a chassis? In my opinion, a frame is just a bare frame complete with crossmembers and without suspension. A chassis is a frame with all the ancillaries, such as the front and rear axles, suspension, shocks, radius rods, etc. A rolling chassis is the same but on wheels.

HOW TO BUILD AFFORDABLE HOT RODS

CHAPTER 5

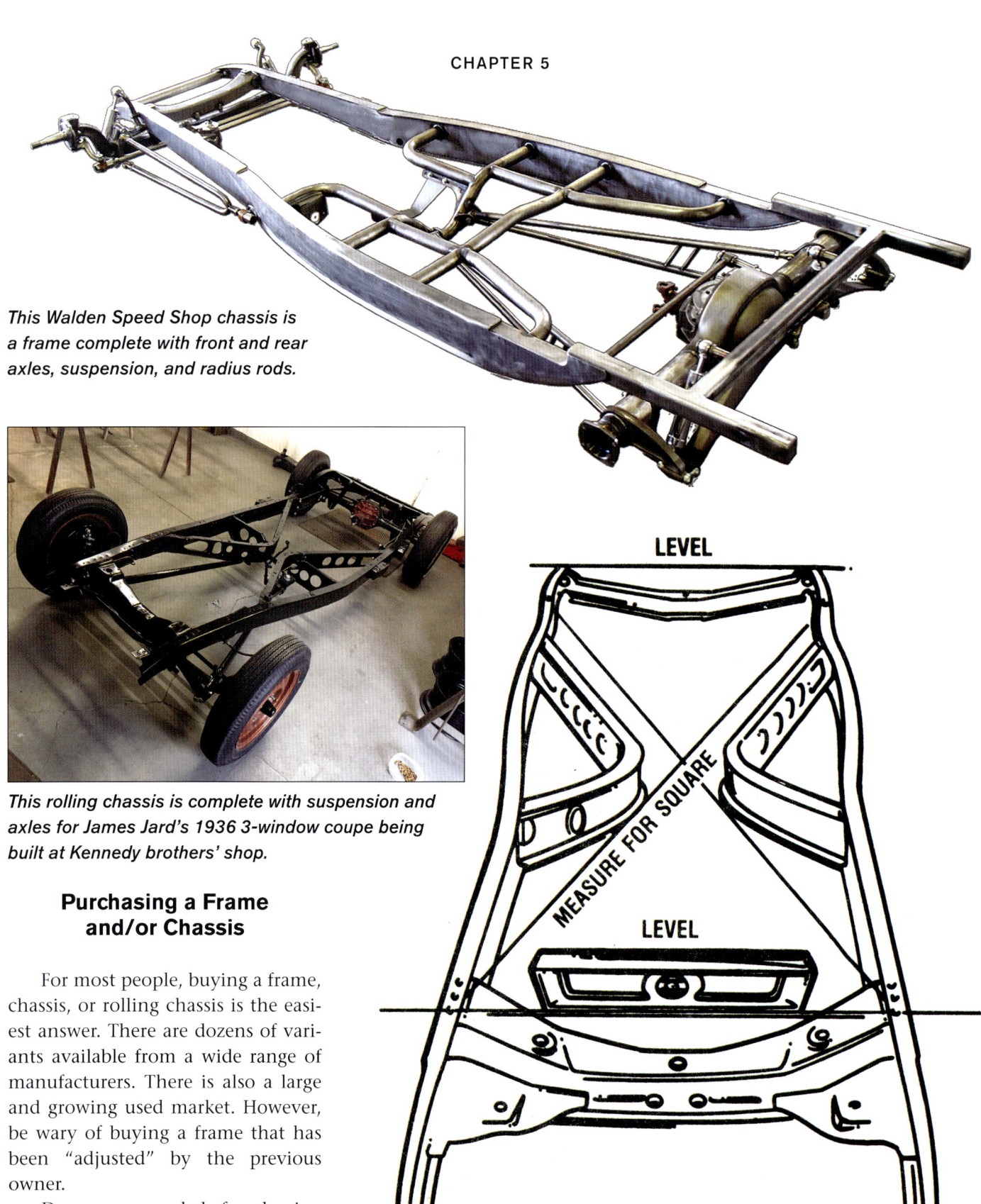

This Walden Speed Shop chassis is a frame complete with front and rear axles, suspension, and radius rods.

This rolling chassis is complete with suspension and axles for James Jard's 1936 3-window coupe being built at Kennedy brothers' shop.

Purchasing a Frame and/or Chassis

For most people, buying a frame, chassis, or rolling chassis is the easiest answer. There are dozens of variants available from a wide range of manufacturers. There is also a large and growing used market. However, be wary of buying a frame that has been "adjusted" by the previous owner.

Do your research before buying a new frame, and even more so with a used frame. Have a clear picture of what you intend to build and look for the frame that fits your needs. Where possible, buy a frame that you

It doesn't really matter whether you're building or buying a new or used frame, it needs to be square and correctly dimensioned. Just because it's new doesn't mean it's correct. (Art Courtesy Pete & Jake's)

44   HOW TO BUILD AFFORDABLE HOT RODS

FRAME, CHASSIS, STEERING, AND SUSPENSION

can see and measure. Be sure that it's square and not butchered. For example, someone may have adjusted the front crossmember to alter the camber. Someone may have cut off the front and rear frame horns for a *bobbed* look. Someone may have cut out the transmission mount or engine mounts for a different transmission or engine combination. Be careful; things are not always as they seem.

You can purchase a frame on the internet, and in many instances that is a good starting point. However, buying a frame without seeing it in person is much like buying a car without seeing it in person, and you wouldn't do that, would you? You hear stories about online purchases that don't work out because what you see is not always what you get.

Building a Frame

As I was putting this book together, there were a lot of rods coming together at Mick's Paint, Troy Ladd's Hollywood Hot Rods, and the Kennedy brothers, where I followed the build of a Model A chassis for Mike Williams, a 1932 for Dick Wade, and a 1936 coupe for James Jard.

Jay Kennedy had Matt Bryant begin Mike Williams' project by step-boxing the A frame. Step-boxing is a style of frame boxing developed by Jim "Jake" Jacobs and adopted by SO-CAL Speed Shop in 1997 and other frame builders. Step-boxing places the boxing plates slightly inside the rails and enjoys the strength of an unground fillet weld on the boxing plates. It also provides increased clearance for brake and fuel lines as well as power cables. Not many builders step-box a Model A, but in this case, it works.

In early examples, step-boxing was simply boxing plates set inside the rails, but in Bryant's version, the step plates are a U-section and slipped inside the stock rails. The two flanges are then spot welded along the length of the frame.

After the rails were boxed, the frame was set up level on jack stands. The frame was set at a 3-degree forward rake, and the front crossmember was flattened 1½ inches to lower the spring-mounting surface and reset in the chassis at an angle of 7 degrees. When the frame is at the correct 3-degree rake, the caster should be about 4 degrees. Ford specified between 4½ and 9 degrees; 5 is optimum, but according to Pete Eastwood, "Anywhere from 3 to 7 will work."

It's important to get this right and not think, "I can fix that later." The reason to get it right now and not later is so that the spring sits at the correct 4-degree angle to match the angle of the other components. If the spring is out of alignment with the angle of the axle, you could encounter some undesirable spring bind causing a lack of suspension travel.

Bob Walden step-boxes his frames in sections with the front section thicker for mounting the shock bosses. The inserts need to be contoured to fit the shape of the frame. The holes are to access body mounts.

Matt Bryant's style of step-boxing uses a U-section of 11-gauge sheet steel bent to fit inside the frame and rosette welded every inch or so. It negates the need for full-length welding.

HOW TO BUILD AFFORDABLE HOT RODS

CHAPTER 5

Another method of mounting an adjustable spring perch is shown here, where the fabricated perch doubles as a spring hanger and a lower shock mount and is mounted through the wishbone.

The mounts used early Ford-style biscuit rubber mounts that are available from a number of suppliers.

One answer to this is adjustable spring perches where the spring perch is mounted so that it can swivel and allow the spring to likewise swivel until it is in alignment with the axle.

Moving rearward, the engine mounts were gusseted, L-shaped brackets were attached to the side rails that will support the engine using early-Ford-style rubber donut mounts, and a U-shaped Hurst-style motor mount cradle were added.

The central crossmember/transmission support was made up of a 5-inch-drop SO-CAL ladder bar crossmember. It is 1¾ inches in diameter drawn over mandrel (DOM) 0.125 seamless steel tubing that is 43¼ inches wide that can be cut to fit. Two fabricated bent legs were attached to the crossmember to form a K-member. The transmission mount was made of 1-inch round tubing bent into a lazy-C shape and fitted with a pair of SO-CAL urethane-bushed rod ends. The urethane allows for a little transmission movement. Best Way Stamping made the tabs, and Jay typically fabs his own K-legs to run parallel to the centerline. "I just don't like trying to drill the various holes on an angle," Jay said. "It's easier when the tubes are square." Jay also prefers to use slotted transmission mount brackets.

Locating tabs for the rear radius

Clevises, Heim Joint, Tie-Rod Ends, or Urethane Bushings?

Until 1974, few choices were available for what to use at the end of your radius rods, but that year Pete and Jake's introduced four-bar link rod ends with urethane bushings. Prior to that, there were clevises, heim joints, or traditional rod ends—none of which had any give. The urethane bushings offered a little give and were quickly copied by the rest of the industry. The bushings also became available for front and rear spring shackles, shock mounts, engine mounts, etc. They were available anywhere that a small amount of flexibility was desirable. ■

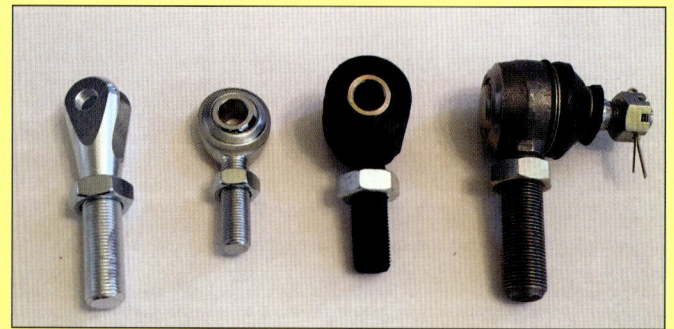

In the early days, the only choice you had for suspension ends was clevises, heim joints, and traditional rod ends, none of which had any give. In 1974, Pete and Jake's introduced urethane-bushed rod ends that allowed a little flexibility in the suspension.

FRAME, CHASSIS, STEERING, AND SUSPENSION

The original Deuce front wishbones were located by a rubber cushioned ball in the middle of the car under the transmission.

rods were fabricated (the SO-CAL ones not being in the right location) and welded to the crossmember. The radius rods are actually 1936 Ford wishbones split and reworked to fit this chassis. Bungs to accept rod ends were welded into the ends of the radius rods. There are some poorly made bungs on the market with some sloppy threads, so be careful when you make a purchase. At the axle end, the radius rods were extensively reworked to fit the flange on the Winters quick-change and have the correct angle toward the center of the car.

On the original early Ford, the wishbone was located in the center of the chassis in a rubber cup. When the wishbone is split and the ends are spread, the angle of attachment at the axle end is altered, which needs to be adjusted. By doing so, you induce some bind because the wishbone and axle are no longer rotating around the central pivot point. It will create some harshness because the Ford wishbone is rubber-mounted and yours will be solid unless you use some type of urethane bushing.

In the rear, the frame was zee'd and kicked up 3 inches. Upon reflection, the kick-up should have had another inch to help accommodate the huge Winters 10-inch quick-change Mike specified. As it is, plans for a Model A transverse leaf spring had to be nixed in favor of coilover shocks, so Matt fabricated upper and lower shock mounts that were welded to the radius rods and the Model A rear crossmember. Because of the size of the quick-change, the crossmember had to be sectioned 3/4 inch for clearance, but once Jay finished the modification, it was barely visible.

All of these components were tacked into place and were not finish welded until everything was correct. It's important that you build the car dry and get all the bugs sorted before you strip it down for finishing.

Front End

When it comes to the front end, there are limited choices because we're not really looking at anything other than an I-beam or tube axle and a transverse leaf spring. Beams and tubes are simple in theory, but in practice, there are some technicalities to be aware of if you want your rod to drive and handle well.

Ts, As, and 1932s all had the radiator, crossmember, spring, and axle stacked on top of each other vertically (as you can see on this completely stock Model T roadster).

HOW TO BUILD AFFORDABLE HOT RODS 47

CHAPTER 5

Except for the dropped axle, the front end on this 1932 is almost stock with a stock uncut crossmember and a stock eye spring.

suicide-style. Mounting the spring behind the axle is also a method of pushing the wheels forward and extending the wheelbase. All of these combinations are okay.

The main thing to remember with any front end is to spend time setting up your car by getting the geometry correct. Your rod will then be fun to drive, and you won't be fighting it.

1. 5 degrees of positive caster is optimum, but anywhere from 3 to 7 will work.
2. Set the Ackerman angle to have a line from your spindle through the steering arm to the center of the back axle.
3. Try to have a line through the kingpin intersect with the center of the tire at the ground.
4. Set your camber at 1/4 to 1 degree.
5. Set your toe-in to be about 1/8 inch.

In many cases, the axle is going to sit directly below the spring, but it can be mounted behind the spring as it was in 1935-and-up Fords. That's also a popular style on Ts and some other radical rods. Occasionally, on certain Ts, the spring is mounted behind the axle

This is a Model A roadster fitted with 1935-and-up split wishbones that put the spring ahead of the axle. In turn, that pushes the axle back behind the crossmember and shortens the wheelbase unless the crossmember is moved forward.

Note that when these 1935-and-later wishbones are split, the spring hangers angle in and must be heated and bent to make them square to the axle.

HOW TO BUILD AFFORDABLE HOT RODS

FRAME, CHASSIS, STEERING, AND SUSPENSION

It is difficult to discern because of the way it is designed, but a 1936 front end has the spring mounted ahead of the axle. To lower the front end, the crossmember can be sectioned, and a reverse-eye spring can lower it some more, but that's maybe too far.

This British-built modified has a suicide-style drilled axle that is suspended on semi-elliptic springs. That is no longer a typical way to go, but it works in this application.

Axles

All early Fords (except the 1937 V-8-60) had a carbon manganese (chrome) alloy forged steel I-beam. There are seven axle types in total, and they have different widths, drops, and spring perch bosses. Research before you make a purchase because the axle you choose needs to be compatible with the spring, wishbones, etc. Incidentally, the 1937 was a hollow forging that was slightly flattened in the front and back. Axles from 1937 onward have a little more *smile* than earlier axles.

Ford's forged steel is tough and versatile, and early dropped axles were usually made by heating and dropping the ends. They were often called *Dago* axles because many were dropped near San Diego by Ed "Axle" Stewart. In L.A., there was Mor-Drop and Okie Adams, who was sometimes associated with Blair's Speed Shop in Pasadena. Okie made dropped axles by cutting off the ends just past the spring perch boss and welding on a new, dropped end. This was a good idea because it meant that the axle end did not get distorted, the kingpin boss and hole were not affected, and the axle retained a nice shape. Unfortunately, these axles are rare and quite expensive.

F.E. Zimmer Co. began advertising Dago dropped axles in the April 1948 issue of *Hot Rod* for $12, and Alex Xydias's So-Cal Speed Shop advertised So-Cal dropped and filled axles in the same issue. Around that time, Bell (the same company that eventually made Bell helmets) offered

Troy Ladd's Hollywood Hot Rods has taken an entirely unusual approach with this parallel, semi-elliptic leaf-spring front suspension on Pat Gauntt's coupe.

CHAPTER 5

On top is a 1928–1931 Model A with a 2¼-inch spring perch boss, and a 1933–1936 is on the bottom. All other early Fords, except the 1937 V-8-60 tubular axle, have a 2-inch spring perch boss.

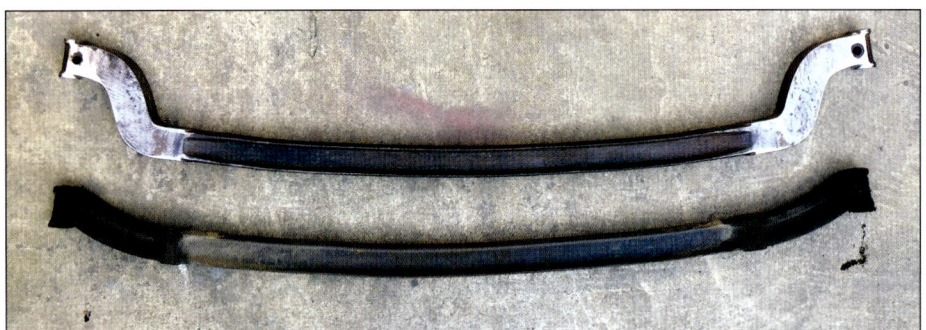

On top is a very rare Okie Adams dropped axle that was made by welding new cast ends just outside the spring perch boss. They were very well made but a little wider than a conventional dropped axle.

The one-year-only 1937 Ford axle was a hollow forging that was slightly flattened through the middle and had 2¼-inch spring perch bosses.

dropped tube axles with cast ends welded to a center tube. That enterprise lasted only about a decade, and brand-new dropped axles were not available again until the mid-1970s, when Jim Ewing started the Super Bell Axe Co. Ewing made his axles in the same way with cast ends welded to a central tube section with a nice smile. The market blossomed, and soon new cast or forged I-beams also became available. The only real difference between the two is that a forged I-beam, like an original Ford axle, will twist a little and perhaps be a little more forgiving than the more rigid tube axle.

There are thousands of axles out there today in almost every imaginable drop, finish, condition, and width. Be careful of what you buy, be sure to check for straightness, and test the boss with a kingpin if you can. If it doesn't fit, there will be some work to do.

Anti-Roll/Sway Bar

As described elsewhere, an anti-roll or anti-sway bar will help stabilize your car, but it might be overkill and clutter up a nice, clean

Jay fitted an aftermarket front sway-bar kit to James Jard's 1936 Coupe. It was mounted ahead of the spring (more or less in the same location as the later stock Ford sway bars).

FRAME, CHASSIS, STEERING, AND SUSPENSION

You can see the linkage of the front torsion bar behind the shock on Jim Busby's road racing 1932 coupe. It's overkill unless you're serious. Notice the fabbed tube shock mounts.

Some traditional-style batwings were designed for clevises. On the left is a vintage fabbed batwing, and on the right is one fabbed from a wishbone end and steel plate by Matt Bryant.

front end on a lightweight rod. Ford introduced a front stabilizer bar in 1940 on some models, so they're nothing new. Front sway-bar kits are available from companies such as SO-CAL.

Batwings

Batwings act as the anchor between the radius rods and axle. However, if you use spilt wishbones, the batwing is built in to the wishbone. If you choose to go with aftermarket radius rods, you have a choice of batwings because there are numerous on the market in steel or stainless steel, fabricated or cast to accept clevises, heim joints, or rod ends. Over the years, batwings have become more versatile and some include lower shock mounts and Panhard bar brackets. They are available from numerous companies, such as Pete and Jake's.

Panhard Bar

A Panhard bar can help prevent lateral movement and your car swinging on the shackles. Typically, a Panhard bar attaches to the axle on one side and the frame on the other. However, it can attach at one end to the batwing that is located by the axle. The Panhard bar has to be able to move up and down with the axle and should be as long as possible and move easily with the use of heim joints, bushings, rod ends, or clevises.

On the left, Pete and Jake developed these modernized traditional-investment cast stainless batwings with built-in lower shock mounts and a Panhard bar tab. On the right, polished stainless batwings for rod ends with urethane bushings are shown. They can also have built-in shock and Panhard bar mounts.

HOW TO BUILD AFFORDABLE HOT RODS

CHAPTER 5

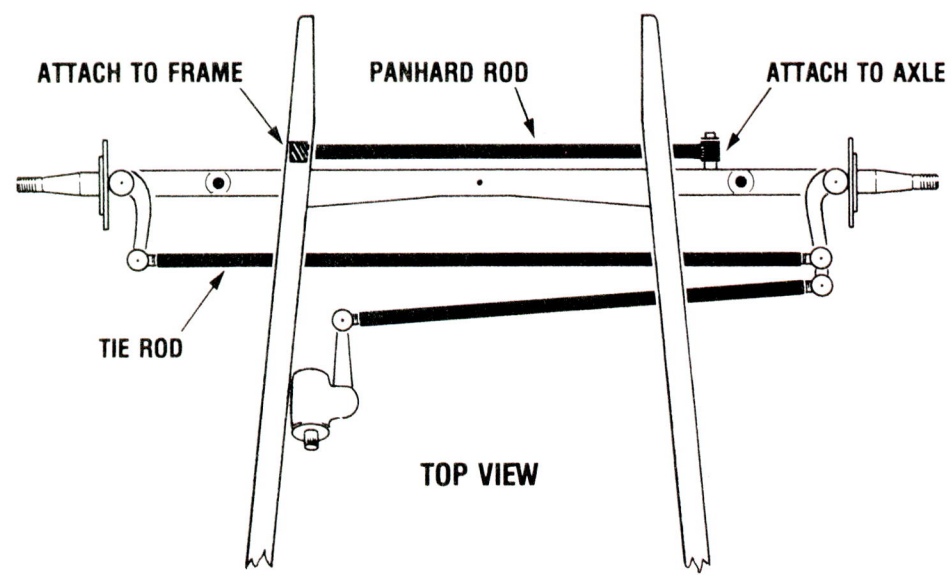

A Panhard bar helps prevent lateral movement by connecting the frame to the axle. The longer the better, and it can mount in front of or behind the axle. (Art Courtesy Pete & Jake's)

This is a typical pre-1935 early Ford split wishbone bolted to the axle. Note that an adjustable spring perch has been mounted to the wishbone behind the axle.

Radius Rods (Hairpins) and Wishbones

Radius rods (often called hairpins because of their shape) are the arms that locate the axle. The simplest approach is to retain the stock Ford un-split wishbone, but not if you plan to lower the car.

The next approach is to split the wishbones and separate them from the central U-shaped casting that locates them in the crossmember under the transmission. Remember that in the stock assembly, the axle moves freely around the ball socket. If you split the wishbones, the axle will not move as freely—possibly a small price to pay. Of course, you can take the split one giant step further and move the wishbones all the way out to the chassis rails.

Obviously, as you separate the wishbones, you put them in bind because they are no longer able to pivot about that central point. However, the more flex you build in to the mounting, the less it will be noticeable—that is, if you use urethane bushings rather than other types of rigid rod ends such as a clevis.

This is the welding table of Matt Bryant, where he's about to begin the fabrication of some split front wishbones, including welding in the plugs for the tie rod ends.

HOW TO BUILD AFFORDABLE HOT RODS

FRAME, CHASSIS, STEERING, AND SUSPENSION

Another reason for a dry build, especially when you're trying something new, is to make sure steering parts interconnect as they should. For example, look at the clearance in the wishbone for the tie rod on this Walden front end.

A similar split wishbone is on the front of Mike Williams's Model A pickup. Stay tuned for the fabrication of the brackets.

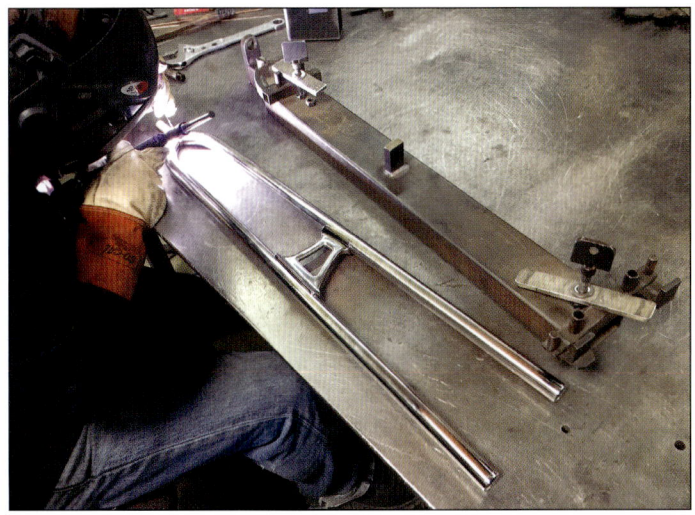

Greg Hirota at SO-CAL Speed Shop welds a hairpin radius rod complete with a neat gusset in the middle. It's one way of decorating and individualizing a hairpin.

Here's another hairpin gusset that is perhaps a little more traditional and simple in appearance. It has that early Ford-style tie rod end with leather wrap.

Brackets for the rear end of the radius rods or the wishbone need to be purchased or fabricated. Matt and Jay first mocked them up with cardboard.

HOW TO BUILD AFFORDABLE HOT RODS

CHAPTER 5

Shackles

Shackles enable the swing action between the spring and the spring perch. They are available in a number of styles from traditional to modern in steel and stainless steel, and most are now fitted with urethane bushings.

Dan Clare fashioned these friction shocks from found parts, made parts, and Model A shock links for a very vintage look.

Troy Ladd of Hollywood Hot Rods installed these British-made Andre Hartford friction shocks on the rear of Pat Gauntt's coupe. They could also be used on the front.

These traditional-looking, cadmium-plated steel front shackles are available from SO-CAL and feature centerless ground steel pins.

Jim "Jake" Jacobs used these original Ford Houdaille front friction shocks on his Model A roadster. You can't get more traditional than this.

Most rodders go for tubular shocks mounted on traditional-style brackets. Most often, they are engineered and styled after the S-shaped Ford F1 shock bolted to the frame.

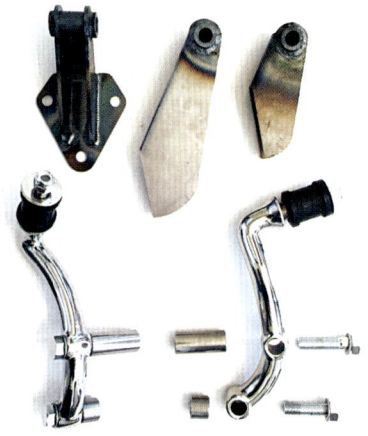
The hot rod parts industry has a number of upper shock mounts available in a variety of sizes and styles from bolt- and weld-on to the polished stainless F1 style.

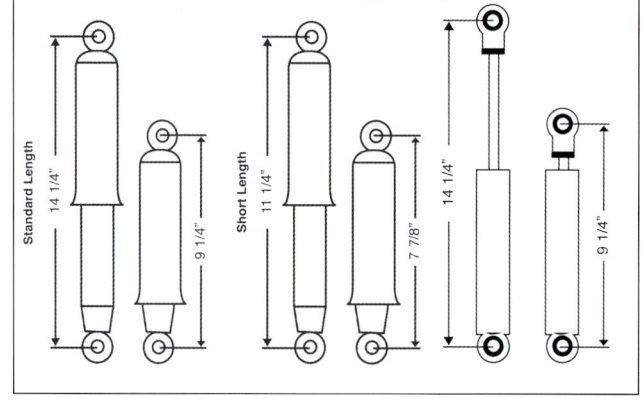

Tubular shocks of various lengths, both covered (shown left) and uncovered with exposed upper shafts are available from many suppliers. Make sure you buy the right shocks for your application. You can always use an old pair for mock-up until you have the correct measurements. (Art Courtesy Pete & Jake's)

Shocks and Shock Mounts

Ford didn't make the switch to tubular shocks until 1948. All early Fords were fitted with lever arm hydraulic dampers made predominantly by the Houdaille Co. However, unless you're really stuck in the past and want that look, I'd recommend tubular shocks. With that being said, Troy Ladd located some British Andre Hartford oil-assisted friction shocks that he used on Pat Gauntt's coupe.

FRAME, CHASSIS, STEERING, AND SUSPENSION

Tapering Steering Arms

This Deuce frame was destined for tubular shocks up front, so Jay had to weld bungs in the frame and fab a lower shock mount. You can see that the Dodge shock brackets were out of alignment with the shocks.

Jay fabricated a traditional-style lower shock mount that was tacked to the axle. It was finish welded once everything was in place and tested to work correctly.

Threaded bungs were welded into the frame so that the lower part of the shock mount had something sturdy to bolt on to.

Although it's still glowing, you can see that Jay successfully bent the Dodge shock bracket to align with the shock. Obviously, you have to get both sides the same.

If you are extremely crafty, you could fashion your own upper shock mount, such as this piece made by Matt Bryant and spotted at Walden Speed Shop.

Springs and Spring Perches

There are any number of new and used springs out there. While those original Ford springs are tough, they are almost 100 years old and may have had a rough life. A new spring from a company such as Posies might be the way to go, depending upon where you started. You must be careful to match the spring to the perches, shackles, and axle. You don't want the main leaf to be so long that the shackles hit the perches or the spring bottoms out on the axle. Springs are usually available in various widths, and you want the shackles to hang at 30 to 45 degrees from horizontal when the springs are loaded.

HOW TO BUILD AFFORDABLE HOT RODS

CHAPTER 5

		SPRING WIDTH	PERCH/ HANGER	SPRING EYE
MODEL T	REAR	2''	3/4''	3/4''
'28 - '31 MODEL A FORD	FRONT	1-3/4''	11/16''	11/16''
	FRONT	1-3/4''	11/16''	3/4''*
	FRONT	1-3/4''	3/4''*	3/4''*
	REAR	2-1/4''	3/4''	3/4''
'32 - '34 FORD	FRONT	1-3/4''	3/4''	3/4''*
	FRONT	1-3/4''	3/4''	7/8''
	REAR	2-1/4''	3/4''	7/8''
'35 - '41 FORD	FRONT	2''	3/4''	3/4''
	REAR	2-1/4''	3/4''	3/4''

As you can see from this spring chart supplied by Pete & Jake's, most early Fords had similar-sized springs made from chrome alloy steel.

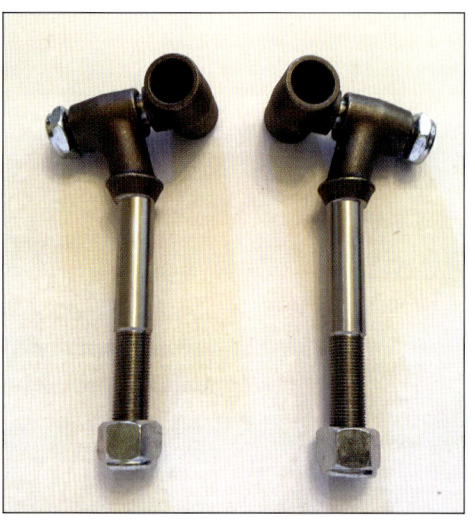

Adjustable spring perches can be extremely helpful when you try to set the caster and find that the front crossmember is not at the correct angle.

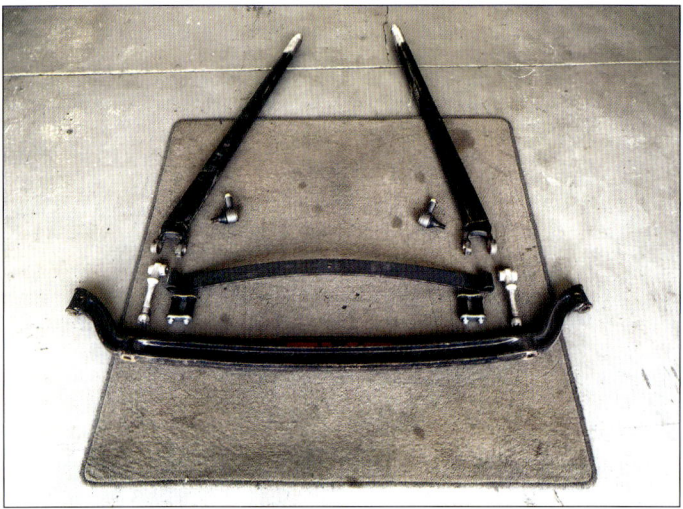

A typical hot rod front end now has a drilled dropped axle and a reversed-eye main leaf, where the eyes roll up rather than down and the spring arch is much flatter.

There's nothing wrong with going for coilovers up front, especially if you're drag racing your Model A coupe like Debbie Davis's Estranged.

You can see the work that Jay puts into shaping and making an original spring look good and slide properly. Note that the shackle is not loaded at this time.

Steering Arms

Pre-1936 Ford spindles had the steering arms cast into the spindle. They are perfect for many applications, but depending on the amount you lower your car, you will probably have to heat and bend the steering arms to clear the wishbones or radius rods. Thankfully, the arms are forged steel and will tolerate the heating and bending process.

From 1937 on, Ford made the steering arms bolt on, which gives the builder more options when it comes to aftermarket bolt-on steering arms.

56   HOW TO BUILD AFFORDABLE HOT RODS

This style of steering arms is designed to bolt on to the 1937–1948 Ford spindles. They are available in polished and unpolished stainless and regular steel from many suppliers in regular and deep drop forms. These arms are often bolted to the spindle with a blind hole, but the through bolt shown is preferable unless you are very careful to make sure the bolt is of adequate length. The hole is well tapped to the bottom, and Loctite is used for security. Be careful when buying components on the internet where the description is obviously wrong and the listing says, "Photo might not be actual product." Really?

Early Ford spindles had the steering arms cast in. You might have to heat and bend the arms to clear other suspension components. They also had the tie-rod end bolt up from the bottom, and you might also have to reverse that for clearance.

For the tie-rod end to bolt in from the top, you will need to taper the hole from the top (but only halfway).

With the top of the steering arm tapered, the tie rod can now be inserted from the top rather than the bottom. As always, test it before you drive it.

Here, the tie rod remains bolted up from the bottom, but note how the steering arm had to be heated and bent to clear the dropped axle.

Note that with some axles (such as the one shown here) the dropped steering arm was too short and interfered with the axle end, so a new, longer arm had to be made.

CHAPTER 5

You can clearly see the aluminum mounting blocks for this steering damper installed in the famed Winged Express AA/Fuel Altered drag car.

The Kennedy brothers favor early Ford worm-and-sector steering from the box through the drag link to the spindle. It works but it can be improved upon.

Steering Damper/Stabilizer

A steering damper can help improve your steering smoothness and eliminate bump steer and shimmy. They are available painted or chrome from a number of suppliers. They should be mounted between the radius rod or wishbone and the steering tie rod. Be sure to test their travel before you go out on the road to make certain that the damper does not restrict steering movement.

Tie Rod and Drag Link

The tie rod does as it says; it ties the two steering arms together. The drag link ties the steering arm to the pitman arm. Early Fords typically have conventional steering with a pitman arm and a drag link connected to the driver-side steering arm. The tie rod then runs across the car to the other spindle. It works fine but can be improved upon. Incidentally, Ford shifted from the drag link to cross steering in 1935.

In the 1970s, rodders discovered the Chevy Vega cross-steering box that helped eliminate some of the Ford's weak points. It's available with a ratio of 20:1 or a Flaming River 16:1.

A typical Vega cross-steering setup on Mick Jenkins's roadster shows the Vega box to the right of the engine, forward-facing pitman arm, plastic-wrapped drag link, and tie rod. Note that Mick's shock mounts double as headlight mounts.

Mike Williams's Build

Mike Williams's intention was to combine two of his dream trucks into one build: Pete Faruga's 1929 Model A pickup and Dean Lowe's 1929 that appeared on the cover of *Hot Rod* magazine in January 1962. Trying

This is a nice-looking tie rod and drag link assembly. However, I'd be concerned about those short studs securing the tie-rod ends. Short self-locking nuts or castellated nuts are preferable, but this may be a mock-up only.

to recreate one vehicle is tough, and trying to combine two is almost too much, especially when you don't have a great reference and you want to go drag racing.

Unfortunately, Faruga had sold his original chassis, and the Lowe truck was in the UK. Consequently, Mike sourced a Model A chassis and shipped it to the Kennedys who intended to replicate the Lowe chassis.

FRAME, CHASSIS, STEERING, AND SUSPENSION

Mike Williams's Model A Frame

Mike Williams's project began with this truck found for him by his lifelong friend David Steele, executive director of the American Hot Rod Foundation. The truck already had a flathead V-8, but there was lots of work ahead for the Kennedy brothers.

Prep work has begun. Notice how the front crossmember has quite a droop to it. That will be leveled out by raising the spring mount and lowering the car.

Matt began by tacking box section steel tube to the frame rails as a fixture to hold it all in place. Notice how the instructions are marked on the frame so that Matt remembers what he's supposed to do.

Matt center-punches the rivet head before drilling the rivets out. Thankfully, early Ford frames were riveted and not welded together, and those rivets are not too tough.

Once all the rivets had been drilled out, Matt was able to remove the crossmember by tapping it toward the rear of the chassis.

Matt used an air-powered cut-off wheel to trim the aftermarket front crossmember because it was a little oversized. You could also use an angle grinder.

HOW TO BUILD AFFORDABLE HOT RODS

With the frame rails level, the front crossmember should be about 9 degrees negative because you are eventually going to angle or rake the frame 3 to 4 degrees to give you an optimum 5 degrees of caster.

Matt has given the rear of the frame a 3-inch kick-up to help lower the rear. He has also installed a boxing gusset plate on the inside to give the kick-up strength.

The transition from the stepped-in boxing plate to the kick-up is cleanly done and will be hardly noticeable under the back unless you look for it.

Once the majority of the basic frame welding was complete, the frame was set up on axle stands at the correct angle.

Once the frame had been set up at the correct angle and ride height, the major mechanical components (such as the quick-change rear axle) could be set in place.

The next stage was to drop in a mock-up block and transmission. At this stage, front engine mounts had been made, and the central K-member had been mocked up.

The engine was set at 5 degrees using a magnetic angle locator and a level set across the block.

FRAME, CHASSIS, STEERING, AND SUSPENSION

It's a little rough around the edges, but this is an original Hurst engine mount that bolts to the front of the block and uses stock 1932 Ford-style biscuit engine mounts.

The tubular K-member comprises of a narrowed, off-the-shelf 1¾-inch SO-CAL crossmember and two forward-facing legs made of similarly sized steel tube. Jay likes these tubes to run parallel to the centerline so that they are easier to drill.

Wooden blocks were used to support the rear of the transmission case while the transmission mount was fabricated.

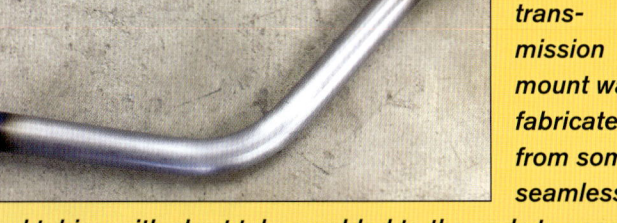

This smiling transmission mount was fabricated from some seamless steel tubing with short tubes welded to the ends to accept standard, rod-end urethane bushings.

The bent tube was offered up under the transmission just to make sure that it was correctly shaped and to see where the mounting tabs would fall.

Tabs from where the transmission mount hangs can be found in many hardware stores and online. The bracket to hold the transmission mount was fabricated from 1/4-inch plate.

61

CHAPTER 5

Rear Radius Rods

Traditional-style split rear radius rods were made from 1940 Ford tubes and 1937–1948 ends. The weld-in bungs are available from companies such as Rod End Supply.

These are the three components of the rear end of the wishbone. From left to right are the 1940 Ford wishbone, the plug, and the 1937–1948 forged steel bracket.

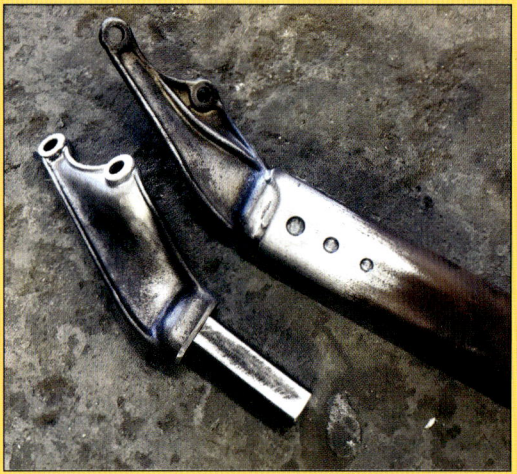

This is a close-up of the axle ends of the radius rods. Matt sleeved the joint between the cast ends and the wishbone legs, and then he drilled holes in the legs for rosette security welds.

The front end of the wishbone had a weld-in, threaded bung welded in the end. Be thoughtful when you order these online because some have very suspect, loose threads.

Crescent-shaped brackets for the rear end of the wishbone were made from 3/8-inch steel plate that will be welded to the rear axle.

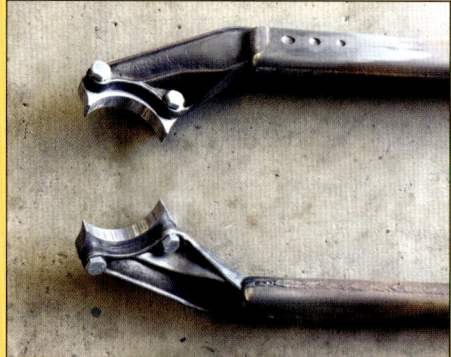

The wishbones are ready to install. Notice the three rosette welds in the wishbone. The bones were drilled through to the plug and welded for security.

For now, the wishbone adapter brackets are tacked securely to the axle ends until the rest of the chassis work is complete because adjustments may need to be made.

Rear Springs

Initially, Mike and Jay's thoughts were to use a 2¼-inch-wide Model A spring, but the size of the Winters quick-change meant that it was not possible. A decision was made to go with SO-CAL coilover shocks mounted ahead of the rear axle. They provide a great, adjustable ride and are unobtrusive when mounted in front of the axle.

After they decided to ditch the leaf spring and go for coilovers, Matt and Jay offer up a SO-CAL coilover to see how it will look and figure out the mounting points.

The upper shock mounts were fabbed from steel plate with studs turned on the lathe. Note how the bracket was contoured to snugly fit the Model A crossmember.

Matt fabbed the lower shock mounts from some steel plate, and the shock studs were machined on the lathe. They were then welded to the wishbones.

The SO-CAL coilover shock was offered up. Nothing was finish welded until everything had been mocked up and checked.

CHAPTER 5

Finishing Up

At this stage, the frame was almost complete in that the major components have all been either welded or tacked into position. Matt just needs to weld it up.

Something not shown in this sequence but added later was a driveshaft safety loop, which is essential if you are running an open driveshaft.

It's not quite finished, but Mike's Model A is coming along with most of the major components from engine to cab mocked into place. There's still plenty to do though.

A Tale of Two Trucks

By Mike Williams

As far back as I remember, the bulletin board in my dad's shop had a Polaroid of the Chevy-powered 1929 Model A pickup that was the fastest car in town when he moved there in 1958 at age 15. It was built by Stan "Pete" Faruga, class of 1955, who still owns it today. The photo was taken in November 1961 when they were on their way to the Niagara Falls airport drag strip. I've never met Pete, but I called him after losing my dad in 2013, and I was nostalgic for stories. Pete told me he'd taken the truck apart to put a modern chassis under it with a crate engine. When I told Dave Steele, my friend since eighth grade, he shot back, "Buy his old frame and engine, and we'll just rebody it!"

Now, I love early Super Stocks (1962 is the pinnacle for me), but I'd been wanting a late 1950s/early 1960s hot rod, something Dad never had. I kept seeing the picture of Faruga's pickup, painted in our high school colors. I pitched Dave's idea to Pete, but he'd already sold the old chassis and drivetrain. Nevertheless, when Dave and I were looking at some hot rod, we'd often remark, " . . . but it's no Faruga pickup."

When Dave called in the summer of 2018 to say that a friend's neighbor was selling a stock, rust-free 1929 Model A pickup for a bargain price, I said, "Okay, buy it and call the Kennedy brothers." We often said that I could just hand Dad's Polaroid to the Kennedys and tell them, "Call me when it's ready." They'd understand completely. While the plan was to recreate the truck's 1961 external appearance, the mechanical inspiration also came from Dean Lowe's red truck that was on the cover of the January 1962 *Hot Rod* magazine and was the 1962 NHRA Winternationals B/Street Roadster-winning RPU. A Lowe family friend, the legendary Frank Kurtis, built the chassis and torque-arm rear suspension.

Soon after the build was done, Dean and his father realized that the roadster's 265 Chevy wouldn't cut it at the drags. They took the advice of another friend, "Dyno" Don Nicholson, and ordered a new 315-hp 283. With a Corvette dual-quad setup from Ak Miller, the crate engine with a T-10 4-speed and 4.46 gears produced 12.30 ETs at 110 mph. The Kurtis chassis allowed high-RPM launches even on the era's pie-crust slicks. I wanted to replicate that same chassis/driveline combo in my pickup. For its national record-setting run of 11.77 at the 1962 Winternationals, Dean had the heads milled and ported by Jocko Johnson, Rochester fuel injection, an Isky 505-B roller cam, and 5.30 gears. However, I wanted something more street-friendly and faithful to Faruga's experience—at least that was the plan.

Dave quickly sourced a standard-bore 1958 short-block and a pair of double-hump cylinder heads from Chris Wickersham. The parts were dropped off at Blair's Speed Shop for proprietor Phil Lukens to replicate a snappy, dual-quad, solid-lifter, over-bored 283 circa 1962.

Faruga's 1958 270-hp 283 was punched out to 301 ci with 11.5:1 Jahns pistons and headers but was otherwise stock. I limited my overbore to 0.060 inch for 292 ci but likewise wanted higher-than-stock compression for an authentic experience. However, if I have to add race gas anyway, why not run straight race gas? Phil happily ordered custom Ross pistons that yielded 12:1 compression with the fuelie heads. Since I was already cheating with the heads compared to Faruga's stock Power Packs, we also sent them to Las Vegas for some porting by Bob Morgan, along with 2.02/1.60 valves. I ordered the stock 097 Duntov cam (Dad loved them), but when it arrived at Blair's, I got a call from Phil. He asked if I knew that it was only 0.395-inch lift and 270 duration, why I bothered porting the heads, and if I realized that we wouldn't be able to run any timing with that cam and 12:1 compression.

I reminded him that this project was about creating an authentic circa-1962 experience and that even 270 hp would be plenty for a Model A. However, the thought of leaving so much power on the table had already gnawed at me, so I relented saying, "I'll run a bigger cam as long as it's an old-school name." Phil likes Engle, so we compromised with a 0.520-inch-lift/288-duration solid-lifter grind, which he further augmented by massaging 1.6:1 roller rockers to fit under the Corvette valve covers for 0.555-inch lift. When I asked if he was sure it had enough low end for Connecticut's twisty, hilly, 25-mph back roads, he exclaimed, "In a Model A? Just let the clutch out, and it'll drive away!"

WCFB four-barrels were sourced from Phil Cancilla, who provided the higher-flowing but still correct-appearing

CHAPTER 5

models used on 250-hp 327 and 348 Chevys. Although they were restored to new specifications, I had them shipped directly to Jimmy Bridges in Nashville, another friend of Dave's who's been winning NHRA races since 1958 and still runs an 8-second SS/B 427 Corvette. He calibrated the carburetors for my engine and provided and rebuilt the 1962 Corvette dual-point distributor.

I ruled out the 1948 Ford 3-speed transmission that Faruga ran (he would hang its broken Zephyr gears from the rearview mirror) and only briefly flirted with the idea of a LaSalle 3-speed before I sourced an aluminum T-10 from Jim Jard. When Faruga's transmission didn't break, the axles in his Columbia 2-speed banjo rear end often did, so I nixed that in favor of a quick-change rear like Lowe. Unwilling to risk scattering a new Winters unit with a clutch dump on a sticky track, I went with the 10-inch Champ version with Ford-style tubes and bells. The fast-revving little Chevy will love the 5.15 ratio at the drags, and my ears will love the 3.30 ratio for the 112-mile drive home.

One of Dad's best friends, Bob Skora of Skora Automotive in Eden, lived near Faruga as a kid and remembers how they'd all jump on their bikes when they heard him start the pickup and hope he'd do a burnout. Bob provided paint to match the look of the 1957 Cadillac Castile Maroon in the photo of the 1929 in the pits at Niagara.

And that, as they say, is all she wrote. At the time this book went to print, the Kennedy brothers were still working away on my truck. I'm hoping for a 2020 completion because my late dad and I are just itching to get on down the road. ■

Visual inspiration for Mike Williams's pickup came from his local hero Stan "Pete" Faruga. It was the fastest car in town in 1958 and was painted 1957 Cadillac Castile Maroon, as seen in this photo of the 1929 in the pits at the Niagara Falls Airport drag strip. (Photo Courtesy Mike Williams)

Mechanical inspiration came from Dean Lowe's January 1962 Hot Rod *magazine cover car that won the B/Street Roadster class at the 1962 Winternationals. At the time, it was powered by a 283 with a Corvette dual-quad setup from Ak Miller and a T-10 4-speed. The truck is now owned by Stephen Hill and is seen here at the Pendine Sands Hot Rod Drags. (Photo Courtesy Keith Harman)*

FRAME, CHASSIS, STEERING, AND SUSPENSION

Dick Wade's 1932 Frame

Perhaps no frame has been rodded or duplicated more than a 1932 Ford, and like the proverbial cat, there are as many ways to skin it.

In the case of Dick Wade's 1932 3-window, it's a simple solution to the age-old problem. Matt Bryant's first task was to remove the original K-member and partially step-box the rails in sections: one from the front crossmember back to the firewall, small sections for mounting the tubular K-member, and in the rear over the kick-up. These boxing plates were made in a U-section and inserted into the rail and rosette welded along the flange. It's a different way of doing the boxing that negates the need to weld the whole seam.

Once the boxing plates were installed, the front crossmember was sectioned 1½ inches by Jay to raise the spring and lower the car. You can buy stamped-steel front crossmembers that are already lowered 1 inch. Beware: we have encountered aftermarket crossmembers that are fatter through the middle and therefore have to be adjusted for the factory spring-mounted U-bolts to be used. It's a simple fix but something else that needs to be addressed.

In the center, the K-member consists of a SO-CAL 5-inch dropped ladder bar crossmember and a pair of dog-leg tubes welded between the crossmember and the boxing plates. Jay prefers to run the K-legs parallel to the centerline because he finds it easier to drill them when they are parallel. The K-member is fitted with slotted transmission mounting brackets and the tabs for the rear ladder bars. There's also bracketry for the pedal and master cylinder assembly.

Moving to the rear, the stock crossmember was replaced with a Model T crossmember that affords clearance for the axle. Note that you never quite know how a spring (old or new) is going to sit until you get weight on it. Springs rarely fall exactly where you want them to, and that fact reinforces the need to perform a dry build before you tear the car apart for finishing. In the case of Mike Williams's truck, it was found that a transverse leaf spring wouldn't work and coilover shocks had to be used.

Jay was already well into Dick Wade's 1932 3-window when I came around. You can see here that the frame is boxed, and the K-member is in.

The top surface of the original factory crossmember was cut out and raised 1½ inches to lower the front. Aftermarket crossmembers that are lowered 1 inch are available, but beware that some are too wide to accept the factory U-bolts that secure the spring. The stock engine mounts were retained.

HOW TO BUILD AFFORDABLE HOT RODS

CHAPTER 5

Matt Bryant step-boxed the stock frame using his method of folding U-sections of steel and pushing them into the stock rails. The boxing plates are then spot welded along their length rather than seam welded.

The K-member is made up of a SO-CAL 5-inch dropped ladder bar crossmember complete with tabs for the rear ladder bars. Jay made up his own K-legs that run parallel to the centerline and have long, slotted adjustable transmission mounts and a master cylinder mount on the driver's side.

The first mock-up front end for Dick's Deuce was this dropped I-beam assembly fitted with a reverse-eye spring and a pair of fabricated batwings for the hairpins.

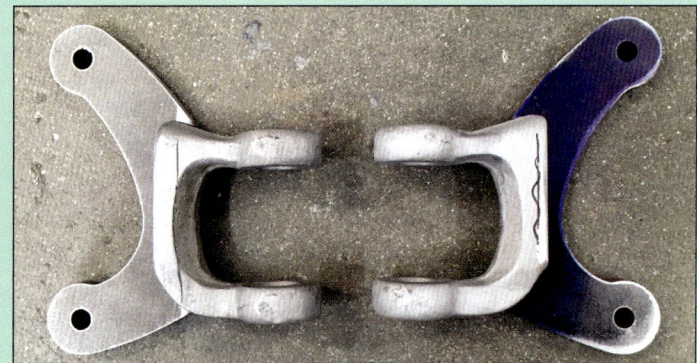

Matt fabbed these simple batwings from some forged steel 1932 Ford wishbone ends and some Jitney Jake Jacobs batwings.

Clevises were attached to the batwings, and the modified SO-CAL hairpins were offered up just to see how it would all look. It's always good to mock things up first.

The modified hairpins look excellent mocked up and will certainly enhance Dick's Deuce. There's nothing wrong with adding a bit of individuality to your ride.

FRAME, CHASSIS, STEERING, AND SUSPENSION

Matt slipped the front end under the frame and got ready to work on the steering and a front spreader bar.

The first task was to try the kingpin in the axle boss. Remember, any old axle is probably 50-plus years old and might not be in the best of shape.

The store-bought hairpin-style steering arms were a couple inches short because the cast ends of the Okie Adams axle are wider than a regular dropped axle.

As a consequence of the wider axle end, Matt fabricated a new through-stud hairpin steering arm (complete with a strengthening gusset).

The Rear

With the front of Dick Wade's 1932 3-window more-or-less sewn up, Jay turned his attention to the rear, where he intended to take a slightly different approach to a traditional assembly by combining the attributes of a stock-based wishbone with the added strength of a ladder bar.

Knowing the early Fords and having a stash of parts are a huge help, and Jay has both knowledge and stuff. He dove into his stash and came up with a solution that used 1937–1940 Ford axle bells and 1935–1936 wishbones that he craftily turned into ladder bars with the addition of a bolt-on top tube secured by clevises.

In the rear, Jay fitted a Model T crossmember and used a Model T leaf spring to clear the center section. In this shot, the spring has a stock eye and does not have a reversed eye that can be used to further lower the car if necessary.

HOW TO BUILD AFFORDABLE HOT RODS

CHAPTER 5

From the stash Jay selected two different wishbones from which he would fabricate the new ladder bar assemblies. The top wishbone with the spring hanger is 1937–1940 and the lower one without it is 1935–1936.

Jay used 1937–1940 Ford axle bells because their spring hangers are conveniently located and won't interfere with other chassis parts during axle travel.

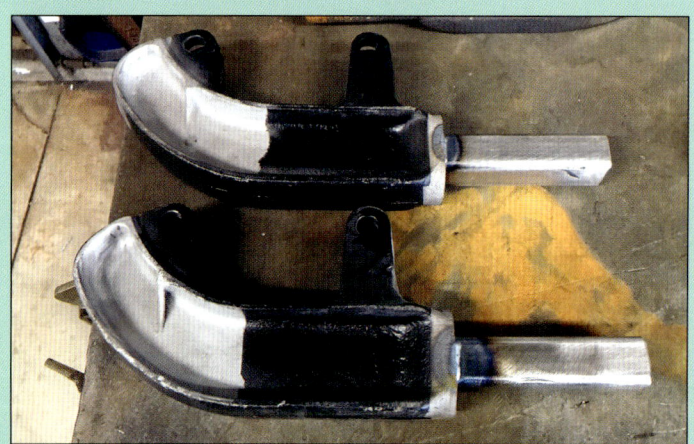

The rear ladder bars were fabricated by using 1935–1936 Ford wishbone ends that were separated from their legs and had their shock mounts removed and ends reshaped.

A cardboard template was used to fabricate these brackets that were welded to the axle bells. Similar axle brackets are available on the internet from companies such as Queen City Fab.

The back end of the wishbones was cut to length and fitted with a weld-in bung. Note the hole in the wishbone for a securing weld and Pete and Jake's urethane bushings.

Jay used 1937–1940 Ford axle bells because their spring hangers are conveniently located and won't interfere with other chassis parts during axle travel. Note the new wishbone brackets.

70 HOW TO BUILD AFFORDABLE HOT RODS

FRAME, CHASSIS, STEERING, AND SUSPENSION

The wishbones have been installed but note the clevises mounted on the upper parts of the crescent-shaped bracket on the axle bell.

Jay fabricated the lower shock mount and welded it to the forged steel end of the wishbone. Remember, that Ford material is great to weld.

The upper shock mounts were made simply by using steel tabs and a threaded bung that was welded to the original Model T crossmember.

Jay decided to turn the wishbones into ladder bars and fabricated support gussets using some steel plate and steel tube.

A close-up of the axle end of the assembly with the shocks mounted and the gusset bolted to the wishbone using an existing hole that is there for the original Ford brake mechanism.

CHAPTER 5

The front end of the ladder bars meet as close together as possible in the middle of the car (as they would have in the original Ford configuration).

The completed radius rod and wishbone assembly looks and works great. It has a very traditional appearance true to the era.

A lot has been accomplished on Dick Wade's 1932 3-window, but there's still some way to go before it can be wrapped up. It's looking tough though.

FRAME, CHASSIS, STEERING, AND SUSPENSION

James Jard's 1936 3-Window

James Jard's 1936 was rodded when it came to the Kennedys' shop, but it needed to be freshened up. The front end was lowered with a 4-inch-drop Super Bell axle and had split wishbones, early Ford steering, and a 1941 Lincoln brake conversion for 1935–1936 spindles from Boling Brothers.

The powertrain was comprised of an aluminum headed Ross Racing 371-ci Oldsmobile Rocket punched out to 393 ci and mated to a Tremec 5-speed with a Ross adapter. Out back was a Ford 8-inch located by four-bar links with clevises at the front and urethane-bushed rod ends in back. The suspension was comprised of a stock leaf spring with conventional shocks.

Jay's worksheet included lowering the back end, removing the four-bar clevises, and a general tidy up. He tidied everything up in the front and installed new steering arms, an anti-sway bar, new shocks, and new brakes. Meanwhile, Joe rewired and repainted the whole car.

Ultimately, James's 1936 was better looking, better handling, better going, and better stopping. Therefore, it was a safer and better-driving hot rod.

James Jard's 1936 3-window is shown just before the body, which had some repairs to the doors and fenders, was removed for Jay to begin the frame work and Joe to begin the paintwork.

With the body removed, you can see that the X-member is virtually stock. However, note that the front wishbones have been split, and the Ross Oldsmobile engine is backed up by a Ross adapter and a 5-speed Tremec.

Jay began by cleaning up all the unnecessary lumps and bumps that will not be needed. Note that the front shocks were mounted on the lower spring shackle.

HOW TO BUILD AFFORDABLE HOT RODS

CHAPTER 5

Front End

The front end of James's 1936 had the stock wishbones slightly split and therefore the spring hangers had been heated and bent to realign with the stock spring and front crossmember. The front shocks were mounted on studs through the lower shackles, which was okay-ish. The existing steering arms were changed out for some steel, deep-drop, bolt-through SO-CAL steering arms with new tie rods and a new drag link. It all worked, but it could be improved.

This SO-CAL anti-sway bar kit that Jay modified to fit was new. It mimics the stock Ford anti-sway bar that was installed as standard on some Fords from 1940 onward.

The front suspension was more-or-less stock, but you can see that the stock wishbones had been split and the spring hangers had been adjusted to realign with the spring.

Having relieved the top of the stock spindle, the new backing plate was now able to fit snugly against the spindle face.

Partway into the process, Jay has installed new shackles and new steel, deep-drop, bolt-through SO-CAL steering arms with a new tie rod and tie-rods ends.

74   HOW TO BUILD AFFORDABLE HOT RODS

FRAME, CHASSIS, STEERING, AND SUSPENSION

Rear End

The rear end of James's 1936 was half-rodded in that it had been fitted with an 8-inch Ford axle located with four-bar links. However, they had heim joints at the front and urethane-bushed rod ends at the rear. The rear spring was stock, and the car had conventional shocks. The whole thing could be lowered several inches by sectioning the rear crossmember and changing out the clevises, and replacing the worn shocks could improve the ride.

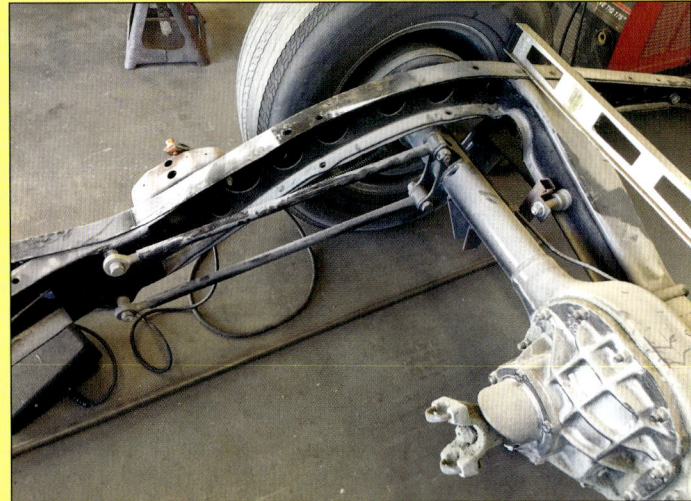

In the rear, James's 1936 had been fitted with an 8-inch Ford axle, four-bar links located at the front with heim joints and with urethane bushed rod ends at the rear. The spring and crossmember were stock, and the car ran conventional shocks.

Some 1-inch square box section tube has been bolted and tack welded to the frame rails to keep them in alignment while the crossmember has been removed.

The rear crossmember on Matt's welding table is about to be seriously sectioned by 4 inches to lower the rear end.

Reinstalled in the frame, the sectioned crossmember will help lower the back of the car by 4 inches. Notice the length of the Panhard bar.

CHAPTER 5

The new brackets bolt to the existing mounting holes that were used to mount the heim joints. Notice that an extra support was added to the center of the brackets.

The new forward brackets for the rear four-bar links are a vast improvement over the old hard-riding heim joints.

The upper rear shock mount is welded to the top surface of the rear crossmember. The lower shock mount has a typical mount that has several mounting holes and SO-CAL shock mounting studs.

This close-up shows how the SO-CAL front anti-sway bar is installed and how the brackets for the links are welded to the front axle.

The pedal assembly shows the use of a 1939–1948 Ford master cylinder and stock pedals. The cylinder has a stop-light switch mounted behind the outlet.

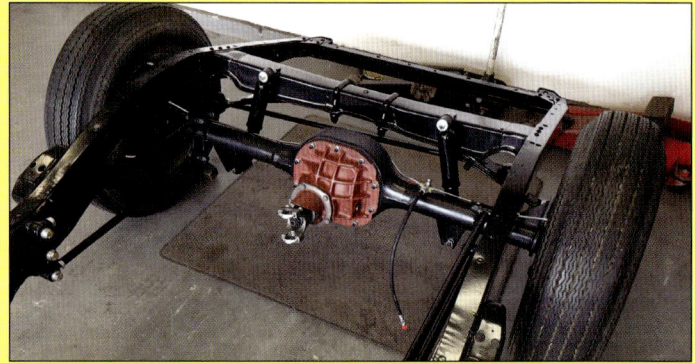

The rear end is much tidier and lower with a sectioned crossmember, new upper mountings for the shocks, new brake lines, and the revised four-bar links.

FRAME, CHASSIS, STEERING, AND SUSPENSION

Jay lowers the Oldsmobile engine and Tremec transmission into the rolling chassis using a large overhead gantry with a load leveler that makes the task easy for one person.

Dropping the engine and transmission into the chassis lowered the front frame horn to 12½ inches, which means the weight of the engine lowered the frame 2½ inches.

The Ross Racing Oldsmobile looks right at home in the refurbished 1936 chassis. With 393 ci, alloy heads, and three Rochester 2Gs on an Offy, it puts out 400 hp and 435 ft-lbs of torque.

Although there is still some work to do, James Jard's 1936 3-window looks a whole lot better than it did when it arrived in Pomona. It will be a great driver.

Torque Arm

Something that Mike Williams wanted that not all chassis builders incorporate was a torque arm/bar similar to the one on Dean Lowe's RPU. Mike found one poor photo of the arm in the 1962 issue of *Hot Rod* magazine, and that was all Matt and Jay had for reference.

A torque arm is particularly beneficial in a chassis with leaf springs or coilovers to help prevent rotation of the rear-end housing during acceleration or deceleration. By controlling pinion rise and axle wrap, the torque arm allows the springs to perform their intended function of supporting the vehicle. It should be noted that the front-most mounting point of the torque arm should be in line with the front mounting points of the wishbones or radius rods—you want it all rotating on the same axis.

In the case of Mike's chassis, Matt used steel tube, a large C-shaped bracket bolted to the quick-change flange, and some clevises to fabricate the torque arm. It's as close to the shape of the Lowe arm as possible.

Most shops have a stack of cardboard handy that can be used for making templates. To paraphrase Lil' John Buttera, "Cut away everything that doesn't look like a bracket."

Once the bracket was finished, it was bolted to the axle housing with new, longer Grade-8 bolts. There's a clevis hanging from the upper part of the bracket.

A phone or an iPad comes in handy when referencing vintage photos or magazines for a build or restoration project. These are photos of Dean Lowe's RPU.

Matt measured his upper and lower tubing lengths. The front end of the torque bar needs to move parallel to the wishbones.

FRAME, CHASSIS, STEERING, AND SUSPENSION

The finished torque bar is as close to the Dean Lowe example as possible given that Matt and Jay only had one poor magazine photograph to go by.

Matt bolted the bracket and the torque arm in place. The front rod end must be in line with the front mounting point of the wishbones, although it doesn't look like it here.

It was decided that the torque bar would be better located using brackets hanging from a tube over the driveshaft rather than being mounted on the transmission crossmember.

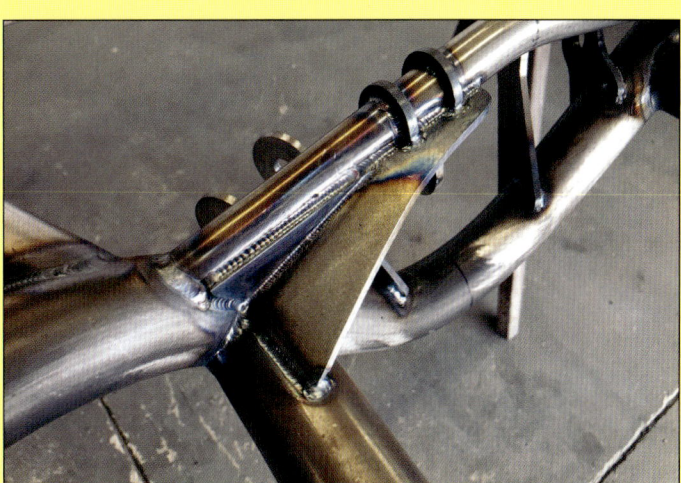

To finish, Matt fashioned a nice gusset plate to support the forward end of the torque bar. It's going to take a lot of force and needs to be secure.

The finished torque arm was painted satin black and installed in Mike Williams's Model A chassis. It's unobtrusive, does the job, and is true to the original.

CHAPTER 5

Torque Tube

Newbies to the rod game might not know what a torque tube is or even what Hotchkiss drive is. They both are means of transmitting drive from the transmission to the rear axle.

Though they were typically found in expensive cars back in his day, Henry Ford favored the torque tube, which is a fixed tube attached to the back of the transmission and the front of the rear axle that contains a small-diameter driveshaft. In "Ford-ese," the tube acted as a radius rod to prevent the axle from rotating up or down when either the power or the brakes were applied. Today, we call it a torque arm or torque bar.

The torque tube is a good device, and the Kennedy brothers use them all the time when they can, but a torque tube can pose a connection problem for some builders when they try to mix and match engines and axles (for example, a GM 4-speed and a Ford axle or a 1939 Ford transmission and a 9-inch Ford).

Let's back up because all torque tubes are not built the same. Ford increased the wheelbase of its cars from the 103.5 inches (the Model A) to 112 inches (the Model 40) to 114 inches (later models). Consequently, the torque tubes get longer, so do some investigating when you make your drivetrain decisions and consider your rear-end setup.

Of course, you can always convert to open drive, and there are several kits on the market from companies such as Flat-o Products and Hot Rod Works. Typically, they are bolt-on kits for 1935–1948 rear ends with a 10-spline pinion. Any modern quick-change will invariably come with an open drive.

Remember, if you convert to open drive, you will have to engineer a way to locate the factory radius rods if you retain them and install a torque bar to replace the torque tube that performed that function. ■

A close-up of the transmission end of the torque tube from the transmission side of the K-member.

This is a close-up of the rear axle end of the 1932 Ford torque tube. The radius rods are bolted to the axle bells, and the spring hangers are incorporated into the flange.

Notice that the wishbones bolt to a bracket on the underside of the torque tube, and the small, gray loop bracket retains the original brake mechanism.

FRAME, CHASSIS, STEERING, AND SUSPENSION

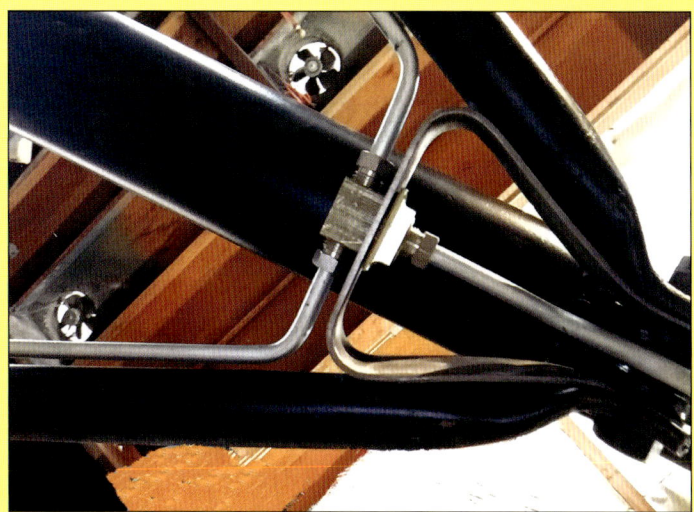

Photographed from the underside, you can see here at Kev's Rod & Custom how the brake line runs under the torque tube and splits into two to go to each rear brake.

Forward of the brake line split there is a bracket and an adapter to convert from a hard line to a flexible line to allow for the movement of the torque tube.

This is what the open drive conversion from Speedway Motors looks like assembled. They say it's a simple bolt-on. (Photo Courtesy Speedway Motors)

If you make the change from torque tube to open drive, you have to find a way to mount the radius rods and install a torque bar to do the job that the torque tube performed.

Chassis, Steering, and Suspension

This section provides key information about components and concepts that are vital to understanding chassis, steering, and suspension systems.

Ackerman

Ackerman steering geometry is the practice of aligning the center of the kingpins, the hole in the steering arms, and an imaginary point at the center of the rear axle. Correct Ackerman prevents your tires from slipping and unnecessary wear. Setting the Ackerman is one of the basic precepts of chassis and steering setup before you go out on the road.

Depending on the components you use to assemble your front end, you might find that your Ackerman is close or not so close. The cure is to heat and bend the steering arms. However, be very careful when doing this. Early Ford steering arms were

HOW TO BUILD AFFORDABLE HOT RODS

CHAPTER 5

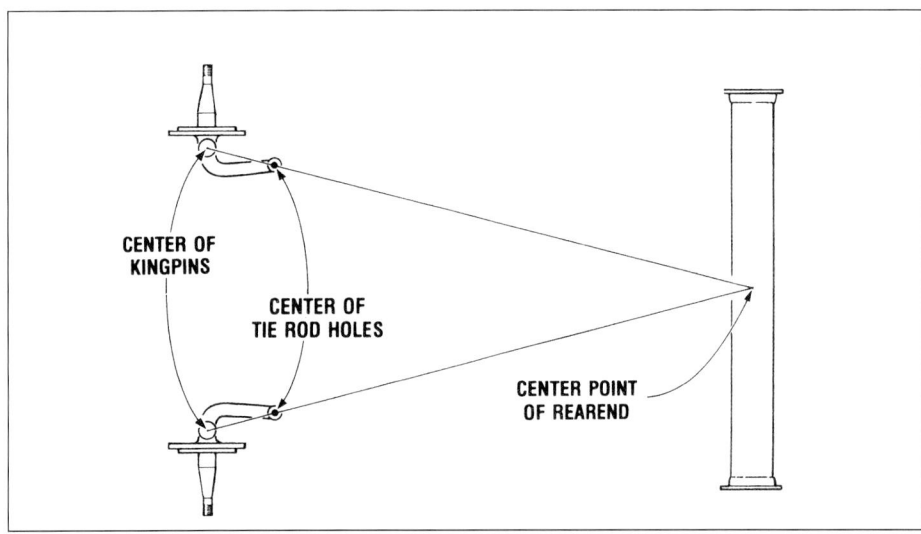

For correct Ackerman, draw an imaginary line through the center of the kingpin, the hole in your steering arms, and intersect at the center of the rear axle. (Art Courtesy Pete & Jake's)

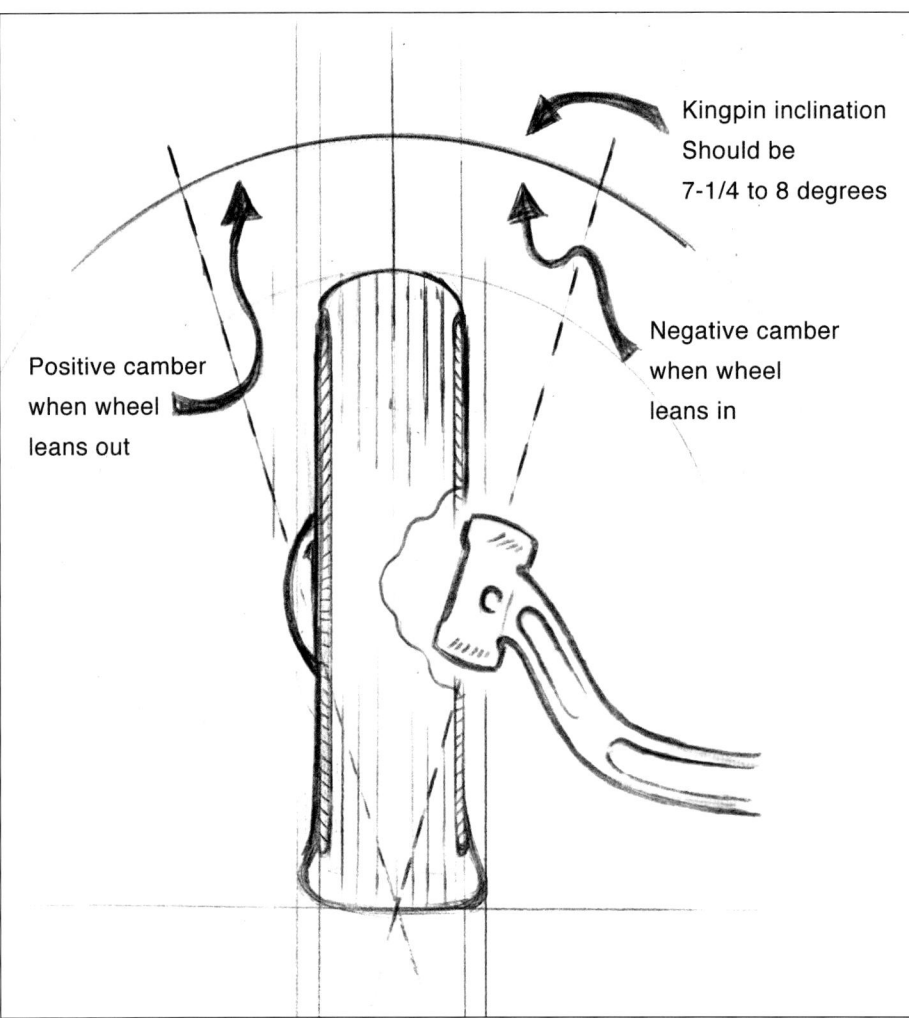

forged steel and can be heated and bent, but unfortunately, some modern arms made of ductile iron cannot be bent.

Camber

Camber is the inward or outward tilt of the wheels. It is measured in degrees from the true vertical when the wheel is viewed from the front. Positive camber is when the top of the wheel leans out; negative camber is when the top of the wheel leans in. Excessive camber causes premature and uneven tire wear. In most rods, the camber should be between zero and 1/2 degree positive. In most cases, the camber is engineered into the axle at the angle where the kingpin hole is machined into the kingpin boss. If your camber is incorrect, a good old-school front-end shop should be able to help.

If you care about all of this, beware when buying an axle (even a new one) to be sure that the kingpin hole is 0.8125 inch. The 1928–1948 Fords all have the same size kingpin. Take a new kingpin with you when you go to buy an axle and make sure that it fits.

Caster

Caster is the backward or forward tilt of the kingpin measured in degrees from true vertical. The rearward tilt of the kingpin is called positive caster, and the forward tilt is negative caster. The angle of caster affects the steering, and positive caster causes

According to Ford literature, the kingpin should be inclined at 7¼ to 8 degrees, and ideally an imaginary line drawn through the center of the kingpin should intersect on the ground with the center of the tire. (Art Courtesy Alex M. Design)

82 HOW TO BUILD AFFORDABLE HOT RODS

FRAME, CHASSIS, STEERING, AND SUSPENSION

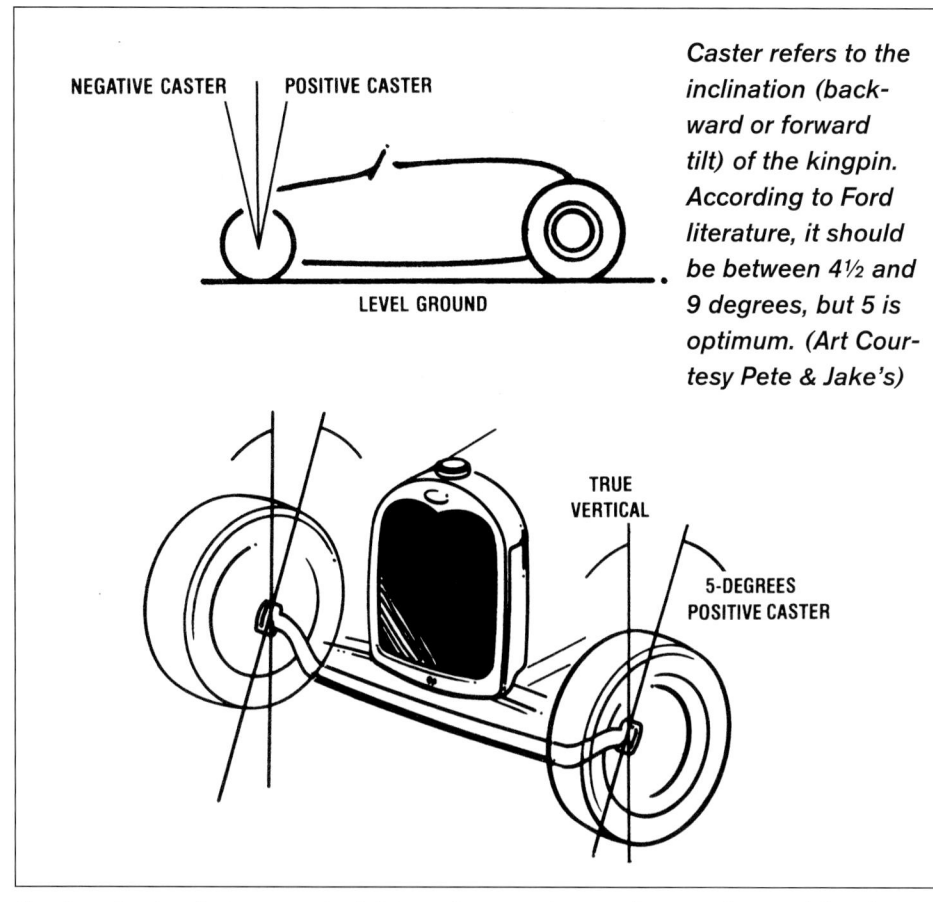

Caster refers to the inclination (backward or forward tilt) of the kingpin. According to Ford literature, it should be between 4½ and 9 degrees, but 5 is optimum. (Art Courtesy Pete & Jake's)

the front wheels to run straight and influences the return-to-center of the steering. Negative caster causes the steering to be touchy and harder to control. Caster can be set by adjusting the radius rods.

Anti-Sway/Roll Bar

Ford introduced a front anti-sway bar (known as a stabilizer or anti-roll bar) on the 1940 Deluxe models, and it also appeared on other models. It was installed to counteract body sway when the 1940 was fitted with longer spring shackles that hung almost vertically to help lower the car. Unfortunately, the bar stiffened up the chassis so much that it caused frame cracks to appear at the firewall. The bar is basically a torsion spring connected to either side of the axle via links and can be effective front and rear.

Panhard Bar/Rod

A Panhard bar or rod is a link that provides lateral location of the front or rear axle. It operates parallel to the axle and connects one side of the frame to the opposite side of the axle. The bar is allowed to pivot at either end. The longer the bar, the better it is.

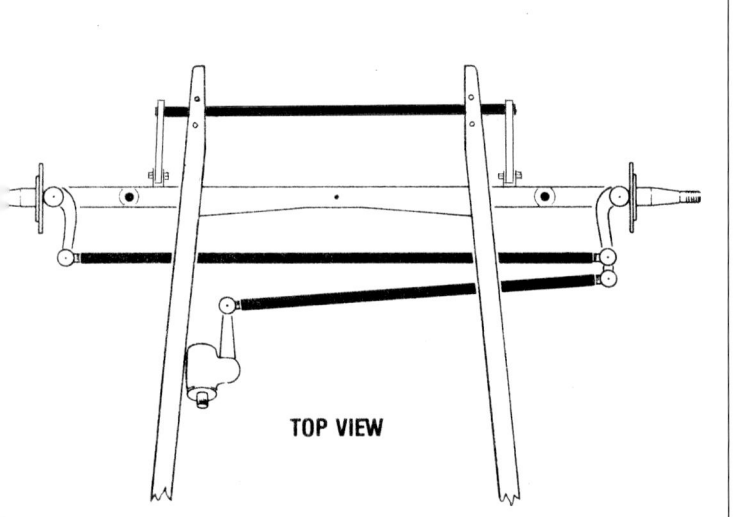

An anti-sway or anti-roll bar was fitted to Ford Deluxe models in 1940. In this configuration, the bar is mounted in front of the axle, but it can just as easily go behind. (Art Courtesy Pete & Jake's)

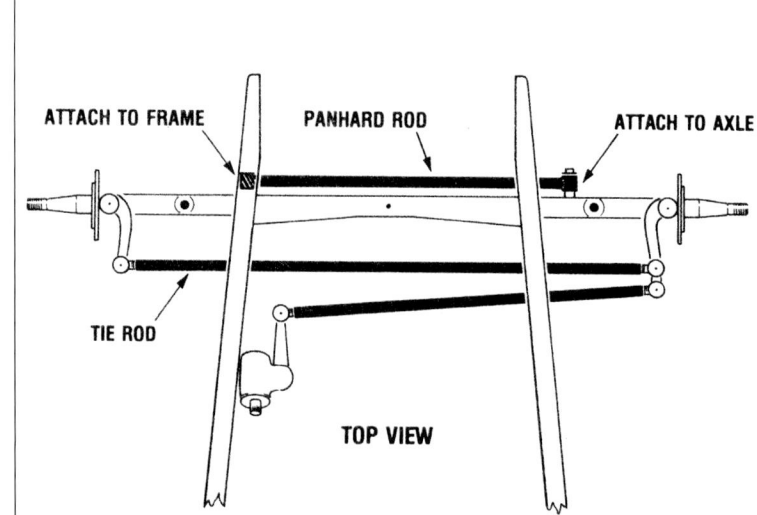

A Panhard bar provides lateral location for the front or rear axle. It needs to travel parallel to the axle and be as long as possible. It can be in front or in back of the axle. (Art Courtesy Pete & Jake's)

CHAPTER 5

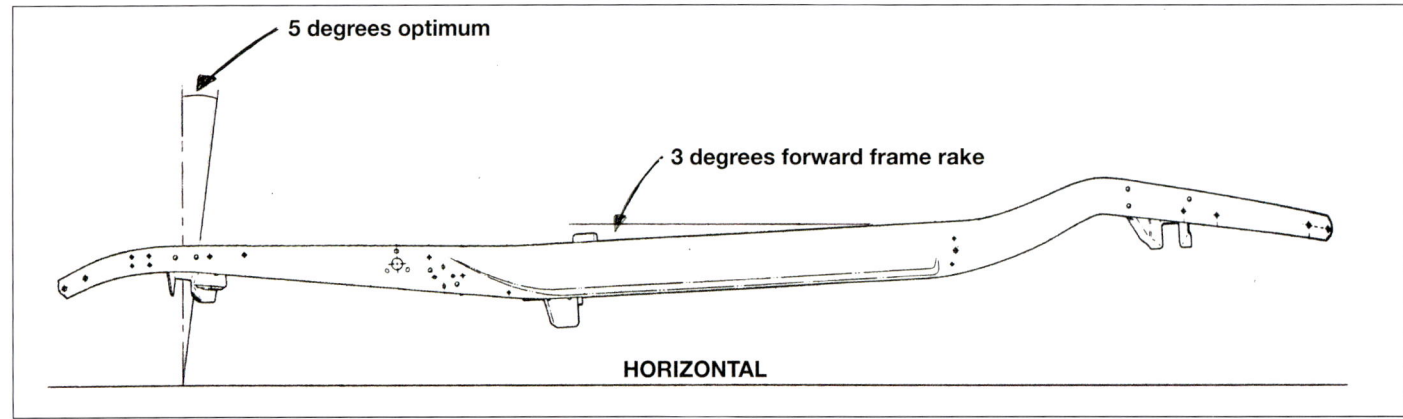

There is no specific measurement for rake, but three degrees of forward rake is a good place to start. Remember that your tire size will affect this and both will affect the caster that ideally should be 3 degrees. All of this should be taken into consideration as you set up your chassis.

Rake

The rake is the angle at which the frame sits compared to the level ground. In the case of most rods, 3 degrees of forward rake is seen as ideal. Although, some builders prefer a more radical rake. In the 1950s and 1960s, some East Coast rods were low in the back and high in the front. They were described as tail- or pan-draggers because of their East-Coast rake.

Rake is typically built into the chassis during construction, but it can be adjusted by installing different-size front and rear tires, and you should figure out tire size and stagger during setup.

Scrub Radius

Builder Pete Eastwood reminded me of the importance of scrub radius, especially if you choose to run deep-dish wheels, such as chrome-reverse rims. Scrub radius affects the car's handling at all speeds and its behavior during braking.

Ideally, with a beam axle, the centerline of the wheel should intersect the centerline of the kingpin below ground, providing a little positive scrub radius. For example, a Model A had a 1/2 inch and Model 40s, 1 inch; so, somewhere in that region is good. A deep-dish wheel with the mounting flange toward the back of the rim will give you positive scrub radius, whereas a wheel with little dish (such as a modern car wheel)

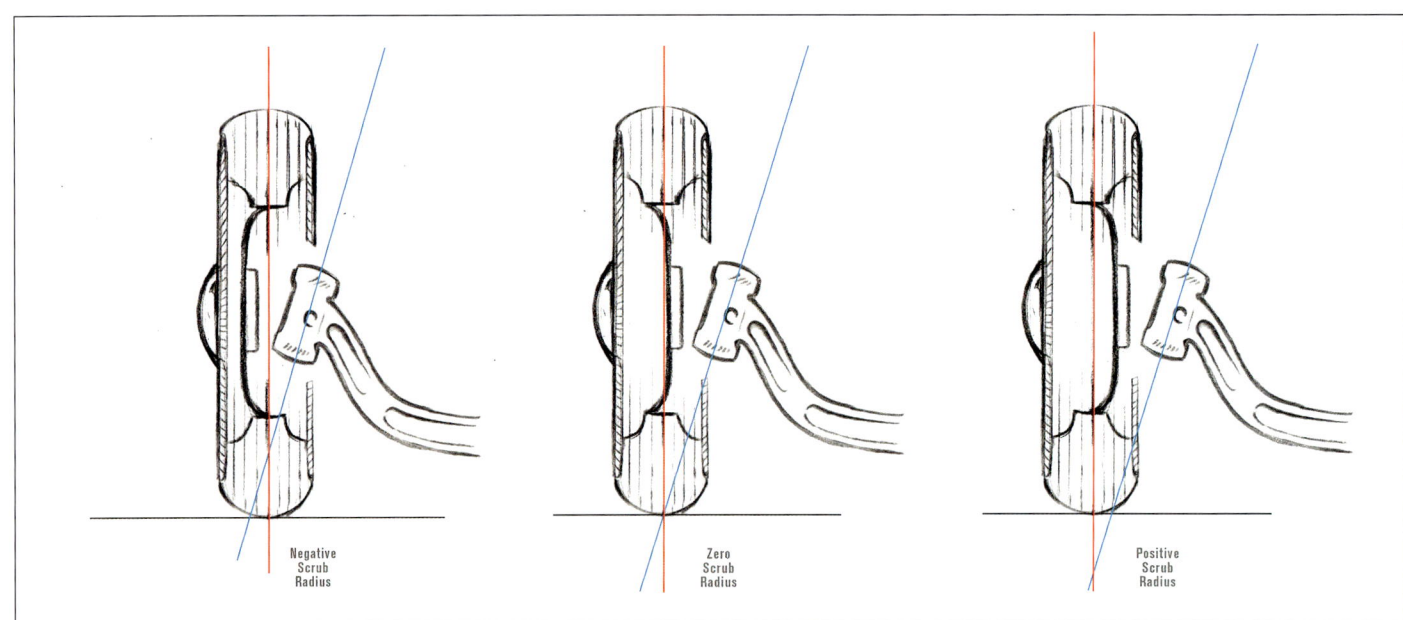

Scrub radius is the term used to describe the scrubbing effect caused by the tire patch and the intersection of the wheel centerline and the kingpin centerline.

FRAME, CHASSIS, STEERING, AND SUSPENSION

will contribute to negative scrub radius. Negative scrub radius helps the wheels straighten after a turn, so a balance is required.

Does scrub radius really matter? If your rod handles okay, then I wouldn't worry about it. If it doesn't and everything else is set up correctly, then it's something to investigate.

Toe-In

Toe-in or toe-out is the angle at which the wheels point when viewed from above. Toe-in is when the wheels point slightly toward each other at the front. Toe-out is when they point away from each other. In my experience, radial tires should be set with 1/8-inch toe-in, and bias-ply tires should be set with 3/16-inch toe-in. Adjustment can be done at an alignment shop or at home by adjusting the tie rod. Ford specified 3/32-inch toe-in on 1932–1936 passenger cars and 1/16-inch on 1937–1948 cars.

Rear-End Redo

Longtime rodder Chuck de Heras arrived at the Kennedy brothers' shop with a Deuce roadster fitted with a 1940 Ford buggy sprung rear end with 1942 Lincoln drums and plug-in 9-inch Ford axles. Chuck wanted an original Halibrand quick-change that had already been fitted with Ford 9-inch axle ends. It had previously been suspended on coilovers and located by ladder bars,

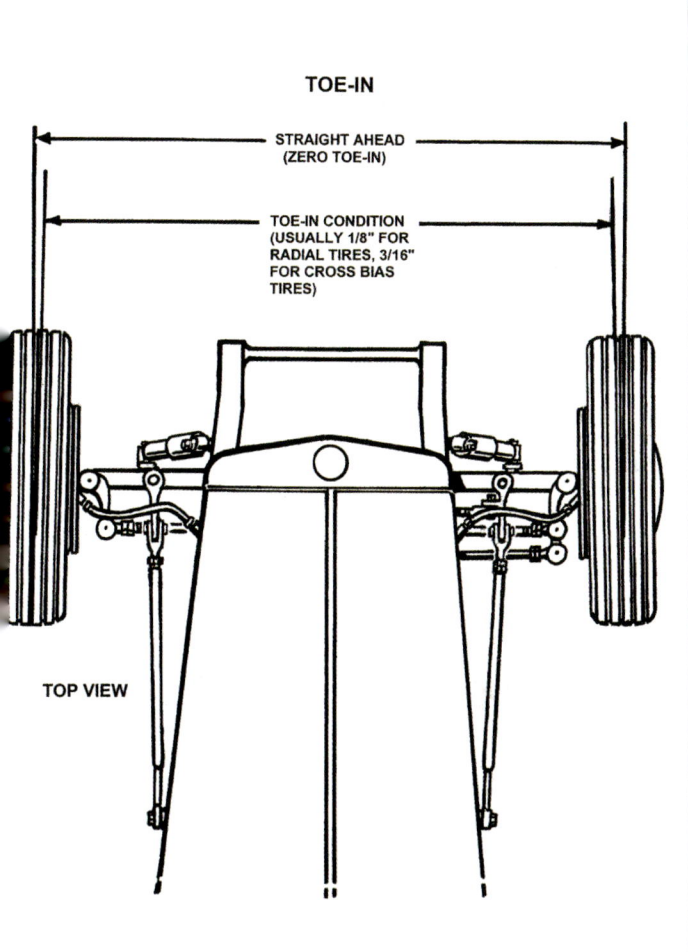

Toe-in is the amount your tires point toward each other when viewed from the top. Ford specified 3/32 inch on 1932–1936 passenger cars and 1/16 inch on 1937–1948 cars. (Art Courtesy Pete & Jake's)

Here's how Chuck's quick-change rear axle arrived at the Kennedy brothers' shop. It was set up for coilovers and ladder bars. It was also fitted with an anti-sway bar at some time.

Greg Hirota at SO-CAL Speed Shop used his fixture to install a pair of SO-CAL's forged rear spring hangers. Note that SO-CAL hangers are almost 1-inch shorter than stock 1940 Ford hangers.

HOW TO BUILD AFFORDABLE HOT RODS

CHAPTER 5

Unfortunately, the ladder bar brackets were not aligned correctly; one pointed up, and the other pointed down slightly. They need to be removed and replaced.

The ladder brackets had to be removed, which was quite a task, and new SO-CAL brackets were installed in the correct location by Greg Hirota at SO-CAL Speed Shop.

Jay installed a SO-CAL 5-inch drop ladder bar crossmember that already had the ladder bar tabs installed. This 43¼-inch-wide tube is extra wide for multiple applications.

After he had installed the Jake-made ladder bars to the axle, Jay slid the axle under the frame and bolted the ladders bars to the axle brackets using clevises.

Jay carefully measured the location of the axle to center it side to side and locate it correctly front to back because the SO-CAL spring hangers are shorter than stock 1940 Ford hangers.

Jay removed the old tubular rear crossmember and tidied up the area in readiness for the stock Model A crossmember.

FRAME, CHASSIS, STEERING, AND SUSPENSION

but Chuck wanted it suspended on a Model A spring using a Model A crossmember, located with ladder bars, and suspended with traditional shocks.

It looked like a fairly straightforward swap until Jay found that the old ladder bar brackets on the quick-change axle had been incorrectly installed. One pointed up, and the other pointed down. This mistake cost time and money to correct because the old brackets had to be removed and new ones installed by Greg Hirota at SO-CAL. Meanwhile, Jay installed a new ladder bar crossmember and an original Model A

Jay slipped a stock Model A crossmember between the Deuce rails. Note the length of square tube welded across the rails to keep them the right distance apart.

Jay didn't want Chuck's roadster to sit too low, so the crossmember was installed at the bottom of the frame and not the top where most builders put it.

With everything in place, Jay installed a Model A main leaf and moved the axle up and down just to make sure everything worked as it should.

The complete quick-change axle assembly is installed with brakes, wheels, and tires, and the spring is secured with factory Model A U-bolts.

Steering

There are really only a few types of steering that you might consider: an original, early Ford-type side-steering box; the post-1935 Ford cross steering; or a more-modern cross-steering box, such as a Vega. Boxes and columns from VW buses, Corvairs, and Ford F-1 (1948–1952) and F-100 trucks (1953–up) remain acceptable if you find one cheap and can deal with the mounting requirements. Note that these are all recirculating-ball-type steering boxes except for the VW, which is like the Ford worm and sector.

Of course, a lot of builders like to retain the factory Ford box because it fits. To some extent, you can mix and match parts to make them perform better. For example, the 13:1-ratio 1932 box will accept the innards from a 15:1-ratio 1933–1934 Model 40 box.

In 1935, Ford introduced cross steering with a 15:1 ratio. From 1936 onward, the ratio was 17:1. Ford changed from worm and sector to worm and roller in 1937.

These early Ford boxes are close to 100 years old and have probably not been well treated, lubed properly, or adjusted. But after they are rebuilt, correctly adjusted, and lubed with SAE 90 gear oil, they will serve another 100 years. Ford recommends they should be checked every 1,000 miles. A resource for refurbishing early Ford steering gear is VanPelt-Sales.com. The website has a link to very detailed steering box and assembly instructions. The EarlyFordStore.com carries complete rebuild kits at $340 that compare favorably with a rebuilt 1955–1967 VW bus column from JBugs.com at $459.95 (for which you must supply your own core).

Whatever steering assembly you ultimately decide on, remember to adjust it properly before you install

Early Ford steering boxes, columns, and wheels are always a good place to start because you know they will fit and work together, but hot rodders always like to make modifications, and that's okay.

Here's a close-up of a 1934 Ford steering box. Note the three-lug mounting flange has one bolt at the bottom, which means it is post-1932.

The steering box has two main internal components: the worm (top right) and the sector (bottom).

Because the frames of early Fords are pinched, the steering box is mounted at an angle. It is square to the car but not square to the frame.

On the left is a stock 1956 Ford F-100 steering box. Note the large mounting flange. On the right is a similar box where the mounting flange has been modified to fit a Deuce frame.

The 1956 Ford F-100 box from the engine side shows the worm (upper right) and the sector inserted into the steering box.

This is how the worm and sector engage within the steering box. These boxes will last for years if they are adjusted correctly, lubed, and maintained.

Jay used a 1956 Ford F-100 steering box in Mike Williams's Model A chassis. Note that the mounting flange has been modified to fit within the Model A frame rail.

Original or repro Chevy Vega cross-steering boxes became ubiquitous when Pete and Jake made them popular in the 1970s. They remain the go-to box for many cross-steer applications.

Look outside the box for a steering box that might work in your application. For example, this inexpensive finned aluminum unit is from a Land Rover.

CHAPTER 5

In his build, Ellis Simmons of Iron Hill utilized this Saginaw recirculating-ball side-steer manual box from Borgeson with a 16:1 ratio.

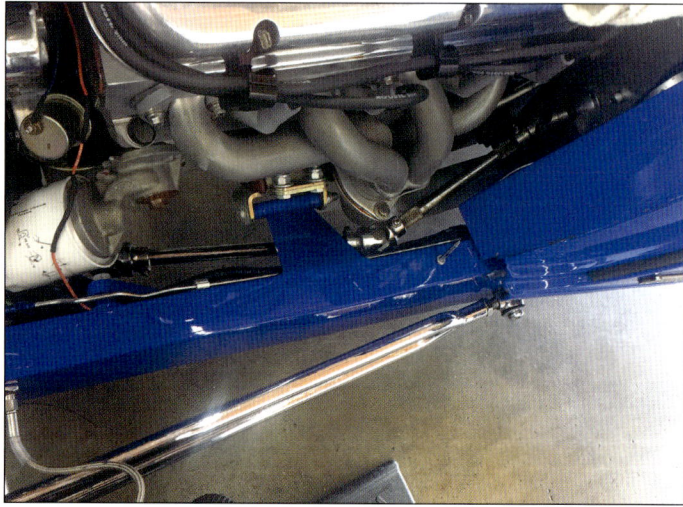

If you have more than two universal joints in your steering shaft (such as this car with three), you need to support the center shaft.

Regardless of whether you choose side- or cross-steering, install a steering damper on the tie rod to help prevent shimmy.

it, lube it regularly, and make sure the retaining bolts are locked.

Brakes

Early Ford brakes were mechanically rod-operated. Henry insisted on "the strength of steel from toe to wheel." However, in 1939, Ford changed to hydraulic brakes. So, opt for the post-1939 brakes.

Scrimping on your brake system seems counterproductive, but you can save some money by choosing steel over stainless lines, refurbishing a used master cylinder, and doing the install yourself. It might take a few tries to master bending brake lines (especially when you have multiple

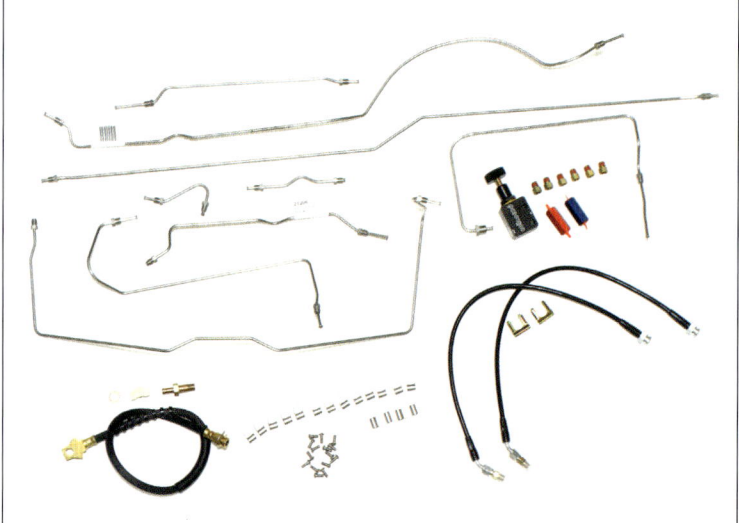

This image of a pre-formed brake line kit from SO-CAL Speed Shop will give you a good idea of the number of components necessary for plumbing a 1932 Ford with drum rear brakes. While it doesn't fit frames other than the SO-CAL step-boxed frame, some components can be adapted. These are not all the components. You will also need the brakes, master cylinder, push rod, pedal, etc.

FRAME, CHASSIS, STEERING, AND SUSPENSION

bends in different directions), but pipe is cheap.

I suggest that you put pen to paper and sketch out the intended system from master cylinder to axles and simultaneously make a list of the various components you're going to need, including frame tabs, hard to flexible adapters, clips, etc. Otherwise, you can just go online and buy a complete kit that has almost everything you need for around $200.

Master Cylinder

Early cars had a single-pot master cylinder that is adequate for an early Ford rod, but if the cylinder goes out or a line springs a leak, you will have no brakes. In 1960, Wagner Electric developed a dual-cylinder brake system, and in 1962, Cadillac added front and rear lines so that if one circuit had a problem, the other would still stop the car. In 1967, the federal government mandated the use of dual master cylinders.

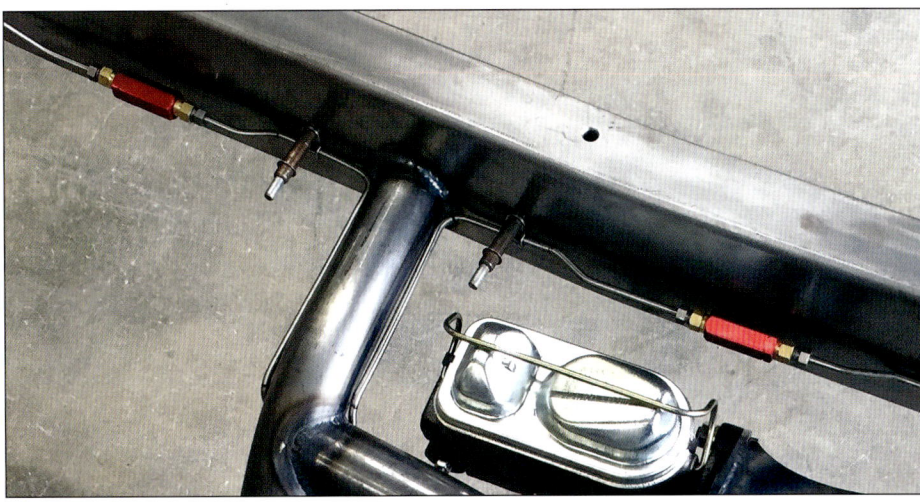

Residual valves are inserted in the brake lines. These are Wilwood 10-pound valves, and you can see that there is one in each of the front and rear lines.

Proportioning Valve and Mounting Block

Proportioning valves (such as those from Wilwood) enable you to fine tune the front-to-rear braking balance by proportionally decreasing the front or rear brake line pressure. Pressure adjustments range from 100 to 1,000 psi. You might need a mounting pad to space the valve away from the frame if you have a step-boxed frame. It depends on the configuration of your frame.

Residual Valve

Residual valves are important because they retain a minimum brake pressure to help eliminate excessive pedal travel in both disc and disc/drum brake systems. Wilwood offers two types: 2-pound (blue) for all-disc systems and 10-pound (red) for disc/drum combinations.

Brake Line Install

Fabricator Pauly Rivera of Mick's Paint installed brake lines on a SO-CAL Model A frame using some pre-formed parts from SO-CAL and fabricated the others. The install was typical with front discs and rear drums. A GM-style master cylinder was used with residual valves, a proportioning valve, and 3/16-inch stainless lines.

This is a 15/16-inch bore, dual GM-style, cast-iron master cylinder with left-side outlets as used by SO-CAL Speed Shop and many others for a disc/drum setup.

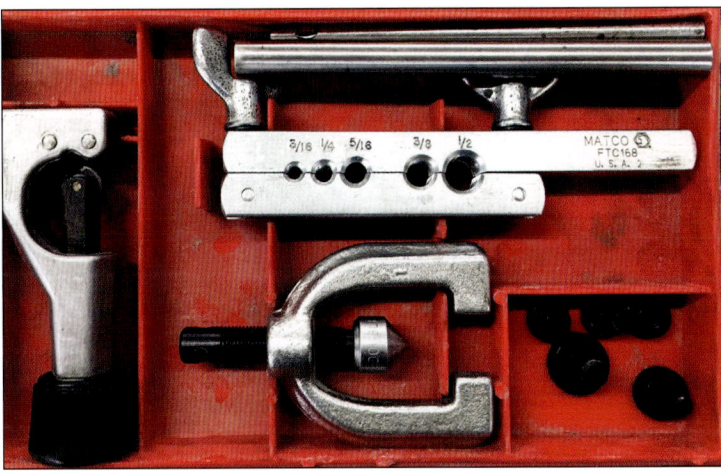

A kit for making brake lines (such as this one from Matco) will be invaluable when it comes time to fabricate your lines at home. Simple kits cost around $70.

HOW TO BUILD AFFORDABLE HOT RODS

Brake-line forming tools are available from a number of suppliers (such as Eastwood) and can cost as little as $20.

The brake tube is inserted in the flaring bar, and the swivel is screwed down to flare the end of the tube. Don't forget to install the nut before you flare, and remember to use some lubricating oil.

On the left, a single flare on stainless steel tubing is used for racing or high-end applications. On the right is a double flare on mild-steel tubing that is primarily used for a street applications.

The master cylinder is bolted firmly to the bracket, and the pre-formed lines are offered up to see how they fit the frame. They fit where they touch, right?

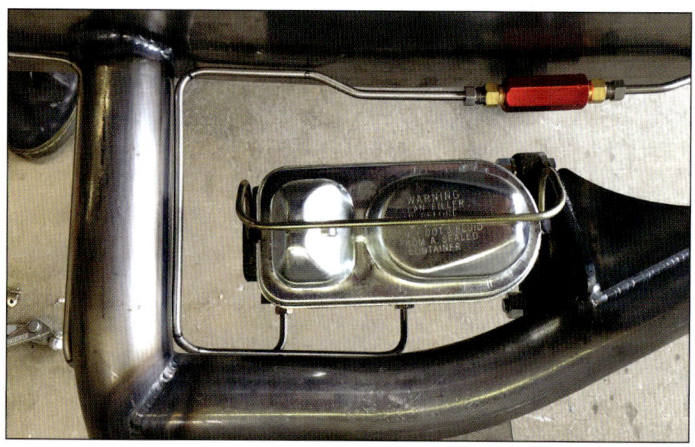
A close-up of the master cylinder shows how neatly Pauly bent the stainless lines to follow the contours of the frame tubes.

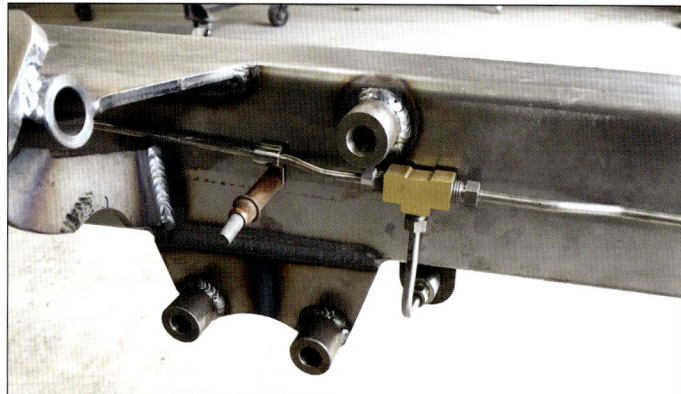
A brass T is inserted in the front line. The down portion goes to the left front brake, while the forward-facing line goes around the front crossmember to the right front brake.

Here is the line that goes inside the frame behind the front crossmember. Note the kink in the middle that is there to clear the front spring retaining bolts.

FRAME, CHASSIS, STEERING, AND SUSPENSION

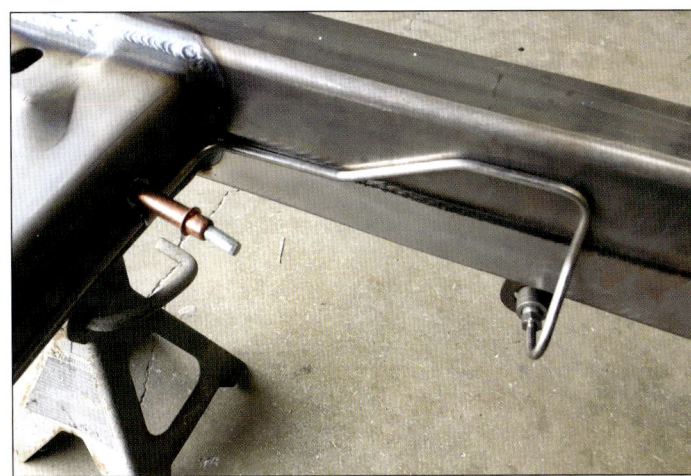

This is the right-hand front brake drop. Note the use of Clecos to temporarily hold the line clamps in position prior to everything being finalized as well as the welded-on frame tab.

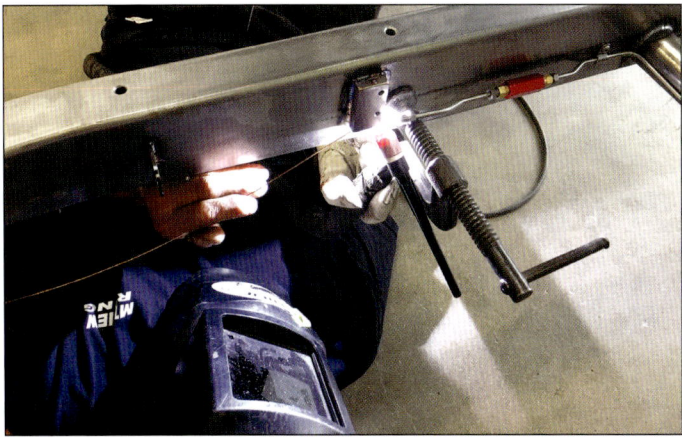

Turning to the rear, Pauly welded on a spacer block for the proportioning valve that is mounted with the adjuster pointing down so that it can be easily adjusted.

The proportioning valve is bolted into position and another tab is tacked to the frame for the fitting that will connect the hard line to the flexible line going to the rear axle.

This is a different frame, but you can see how the flexible line is connected to the hard line on the frame and the T junction on the axle.

Once Pauly had all the lines installed and was happy with their location, he removed the Clecos and tapped the holes for the brake line clamps.

Once the holes were tapped, the stainless brake line clamps from Kugel Komponents were installed. Clamps are available in a number of styles and sizes.

HOW TO BUILD AFFORDABLE HOT RODS

CHAPTER 6

POWERTRAIN CHOICE

With Help from Mike Herman, H&H Flatheads

The heart and perhaps the essence of a hot rod lies in the engine compartment, where pretty much anything goes these days. You can power your rod with anything from a hopped-up Model A engine to a V-12 Lincoln, Y-block Ford, or W-head Chevy, and everything in between. No doubt the only place you don't want to go is to a modern GM LS engine. While they are undoubtedly lightweight, good, and powerful, they look entirely too modern and cluttered compared to a cool, vintage engine. However, they can be made to look old.

Choosing a traditional engine is often a matter of passion rather than sensibility. The decision as to what to use might be as simple as what's in your yard or what someone gave you.

Mock-Up Block and Transmission

A plastic mock-up block and transmission, such as those from P-Ayr Products (mockupmotors.com), are not for everyone because they typically cost around $400. However, if

Lucas Oil makes a range of products to help keep your hot rod running from High Zinc Hot Rod & Classic Car Oil to Ethanol Fuel Conditioner with stabilizers.

This plastic mock-up small-block Chevy and Turbo 350 transmission was put to use at Rick Lefever's shop on his amazing frame table where he began to mock up his son Rayce's Model A coupe. These blocks may be a good investment if you intend to build more than one car.

you might do this more than once with the same engine and perhaps even the same transmission, it may be worth the investment. They even have a plastic flathead Ford V-8 with Ardun heads. Of course, you might be able to find a used one for sale, you might be able to borrow one, or you might be able to share one with some buddies. They typically weigh between 20 and 35 pounds, so they are so much easier to fling around compared to a 400-plus-pound iron block. They also come with threaded inserts in all the accessory mounting holes, so you can be certain that everything fits before you tear it apart for final assembly.

Ford Model A and B and the Russian B

After more than 100 years since their introduction, the Model A and B Ford engines that were derived from the Model T engine continue to be popular. In stock form, the Model A banger only produced 40 hp, but like the 20-hp T, it helped initiate a market for speed equipment. Soon names like Gemsa, HAL, Rajo, Riley, and Winfield became commonplace.

Late in the summer of 1931, Ford introduced the improved Model A, known as the Model B. Still with 200.5 ci, it produced a whopping 50 hp except in the UK, where it was restricted to a maximum of 24 hp. Meanwhile, in the US, Ford engineers believed they had the perfect four. It was okay, and many rodders continue to favor its traditionalness, but

Fuel and Oil

Something to consider when selecting a vintage engine is that technology has moved on, and there are reasons those engines were superseded. Casting and metallurgy technology have evolved, as have materials for bearings, valve seats, valves, pistons, etc. Fuels and oils have changed too.

Remember, those old engines were designed to run on leaded fuel, and that's not easily obtainable anymore. Gasoline as we knew it is now mixed with 10-percent ethanol (E10), ethanol absorbs water, and studies have shown that ethanol is bad for vintage engines. A small amount of water might be acceptable in modern cars but not in a vehicle with a steel gas tank that is not driven on a daily basis. The mixture of water and ethanol can accumulate in the bottom of the tank and cause corrosion. Ethanol, which eventually separates itself from gasoline and binds with water, also eats away at rubber fuel lines, gaskets, and some plastic parts.

Clive Prew, president of Stromberg-97.com said, "The best advice is to buy ethanol-free gas if you can." We researched websites such as Buyrealgas.com and Pure-gas.org and found 14,113 stations that sold ethanol-free gas in the US and Canada. That seems like a lot but not for the size of the two countries. Buying ethanol-free gas is not as easy as one would hope, and I doubt it's going to get any easier.

Colby Martin, director of SEMA Action Network, said that SEMA is in a constant battle with this constantly changing issue and pushes for precise labeling at gas pumps, but it's a hit-or-miss situation.

You can purchase fuel conditioner and stabilizer products from Lucas Oil or STA-BIL that prevent fuel degradation during storage. There are several similar products on the market, but it does not appear that they have any negating effect on the ethanol.

Just as they have been putting ethanol in our fuel, the oil companies have been removing zinc and phosphorous from our oil. The compounds were put there originally as anti-wear ingredients that are particularly important for engines with flat-tappet lifters to provide lubrication during engine start-up when it is essential.

Car manufacturers are happy about the reduction of zinc di-thiophosphate (ZDTP) and zinc dialkyl dithiophosphates (ZDDP) because both compounds lead to the degradation of catalytic converters, and phosphorous increases carbon buildup. These are consequences that hot rodders don't worry about too much.

As another consequence of the zinc and phosphorous reduction, there are now additives on the market and special oils from companies such as Lucas Oil. Incidentally, many aftermarket manufacturers now recommend or require that additives are used during the initial break-in and even for regular use.

Lucas Oil offers three different oil weights in its high-zinc Hot Rod & Classic Car oil line: 10W-30, 10W-40, and 20W-50. According to Tom Bognor of Lucas Oil, "Our Hot Rod oils are manufactured with the highest-quality paraffinic base oils and are fortified with a unique additive package containing high levels of zinc, molybdenum, and phosphorus, which provides a tougher, thicker additive film for maximum protection."

Other companies that make high-zinc oil include Castrol, Marvel, Royal Purple, and Valvoline. ■

CHAPTER 6

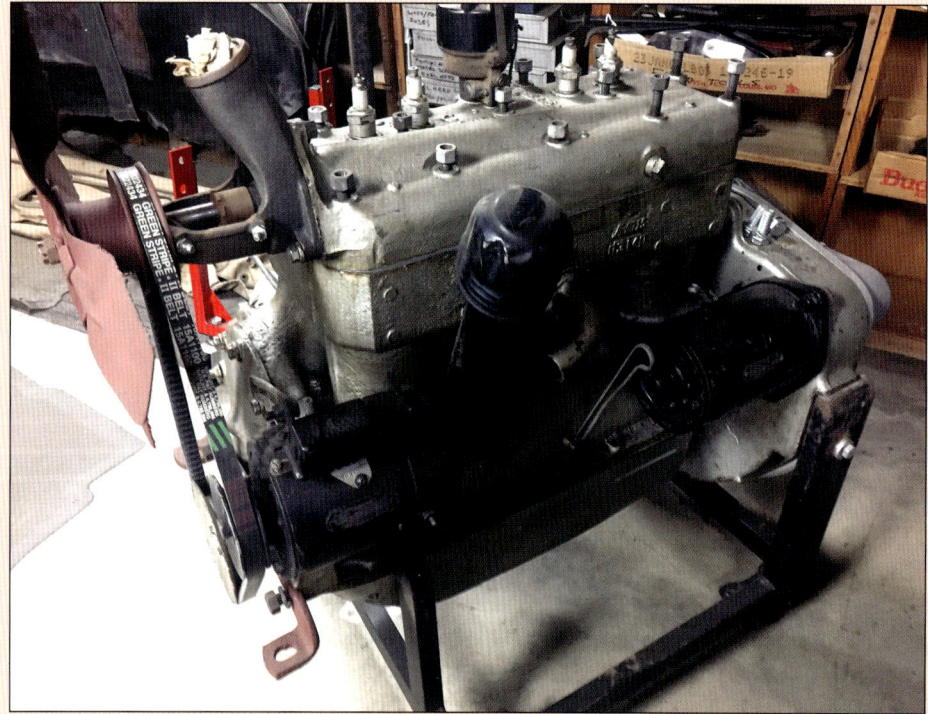

This Russian derivative of the Model A banger (the GAZ Model B) was photographed at Jim Gordon's Early Ford Parts in Rosemead, California. They have a large letter C cast into the head, which adds confusion to the whole Model C saga.

it's a tall, heavy anchor that weighs approximately 464 pounds with the clutch and transmission.

Production of A/B-based four-cylinders continued in Germany and Russia long after 1932. In Germany, the engine was redesigned in 1942 to include a pressurized oiling system, shell main, rod bearings (to replace the poured Babbitt type), fuel pump, and counterbalanced crank. Production continued until 1958 for industrial and truck use. Farther north, in Russia, the GAZ Model B was produced well into the 1950s. Unlike its German counterpart, it does not appear to have been improved at all. That said, it had 18-mm spark plugs compared to the 7/8-18-inch US plugs.

The banger is a great engine for many traditional applications but it's not for everybody.

Ford Flathead V-8 and the French Block

Ford's answer to the banger was the mono-block, 21-stud flathead V-8 introduced for the 1932 model year. The flathead was produced with no major changes for 21 years. However, it was not without its issues. Ford had trouble with the main bearings, and a service letter went out to dealers with fix-it instructions and tools. There were cam problems, lubrication problems, and the engine overheated. Despite producing 65 hp, the 221-ci 1932 engine was never popular.

For Ford, it was a process of continuous development that used the public as its test dummy. The cooling issues were not fixed until 1937 when engineers were finally were allowed to relocate the water pumps from the heads to the block, where they could literally push rather than suck.

The 1937 flathead (flattie) was a one-year-only engine because Ford bumped the number of head studs from 21 to 24 in 1938. In 1940, it introduced the larger-bore 239-ci Mercury V-8, which became a hot rodder favorite because it produced 95 hp rather than the Ford's 85.

Between 1946 and 1948, Ford produced the 59A that is usually identified by the embossed numbers 59 cast into the integral, cast-on bellhousing. The stock heads are often (but not always) embossed 59A or 59AB. These 59A engines remain fairly desirable and are recognizable by the front-mounted crab-style distributor that was on all 1932–1948 engines.

The last-generation flathead was the 1949–1953 8BA. It was chiefly recognizable for car (rather than truck) applications; it now had a bolt-on stamped-steel bellhousing and not the previous cast-in bellhousing. It also had new side-mounted, conventional-looking distributors.

If you're flathead mad, go for the 8BA. However, if that sticky-out distributor bothers you, go for the 59A. All flatheads weigh approximately 615 pounds with the clutch and transmission.

Although Ford ceased flathead engine production in the US in 1953, overseas production continued. For example, flatheads were produced in France for military use until 1990. The French block is similar but not exactly the same as an 8BA because it retains the cast-in bellhousing. They're kind of a hybrid 59A and 8BA and are not a direct or easy swap into a stock old Ford. With that being said, they are more-or-less brand new, rust-free, strong, and have no cracks

POWERTRAIN CHOICE

Manufactured until 1990, the French military flatheads were a combination of 59A and 8BA Ford designs. Stronger than the originals, they are now hard to find.

This is a typical flathead Ford V-8 8BA from H&H Flatheads complete with Navarro heads and intake, a brand-new S.Co.T. supercharger, a pair of Stromberg 97s, and a Taylor Vertex magneto. It makes for a nice package.

that most flathead Fords have. If you're building a rod where originality doesn't matter, then go French.

Ardun

In 1947, Zora Arkus-Duntov, the so-called "father of the Corvette" was commissioned by Ford to improve the output of its aging flathead V-8. Zora, his brother Yura, and designer George Kudasch developed an overhead valve (OHV) conversion for the Ford V-8 that featured hemispherical combustion chambers. Tagged "the Ardun," which was a contraction of Arkus-Duntov, the OHV heads looked

This S.Co.T.-blown Ardun with twin copper-plumed Stromberg 97s was built by Mike Herman at H&H Flatheads for Brian George. It's an impressive, if somewhat expensive, package but definitely shouts traditional.

great and increased the power, but they were somewhat temperamental.

Only about 200 sets were made in the US before Arkus-Duntov moved to work with Sydney Allard in the UK, where a few more sets were made for Allard's J2 sports car. Ardun heads were a much-sought-after hot rod accessory until the mid-1990s, when Don Orosco began to reproduce them. Orosco made about 30 sets before the tooling was sold to Don Ferguson, whose family continues to produce the heads, albeit they have been updated with some modern technology along with a compatible cast-aluminum block. Companies such as H&H Flatheads are known for building complete Ardun engines and offer a range of intakes for various induction systems, including blowers.

Ford Y-Block

First introduced in 1954, the Ford Y-block earned its name because the Y section had long skirts that cradled the crankshaft much like a modern race engine. With 239 ci, the engine produced 139 hp and 193 ft-lbs of torque (25 percent more than the flathead it replaced).

The following year, Ford upped the capacity to 272 and then 292 ci. The 272 produced 162 hp and 258 ft-lbs of torque, while the 292 produced 193 hp and 280 ft-lbs in Thunderbirds and Mercurys.

The horsepower race was on, and in 1956 Ford again increased the capacity to 312 ci and bumped the horsepower to a factory max of 245. That same year, the Mercury division offered a performance kit with cam, heads, and two fours that increased horsepower to 260. Then, in 1957, the factory offered a Paxton centrifugal supercharger that supposedly produced 300 hp and 300 ft-lbs of torque.

The Y-block weighed in at a hefty 625 pounds, had a rear-mounted distributor, and suffered some valvetrain lubrication problems that were solved with an aftermarket oiling system. It also had a maintenance issue due to its solid (rather than hydraulic) lifters. Nevertheless, in the right application, why not choose a Y-block? There are, after all, some cool accessories, such as those neat finned 1956 T-Bird valve covers.

Ford 289

The Ford 289 is a rather forgotten engine in the hot rod world but not in the Cobra, Mustang, and kit car realms. Therefore, it is worth considering because it has history and an abundance of speed equipment. Besides, it's compact, plentiful, and weighs only about 460 pounds.

Ford General Manager Lee Iacocca pushed Ford toward more youthful, performance-oriented vehicles, and in 1962 it introduced the 221-ci V-8 in the Fairlane. That was soon replaced by the 260, which was replaced soon thereafter with the 289. We know the 260 because one went into the first Shelby Cobra and the 1964½ Mustang before it was powered by the 4.0-inch bore 289.

Rod builder Roy Brizio had a long

The Y-block Ford is fairly popular, but its downsides are that rear-mounted distributor and a weight of 625 pounds. It does have those cool ram-horn manifolds. (Photo Courtesy HandHFlatheads.com)

The beauty of a small-block Ford is that it can be dressed up with a large range of Shelby Cobra accessories, such as valve covers and that wicked induction system.

association with Ford. For many years, he proclaimed, "Put a Ford in your Ford." Some people think that's cool, and it only became so when a shorter-than-stock, aftermarket water pump became available along with a short, relocated oil filter. The advantage was that the distributor was mounted in the front and not in the back like a Chevy, which made it unnecessary to recess the firewall.

Personally, I like the 289 Ford and all those cool Cobra accessories; everything from aluminum Cobra oil pans up through the valve covers to the plentiful induction systems.

Buick Nailhead

Produced from 1953 through 1966, the Buick Nailhead is one of the most recognizable OHV engines because of its horizontal valve covers. It got its nickname because the valves were relatively small, were installed vertically, and resembled nail heads.

Made popular by the likes of "TV" Tommy Ivo in his seminal T-bucket, the Nailhead initially displaced 264 or 322 ci. The 322 had a 8.5:1 compression ratio and produced 188 hp. Despite the restrictive valves and some funky exhaust ports, these engines produced lots of torque at the expense of top-end horsepower.

For the 1957 model year, Buick increased the displacement to 364 ci. With a 9.5:1 compression ratio, it produced 250 hp. With a 10:1 compression ratio, it produced 300 hp. However, it was a different engine to its predecessor and shared few parts.

In 1959, Buick introduced the 401 that produced 455 ft-lbs of torque. More power came in 1963

"TV" Tommy Ivo's 1925 T-bucket set the hot rod world on fire in 1957 when it appeared with a 402-ci Nailhead Buick V-8 shown here with Hilborn fuel injection. It ran the quarter-mile at around 11 seconds with top-end speeds of around 120 mph.

with the introduction of the 425-ci Wildcat 465 that was rated at 340 hp. Further increases happened in 1964 with the twin-Carter carbureted 360-hp Super Wildcat. Steel cranks, wild cams, and high compression endeared the Nailhead, but it weighed 485 pounds.

Lightweight Buick /Oldsmobile/Rover

In 1960, GM introduced a lightweight, all-aluminum 215-ci pushrod V-8 that weighed under 320 pounds. The most powerful version produced 200 hp, while the turbocharged Oldsmobile Jetfire produced 215 hp. In just three years, GM produced almost 800,000 215-powered Buicks and Oldsmobiles. There were even a few 215-powered Pontiacs, hence its nickname "BOP 215."

Despite a few cooling problems, the 215 had its extremely long life extended when GM sold the tooling to the UK's Rover Group in 1965. The Rover V-8 was used in Rover cars, Land Rovers, and some other limited-production British sports cars (such as MG, Morgan, and TVR) and became the stalwart of the U.K. rodding scene. There wasn't a huge amount of speed or dress-up equipment, but John Woolfe Racing worked with Offenhauser to produce an intake that used a single 4-barrel carburetor instead of the stock twin SU carburetors. Of course, a blower or turbo can also be installed. Replacement blocks were made until around 2008 by Coscast in the UK.

The aluminum Buick/Rover is an off-the-wall choice in the US but is quite acceptable in Europe, Australia, and New Zealand.

CHAPTER 6

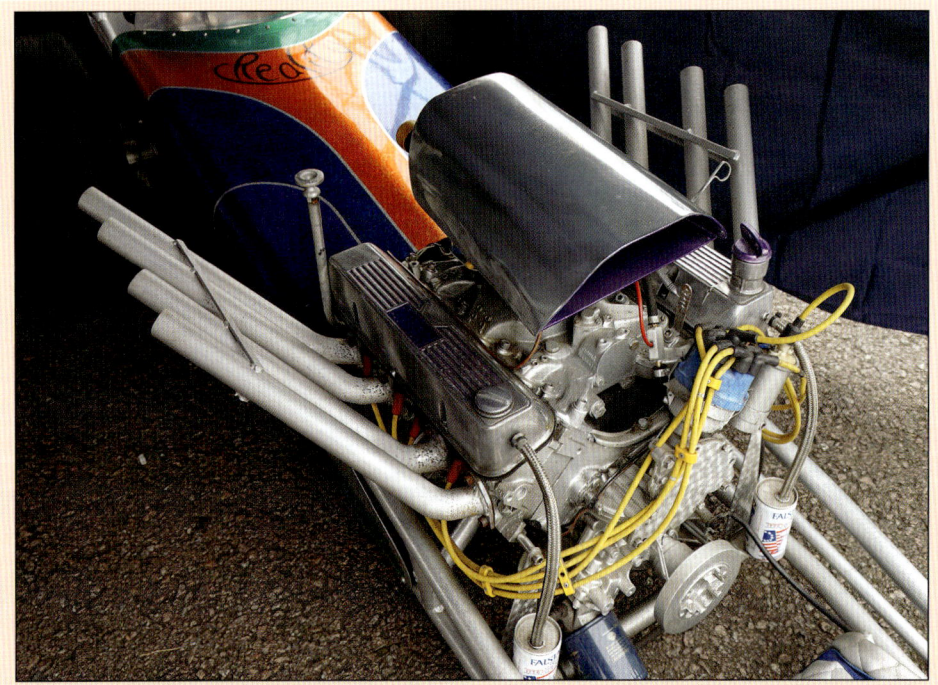

Seen here in a British dragster, the Buick/Oldsmobile/Pontiac-derived aluminum Rover V-8 was the engine of choice for Rover. Hundreds of them found their way in British hot rods as a cheap-and-easy answer to the V-8 question.

Cadillac 331 Series

Cadillac has a long and venerable history with many innovations, but it wasn't until 1949 that it came out with an OHV V-8 that was a design shared with the Oldsmobile 303. The early engines featured a partially integral cast-iron clutch housing. In 1955, it changed to a lighter flat back that bolted to a conventional clutch and flywheel housing.

In 1956, the bore and stroke were increased to 365 ci, but the 1958 Eldorado engine with 3x2s was the one to get because it produced 335 hp. A longer stroke in 1959 pushed displacement to 390 ci, yielding 325 hp, while the Eldorado Tri-Power produced 345 hp.

For 1963, Cadillac re-tooled the engine to make it more compact and 1 inch lower, 4 inches narrower, and 1.25 inches shorter. The power output remained the same as the previous 390. For 1964, displacement was bumped to 429 ci to produce 340 hp and 480 ft-lbs of torque. While 50 pounds was shaved off the weight, these engines are heavy. The pre-1963 units weighed around 700 pounds.

Chevy Big-Block W-Head

Chevrolet's first big-block appeared in 1958 and is distinguishable by its unique W-shaped heads and valve covers. It's a good-looking engine that shouts nostalgia. The first Turbo-Thrust version had a capacity of 348 ci and featured a wedge-shaped combustion chamber where the chamber was in the upper part of the cylinder (not in the head). The plugs were set vertically in the quench area that improved combustion. With a 4-barrel carburetor, the base engine produced 250 hp, the 3x2 Tri-Power setup called the Super Turbo-Thrust produced 280 hp, and the Special Turbo-Thrust increased it even more to 315 with the Tri-Power.

For 1959 and 1960, high-output versions produced 320 and then

This neat old Cadillac has an original Edmunds intake and twin 97s in a heavily hammered, lakes-style coupe built originally by Mike Whitney. A rear-mounted distributor (in this case a magneto) may necessitate a notch in the firewall.

Colby Martin, director of the SEMA Action Network, and his dad Al chose this 1958 Chevy Impala 348 ci W-motor for Colby's 1931 Model A coupe project. The engine was donated by Steve Lenain and was salvaged from a ski-boat.

What can you say about a small-block Chevy in a Model A roadster by Shug Hanchard other than it fits and it's easy to work on? The firewall may have to be notched to accommodate the Chevy's rear-mounted distributor.

335 hp. In 1961, the power was yet again raised to 340 with a single 4-barrel carburetor and 350 with the Tri-Power. Also, Chevrolet upped the ante and released a 409-ci version of the W-head, which at its peak produced 425 hp. Powerful and uniquely good looking, the W-head weighed in at a hefty 665 pounds.

Chevy Small-Block

What can be said about the small-block Chevy that has not already been said? They are commonly known as Gen I engines, which differentiates them from the Gen II LT family and the most recent Gen III/IV LS family.

Production of the Turbo-Fire or High Torque V-8 that was nicknamed *Mighty Mouse* began in the fall of 1954 with 265 ci; it was available in the Corvette and Bel Air. The engines weighed just 575 pounds and produced in the region of 200 hp. In 1957, the capacity was increased to 283 ci, and when fitted with Rochester injection, it became one of the first production engine to produce 1 hp per cubic inch of capacity in the Corvette. Unfortunately, there was no internal oil filter, so an external filter had to be used.

For 1957, the block was re-cast with thicker walls to accommodate a $3^7/_8$-inch bore. This resulted in a power increase from a base 185 hp to 315 when fitted with fuel injection.

Five years later (in 1962), Chevy introduced the 327 with a 4-inch bore and 3¼-inch stroke. Power jumped from 210 hp to a healthy 375 when fitted with a Duntov solid-lifter cam and fuel injection. Finally, with a 3.48-inch stroke, the small-block was out to 350 ci.

Meanwhile, to meet SCCA Trans-Am regulations, Chevy produced a 302 by mating a 283 3-inch-stroke crank into a 4-inch-bore 327. It was the engine that was installed in the Z/28 Camaro from 1967 to 1969.

Chrysler/Dodge Hemi

The Chrysler FirePower Hemi first appeared in 1951 as standard on the Imperial and New Yorker and optional on the Saratoga. The capacity was initially 331 ci due to an oversquare 3.81-inch bore and 3.63-inch stroke. With a 7:1 compression ratio, it produced 180 hp and 312 ft-lbs of torque but weighed a whopping 745 pounds (one head alone weighs almost 120 pounds).

In 1955, Chrysler claimed a dual 4-barrel Carter version as the first production car to produce 300 hp. The displacement was increased in 1956 to 354 ci, and the engine now produced as much as 355 hp and became the first American engine to produce 1 hp per cubic inch.

The 392 version was introduced in 1957 and was almost square due to its 4-inch bore and 3.906-inch stroke. It had a taller raised deck compared to previous engines. However, the heads were cast with wider ports so that earlier manifolds could be used with the new heads on the new block.

The following year, a single-carburetor version with a 9.25:1 compression ratio was rated at 345 hp, whereas the dual-carburetor version offered 375 hp. By 1958, the 392 had reached the end of its life but produced 380 hp.

Meanwhile, Dodge and DeSoto both produced their own smaller versions of the Hemi: DeSoto in 1952 with the 276 Fire Dome, and Dodge in 1953 with the 241 Red Ram. In the case of the Dodge, the early low-compression Hemis produced 150 hp, which gradually improved with the 1955 270 version and the 1956 315. A special, race-only

CHAPTER 6

The big Chrysler and Dodge Hemis came out in 1951 initially with a 331 and later a 392. They revolutionized the hot rod world with their power and are so much easier to work on than a Chevy. (Photo Courtesy HandHFlatheads.com)

D-500-1 package had an aluminum dual 4-barrel intake and Carter carburetors. The final iteration was the 1957 325 ci.

Over at the DeSoto division, the initial 271 grew into the 291 for 1955 and a 330 for 1956. However, Adventurers and 1957 Firedome and Fireflite models had a larger 341 ci Hemi that produced 343 hp when fitted with dual Carters. The year 1957 also saw a 345-ci version that was rated at 345 hp and also had dual carters.

Personally, I have a soft spot for the little Hemi, if only because it weighs 100 pounds lighter than its big brother Chrysler.

Lincoln Flathead V-8

While the flathead Ford was nearing the end of its life, Lincoln Division introduced its own big 337-ci flathead in 1948. A heavy beast and around 850 pounds, the 8EL engine was used in Lincoln cars, while the 8EQ was used in Ford F-7 and F-8 trucks.

The maximum horsepower for 1951 (the last year of production) was 154 at 3,400 rpm, while torque was 275 at 1,800. Hydraulic lifters and forged steel cranks made the 8EL a player. While not a hugely popular hot rod engine, the availability of replacements parts and some Austin speed equipment, such as finned cylinder heads and 2x2 and 3x2 intakes, made people take another look at this engine.

Lincoln Flathead V-12

Although first produced alongside the Ford flathead V-8, the Lincoln H-series L-head V-12 is quite a different engine with its 75 degrees V rather than the Ford's 90 degrees. Initial power was quoted as 110 at 3,900 rpm with 180 ft-lbs of torque available from 400 to 3,500 rpm.

I was always a fan of the small Dodge Red Ram engine seen here in Lynn Byrd's 1932 3-window. They're available in 271, 291, 330, 341, and 345 ci capacities. They have a rear-mounted distributor, but it is nevertheless a compact Hemi.

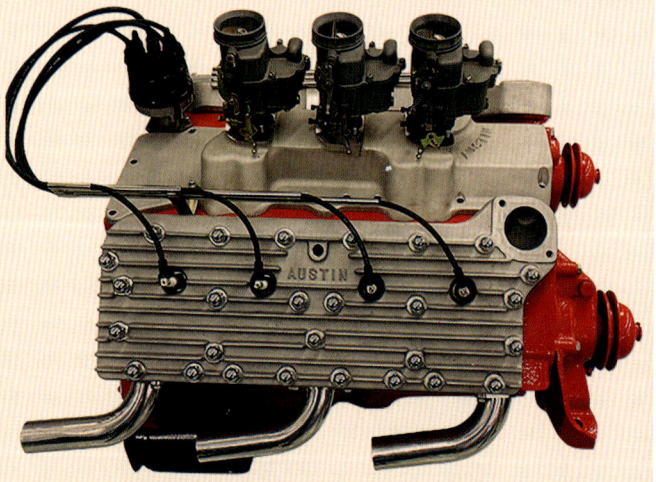

The 337-ci Lincoln flathead V-8 built between 1948 and 1951 weighs a ton, but if you're looking for something different, it's different. Austin has some speed equipment available from H&H Flatheads, and a supercharger would look good on there. (Photo Courtesy HandHFlatheads.com)

POWERTRAIN CHOICE

In 1936, the capacity was 267 ci, and the engine was fitted with hydraulic lifters beginning in 1938. For 1940, the engine was enlarged to 292 ci but fitted with cast-iron heads to aid cooling, and it stayed that way until 1942 when a small run of 306-ci engines was made. The 306, rated at 130 hp, was made for a short time after World War II, but the factory reverted to a 292 for the end of 1946 through 1948 because the large bore caused too many problems.

The Lincoln V-12 did not enjoy a huge hot rod history, but the introduction of heads and intakes put this long-forgotten engine in the limelight. The Lincoln V-12 weighs a staggering 900 pounds, and while it may not outperform the V-8 Ford, it does have cool factor in the looks department.

Oldsmobile

Arguably America's first muscle car, the 1949 Oldsmobile Rocket 88 was powered by a 303-ci Rocket V-8 that produced 135 hp. It rocketed Oldsmobile to the top of the NASCAR tree with six wins out of nine late-model division races in 1949. By 1951, all Oldsmobiles were powered by the Rocket, and by 1952, Super 88s came with a new 4-barrel carburetor, which increased output to 160 hp.

For 1954, the Rocket's capacity was increased from 303 to 324 ci and produced 170 hp with a 2-barrel carburetor, while the 4-barrel version put out 185 hp. Horsepower increased again in 1955 with 185 for the 88 models, and 202 for the Super 88s; and again in 1956 with 230 for the 88s, and 240 for the Super 88s.

The third generation appeared in 1957 when the 371-ci J2 option offered a Tri-Power setup that produced 277 hp. In the wings was the big 394-ci version that was rated at 315 hp with a single 4-barrel. Finally, for the fifth generation, Oldsmobile upped the ante and the Starfire offered the 394 with 345 hp.

Troy Ladd of Hollywood Hot Rods was lucky enough to find this forgotten 1932 3-window that was put away circa 1963, complete with its original 371-ci Oldsmobile from a 1959 Oldsmobile Dynamic 88. It's topped by three Rochester 2Gs on an Offenhauser Tri-Power intake.

The flathead Lincoln V-12 has gained popularity due to H&H Flatheads offering a variety of heads and speed equipment, including blowers. It's a fairly big, heavy engine that doesn't produce a lot of power, but it has all those plugs to get people's attention.

Engine Weights (Approximate)

Engine	Weight
Model A/B Ford 4-cylinder with clutch and transmission	464
Ford Flathead V-8	540
Ford Flathead V-8 (with Ardun head)	800
Ford Y-Block	625
Ford 289	460
Buick Nailhead 401	685
Buick/Rover Lightweight 215	318
Cadillac 331/390	700
Chevy W-Head	650
Chevy Small-Block	550
Chrysler/Dodge Hemi 331	700
Lincoln Flathead V-8 337	850
Lincoln Flathead V-12	750
Oldsmobile 304 Rocket	620
Pontiac 389	675

CHAPTER 6

Transmission Background

The good news about building any kind of rod with a traditional powertrain is that many of the transmission questions were answered many years ago when these components were new.

Of course, the early flathead-powered gow jobs typically had a stock 3-speed Toploader transmission with Lincoln Zephyr gears, or they were upgraded to the beefier LaSalle or complete Lincoln transmissions. Traditional as they may be, those old transmissions are just that: old. The 1932–1938 boxes had no synchronization for first and reverse, and things have moved on since then.

Mitchell Overdrive Manufacturing sells a second- and third-gear synchromesh assembly that fits in original 1928–1931 Model A transmission cases.

As rodders moved away from the flathead and began to adopt the various OHV engines (such as the Oldsmobile, Cadillac, and the Chrysler Hemi), new adapters had to be developed. Indeed, Cragar had numerous adapters to fit early or late Ford transmissions to almost every popular American V-8 for about $60 each.

It's almost impossible to find any reference to early transmission builders, but Stelling began advertising its in-out race boxes in *Hot Rod* in May 1948, as did F.E. Zimmer Co., which advertised Ford and Zephyr transmission gears as well as chopped and balanced flywheels and brand-new column transmissions for $57 exchange. That May issue of *Hot Rod* also had a small ad from Sower's Engineering in Burbank, California, that advertised quick-change rear ends, axles, and U-joint assemblies. In August, Pat Warren at Downey Machine Shop began advertising quick-change rear ends.

One of the first major speed equipment manufacturers to get into the transmission business was Harry Weber, who in 1948 began to manufacture aluminum flywheels advertised in the May 1948 issue of *Hot Rod*. In the early 1950s, Weber made bellhousing adapters to mate early OHV engines to Ford transmissions.

Today, many rodders want to adapt an early engine to a later, more efficient transmission. They either want a better automatic (such as GM's 700-R4) or a 4-, 5-, or 6-speed manual. Each pose their own problems. For example, an auto might need a custom flexplate, whereas a manual might need a custom flywheel, special pilot bushings, special throw-out arms, and bearings. It gets complicated, and you also need to consider where the shift lever of a manual might fall. Some modern 5- or 6-speed transmissions place the shifter uncomfortably far back in a rod application. Incidentally, the Tremec T56 6-speed, for example, offers three shifter locations for your convenience. You also have to give thought to the starter and its position and alignment with the flywheel and mechanical or electrical speedometer drive (if you care, that is).

Although lots of traditional rodders like the nostalgia of a manual transmission, space has to be a consideration. While the manual gearbox itself is usually small and more compact than an auto transmission, the necessary mechanical components (such as the clutch pedal and mechanism) need to be taken into consideration.

For those who want to go with an early Ford transmission, VanPelt Sales has recently introduced *The Ins and Outs of Early Ford Transmissions*, which is marketed as a complete Ford Toploader transmission how-to manual with more than 60 pages and over 140 photos.

Another factor to consider is the type of driveshaft you will end up with. Early Fords had a torque

Conversion kits (such as this one from HotRodWorks.com) convert 1935–1948 Ford banjo axles with torque tubes to open drive using a standard number 1350 U-joint and a 10-spline pinion. (Photo Courtesy HotRodWorks.com)

POWERTRAIN CHOICE

tube that is basically a fixed external tube between the transmission and the rear axle that fully enclosed the rotating driveshaft. It used only one universal joint (U-joint) at the transmission end, whereas a modern conventional driveshaft is not enclosed and uses two U-joints (one at each end). Note that Ford light trucks from 1942 to 1952 had an open driveshaft.

If, as many rodders do, you select a modern transmission and an early Ford rear end with a torque tube, you will need to resolve the issue of how to join the two. One answer is a kit by Flat-o Products that replaces the torque tube of an early Ford rear axle with an open drive assembly.

Another company that makes Ford open driveline conversion kits is Hot Rod Works. It produces various kits for 1932–1948 Ford axle and quick-changes under its Rodsville brand.

You need to give some thought to the depth of the water here before you jump in. Converting to an open drive is a little more complicated than it appears on the surface. For example, the forces exerted on factory wishbones might be more than they were designed to handle. The post-1936 wishbones are quite thin and might not be up to the task if you don't align everything correctly.

Because of the dangers of getting it wrong, it is highly recommended that you test it and move the axle up and down through its complete arc using a floor jack as you assemble your rear end. Do this without the springs and shocks in place but with the locating arms and driveshaft installed to see whether those arms (wishbones, ladder bars, or four-bars) work correctly without binding.

Adapters

A transmission adapter assembly usually (but not always) consists of an adapter plate that bolts to the back of the engine block, an adapter bellhousing that bolts to the plate or the block, and the transmission that bolts to the bellhousing. Of course, you're also going to need the flywheel, clutch disc, clutch pressure plate, and any associated mechanical parts, such as pilot bearing adapters and extensions.

If you're mixing and matching transmissions and are not familiar with the operation, be sure to mock it up before you do any major fabrication that might need to be undone when you find out that it doesn't jive.

One of the oldest and most prolific adapter companies is Wilcap Company. Founded more than 50 years ago by Red Wilson and Tony Capanna, the company offers more than 70 different adapters. Its website (wilcap.com) has a great chart that lists early engines, such as the 1954–1964 Ford Y-block, and the possible adaptations to transmissions, such as GM TH350 and BorgWarner T-5. It's a great starting place.

Another company started about the same time as Wilcap is Trans-Dapt Performance Products that is now part of Hedman Performance Group. Two adapter plates are offered to adapt 1962-and-up Chevy engines to a range of GM transmissions. The limited selection is common when you search for others on the internet. Speedway Motors has a few, but the pickings are slim with the big distributors.

Bendtsen's Speed Gems is worth checking out because it lists adapter kits for a number of engine and transmission combinations, including flathead Ford to Chevy automatic, 1964–1966 Buick Nailhead 401/425 to Chevy automatic, Y-block Ford to Ford 4-speed automatic transmissions with overdrive, 1957–1964 Oldsmobile to Chevy automatic, and a 1949–1953 Cadillac to Chevy manual. The list goes on and is well worth checking out.

Adapting a different-than-stock transmission to your engine usually means locating a transmission adapter that might consist of an adapter plate that bolts to the block and an adapter bellhousing that bolts either to the plate or directly to the box. (Photo Courtesy Wilcap.com)

The company has very thorough installation instructions.

Another company worth checking is Centerville Auto Repair. The website (centervilleautorepair.com) lists a number of new and used transmission adapters, such as an adapter for an S-10 5-speed to a Buick Nailhead, or a Chevy automatic or manual transmission to a 365–390 Cadillac.

Besides its open drive kit, Flat-o Products also makes some adapters. For example, it has a kit to adapt a Ford C-4 auto to a flathead. There is also an adapter to put an S-10 5-speed or a Borg-Warner T-5 5-speed behind all flathead V-8s, as well as V-8-60s and V-12s. Flat-o can also supply compatible clutch discs, pilot bushings, etc. Incidentally, Flat-o offers a version of the C-4 that has a 12-inch-shorter output shaft for short-wheelbase cars.

If you're contemplating a Tremec, check out Silver Sport Transmissions, which took over Keisler. Its website has a wealth of information and even a street rod section complete with a downloadable installation manual. Incidentally, for a comprehensive guide to BorgWarner T5 transmissions, visit britishV-8.org/Articles/Borg-Warner-T5-ID-Tags.htm.

Holley is another source worth checking because it has taken over several old transmission-related brands, including B&M, Hayes, Hurst, Lakewood, and Quick Time. While it offers no specific kits, you should be able to mix and match to get what you want.

Hot Rod Works offers a number of adapter plates, including an adapter that facilitates bolting a GM T-5 with a Ford bolt pattern to a Chevrolet car or pickup bellhousing.

PowerPlayHemi.com, a division of Hot Heads Research & Racing offers a number of kits and parts to adapt various transmissions to early Chrysler Hemis. For example, it has a full-radius, hardened-aluminum adapter to bolt any GM 3- or 4-speed manual transmission behind a 1951–1953 Chrysler engine. This adapter works with both manual and modern hydraulic throw-out bearings. It even has an adapter to bolt a 1948-and-earlier Ford transmission to a Chrysler. It also carries a lot of associated parts.

Finally, Tanson Enterprises specializes in Oldsmobiles and Cadillacs and offers a system to install a TH350, TH400, 700 R4, 200 4R, 4L65E, 4L80E, or Powerglide to a 1949–1964 Oldsmobile 303, 324, 371, or 394 and the 1949–1954 Cadillac. It sounds a little complicated because about 3 inches are cut off of the front of these newer transmissions and a new flange is welded on to keep the transmission from getting longer. Nevertheless, it might be an answer for someone.

An adapter is nothing more than a device (usually an aluminum casting) to mate an engine to a transmission it's not designed from the factory to fit. This was often done in the late-1950s after the introduction of the small-block Chevy, when hot rodders wanted to swap out their flatheads for a new OHV Chevy but didn't want to bother changing transmissions.

Adapter Plate

If an adapter to mate a particular engine and transmission is not available, you may need to fabricate an adapter plate to adapt the engine to a suitable adapter. You can buy adapter plates from several manufacturers for

H&H Flatheads supplies this kit to adapt a flathead Ford V-8 to a Chevy T-5. The kit includes a cast-aluminum bellhousing, clutch disc, fork, cross shaft, etc.

POWERTRAIN CHOICE

Ross Racing Engines makes this adapter to mate one of its Oldsmobile Rocket engines to a Tremec TKO500. It went into James Jard's 1936 3-window built by the Kennedy brothers.

the more common adaptations, such as a small-block Chevy to other Buick, Cadillac, Oldsmobile, and Pontiac TH350 or TH400 transmissions. Danchuk Manufacturing makes a plate to adapt later transmissions to early '55 and '56 Chevy engines that do not have a block-mounted starter.

As always, if you purchase a part on the internet, be sure to do as much research as you can before you buy. Be certain that the plate is meant for your particular requirement and be sure to understand what is and is not included, such as hardware.

Bellhousing, Clutch Can, or Scattershield

The terms bellhousing, clutch can, or scattershield are the common names used in racing for the engine-to-transmission adapter that encloses the flywheel and clutch. They were initially fabricated but eventually Joe Schubeck developed one-piece, hydro-formed aluminum cans that he was soon able to make out of stronger steel.

If you intend to race your rod with a manual transmission, a steel bellhousing is recommended. Be sure to check with the sanctioning body to see if the bellhousing needs to be SFI certified because not all bellhousing are.

This Speedway adapter bolted to a fabricated adapter plate that in turn is bolted to the Lincoln K series V-12 was spotted at Troy Ladd's Hollywood Hot Rods. The transmission is a T-5.

Lakewood, now a part of Holley, produces a range of bellhousings that can be used between big- or small-block Chevy engines and Muncie, BorgWarner T-10, Saginaw, and Tremec transmissions. Not all bellhousings are SFI approved.

CHAPTER 6

Clutch Pressure Plate and Disc

The clutch pressure plate is the mechanism that clamps the clutch disc to the flywheel. By doing so, it transfers engine torque to the transmission input shaft through the clutch disc. In our world, there are primarily three types: a long style with nine springs and three levers, which is used mostly for racing; a Borg and Beck style with nine springs and three levers that are typically wider than the first narrow-type levers for street driving; and the diaphragm style that has a Bellville style of spring that puts an even load onto the pressure plate to the flywheel and requires less effort from the driver.

Flexplate

A flexplate is the stamped-steel disc that bolts to the end of the crankshaft and the face of the torque converter to connect the two parts. More often than not, there is a ring gear on the outer edge that engages with the starter motor. The holes in the plate enable access for the mounting bolts. Note that lightweight, chrome moly steel flexplates are available, as are SFI-approved plates for racing applications.

When installing a flexplate, be sure to use ARP Grade 8 bolts that are the correct length to prevent misalignment. Be sure to follow all instructions relating to the hardware and the starter. If you're assembling your engine on a stand, remember that it will have to be removed from the stand to install the flexplate because it bolts to the back of the engine first. Remember to get a plate of the right diameter and the ring gear to align with your starter.

Flexplates, such as this SFI-approved B&M example from Holley, is designed to fit externally balanced 1986–1997 small-block Chevy engines. It has a single, 10.75-inch bolt pattern and a 153-tooth ring gear.

This Holley/Hays Classic clutch kit is designed to work in conjunction with a 26-spline clutch disc and modern 5- or 6-speed transmissions. The alignment tool is included.

Flywheel

A flywheel does the exact same job as a flexplate but is more often used to connect the engine to a manual transmission. Unlike a flexplate, a flywheel is an integral part of the clutch assembly because the clutch disc is clamped against the flywheel by the pressure plate to transfer torque from the engine to the transmission.

The flywheel is made of steel or aluminum with an outer ring gear of steel teeth that engage with the starter motor, and it is essentially an inertia device that reduces vibration by smoothing out the rotation of the crank. It stores energy to propel the vehicle and provides a surface for the clutch disc to be clamped against.

It stands to reason that a heavier flywheel carries more momentum, but in our world, we want to reduce that mass for the engine to rev more freely. That said, a balance is needed between a quick-revving engine and drivability. You should also get your flywheel and pressure plate assembly balanced, even if your supplier says the pressure plate is already balanced. Typically, the flywheel is balanced first, the pressure plate is added, and the assembly is re-balanced. Note that it is essential to mark the two components so that they are assembled in the same relationship as they were balanced.

SFI

In the early days of the development of drag racing and the performance industry, there became a need for speed equipment to be tested and certified. Initially, what was then the Speed Equipment Manufacturers Association (SEMA) did that under

POWERTRAIN CHOICE

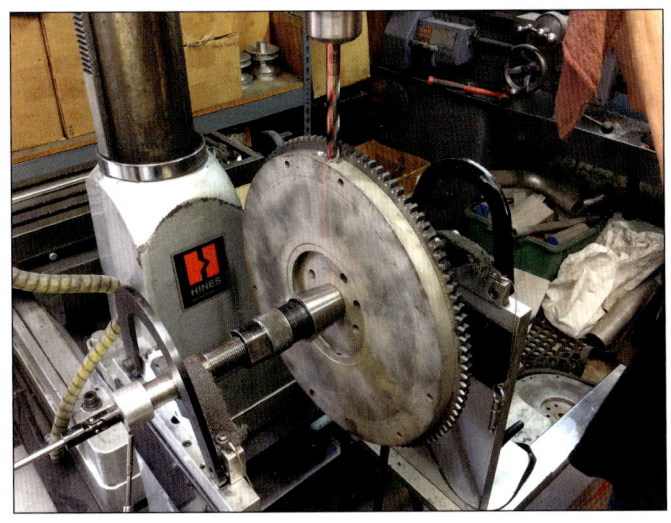

Mike Hermann at H&H Flatheads balances the flywheel first so that if the clutch has to be replaced, the flywheel does not have to be balanced again.

the SEMA Foundation banner. However, in 1978 SFI became its own organization, and it continues to issue and administer quality-assurance standards for specialty performance and racing equipment.

Transmission Options

Rodders have an amazing number of options when it comes to transmissions. There's everything from the original Ford 3-speed Top-loader, or even column shift, to a wide array of automatics and modern 4-, 5-, or 6-speed manuals. The choice is yours, and the deciding factors are preference, space, availability, and cost.

If you're going down the traditional road, the Ford box is the only real choice; you just have to pick the right box. There was a time when those boxes were regarded as weak, but you need to put that opinion into context and remember that they were designed to function behind 100-hp engines in less demanding conditions. Hot rodders doubled the output of their flatties and then switched to small-block Chevys, Cadillacs, and even Hemis and expected Ford's three-some to cope. Ford's box was not designed for that, and it failed. Back then, a failure was easily remedied with yet another wrecking-yard box. Today, with the resurgence of interest in period-correct rods, the venerable 3-speed has found renewed favor.

Of course, back in the day, rodders installed Lincoln-Zephyr (LZ) gears in the Ford boxes or they opted for a 1937 Cadillac-LaSalle (CL), which was regarded in its day as without equal on the drag strip. The CL offered a slightly lower ratio (2.39:1) compared to the 26-tooth LZ (2.33:1); second gear was 1.53:1 for the CL, and 1.58:1 for the LZ. As it was a one-year-only transmission (with the CL moving to column shift in 1938), these boxes fetch a premium unless you're lucky and find one for the right price.

If you stick with the Ford 3-speed and want to mix and match for the best options, then the 1937–1952 case with a 1978 casting mark on the back is the case to find. You can then install later gears, but a preferable option (if you can handle the work) is to use the 1939–1949 pickup case fitted with 1942–1948 passenger-car internals or preferably the LZ close-ratio gearset that will set you back almost $900 from Eckler's Automotive Parts.

In 1941, BorgWarner produced an overdrive unit that bolted on the back of the Lincoln Zephyr box. It became optional on Ford and Mercury cars in 1949. It effectively offered five forward speeds: first, second direct, second overdrive, third direct, and third overdrive. The BorgWarner overdrive units can be found, and restoration parts are available from VanPelt Sales.

Gear Vendors also makes open drive overdrive units that bolt to the back of an early Ford transmission or one that installs in the torque tube. Gear Vendors will supply you with directions to install it in the torque tube or it can make the modifications if you send in your torque tube and shaft. For engines that produced more than typical flathead power, an overdrive from Gear Vendors is probably the strongest solution.

If you have a torque tube rather than an open drive, you can purchase brand new, warrantied overdrive units for both Model A and 1932–1948 models from Mitchell Overdrive. Mitchell's installation kits include new front and rear torque tubes, drive lines, a speedometer cable extension and gear, a shifter and linkage, or cable shift. The overdrive unit that fits in the torque tube features Mitchell's synchromesh technology, which means any gear can be split at any speed to give you six forward gears instead of three. Shifting is manual with a separate shift stick mounted next to the standard stick or an optional push-pull cable shift. It's certainly a solution for some situations.

If you are using or considering the early Ford transmission, I strongly recommend that you visit

CHAPTER 6

Start with the Ford case that is stamped 78 in the bottom-left corner. Better still is the 1939–1949 pickup case fitted with 1942–1948 passenger-car internals.

For high-horsepower applications (more than a hot flattie), overdrive units from Gear Vendors might be the hot ticket. This one bolts to the back of the Ford box, while another is spliced into the torque tube.

VanPelt Sales's website (vanpeltsales.com) for an overdose of Ford 3-speed transmission information. More good information on manual transmissions can be found in the excellent SA Design book *How to Build and Modify High-Performance Manual Transmissions* by Paul Cangialosi.

Other things to think about when you are making decisions about which transmission to use are the physical size of the box (whether it will fit) and how big of a transmission tunnel you will have to make. You need to think about where the shift lever will fall and if it will be comfortable. You will probably need to get a box that has a mechanical speedometer drive. You need to think about the availability of different gearsets in case you get it completely wrong. Finally, you should invest in a new gearbox mount. You just don't want to use a worn-out mount.

BorgWarner T-10 and Super T-10

The history of the BorgWarner T-10 transmission can be traced back to the 3-speed T-85 originally used in the 1935 Chrysler Airflow. In fact, the T-10 shares the same case design, gear centers, and 3-4 synchronizer as the T-85.

The T-10 first appeared in the 1957 Corvette, but it was used by AMC, Chrysler, GM, and Ford. For this reason, they are fairly easy to find. The Corvettes all had aluminum cases, but the GM full-size cars used a cast-iron case until 1960, after which all cases became aluminum. They are tough and period correct for a 1960s-inspired rod, and the box to look for is the Power Brute Super T-10 that was used in the 1974–1982 GM A- and F-Body cars. These Super T-10s featured a 26-spline input shaft and 32-spline output shaft (same as the TH-400 slip yoke) and were built to withstand high-performance applications with hardened gears and

Wanting a period-correct, 1960s-style Model A pickup, Mike Williams opted for a BorgWarner Super T-10 to back up his 1958 283 built by Phil Lukens at Blair's Speed Shop.

110   HOW TO BUILD AFFORDABLE HOT RODS

cases and additional ratios. Super T-10s can be identified by their M-18, M-21, or M-24 GM data tags.

Ford C4

Introduced in 1964 in the Fairlane and some Lincolns, the Ford C4 automatic transmission replaced the Ford-O-Matic that had a cooler name but was only a 2-speed compared to the 3-speed C4. The C4 was lighter because it was simpler and aluminum. In 1965, the C4 became available in the Falcon, F-Series, Mustang, and Ranchero. In 1970, the C4 went from a 0.788-inch 24-spline input shaft to an 0.839-inch 26-spline shaft that also included a matching 26-spline clutch hub. The following year, Ford went to a 26/24-spline input shaft, which means the torque-converter side is 26 spline and the clutch hub is 24 spline.

In its day, the C4 was a popular, low-cost, readily available transmission that was tough enough, but it was discontinued in 1981. That's almost 40 years ago, so it's not really worth bothering with unless you were given one.

Muncie 4-Speed

In 1963, General Motors introduced a 4-speed manual on the Corvette and its full-size cars. Made at GM's Muncie, Indiana, plant, the design resembled the earlier BorgWarner T-85 3-speed and the later T-10. Indeed, the Muncie evolved from the T-10, and they are very similar.

Because of its strength and availability, Muncie became the byword of racers. There were three types: M20, M21, and M22.

In the early 1980s, BorgWarner sold the T-10 to Doug Nash. It was then sold to Richmond Gear, and in 2012, Richmond was acquired by Motive Gear, but I could find no mention of the T-10 on its website, motivegear.com. I did, however, find Richmond ST-10s for sale at 5speeds.com.

BorgWarner/Tremec T-5

Without a doubt, one of the most popular manual transmissions out there is the BorgWarner T-5. Developed from the BorgWarner SR-4 and T-4, it was introduced in 1982 in the AMC Spirit and Concord models. However, it was quickly adopted by GM in 1982 in the S/T pickups, Blazers, and Astro vans. In 1983, Ford put them in Mustangs and Thunderbirds, while GM put them in Camaros and Firebirds. Nissan even used them in the 280ZX and 300Z cars.

Besides having an internal shifter linkage, this robust 5-speed has (for the most part) interchangeable internals, so pick your case and pick a gearset that meets your needs. It's a very versatile transmission. There are two generations: 1982–1985 Non-World Class (NWC) and 1985-and-later World Class (WC) that had several design improvements, so go for the later boxes listed below when possible. Note that the different manufacturers used different size and spline input and output shafts, so do your research before you buy and be sure to look for a box with a mechanical

The legendary Muncie 4-speed was used by GM from 1963 to 1975. For the full story, read Paul Cangialosi's book Muncie 4-Speed Transmissions: How to Rebuild and Modify *from SA Design.*

When it first arrived at the Kennedy brothers' shop, James Jard's 1936 3-window had a C4 with a Wilcap adapter to the Oldsmobile, but it was removed.

CHAPTER 6

Chuck de Heras had an early Ford Toploader in his Ardun-powered Deuce roadster, but Jay Kennedy swapped it out for a more robust 5-speed T-5. The stock K-member was retained but had to be cut to accommodate the transmission.

A Tremec TKO 500 5-speed transmission with multiple shifter locations was installed in James Jard's 1936 3-window after the removal of the Ford C4.

speedometer drive if that's what you want.

The more popular WC units were used in the original vehicles listed below, and the most popular is the GM F-Body T-5 that had a 2.95:1 ratio. The transmission should be tagged, and you can research them at 5speeds.com: late 1985–1996 Mustangs, Cougars, and Thunderbirds, 1988–1996 Camaros and Firebirds, 1993–1995 Chevy and GMC S/T series trucks, 1994–1996 Honda Passports, and 1991–1997 Isuzu Rodeos.

Tremec was founded in 1964 by Ford supplier Clark Transmission and two Mexican companies to meet the need for a transmission built entirely in Mexico. Soon, Tremec was not only supplying the local market but also exporting to the US. In the 1990s, Tremec acquired BorgWarner's manual transmissions, including the rights to the 5-speed T-5, the 6-speed T-56, and the revered T-170 Ford Toploader. This enabled Tremec to launch a line of transmissions for the aftermarket in the late 1990s.

One has to admit, Tremec was very cognizant of the market and quickly offered the T-5 5-speed, TKO 5-speed, and Magnum 6-speed. In 2012, it offered the Magnum XL 6-speed. While the Tremec is the go-to transmission for the performance industry, it might be regarded as too modern for traditional rods. But as you can see, it can be found in many traditional rods. From a performance aspect, there probably isn't a better 5-speed.

GM Hydra-Matic TH350 and TH400

Introduced in 1969, the 3-speed GM Hydra-Matic TH350 replaced the GM Powerglide. It featured a one-piece aluminum casting with an integral bellhousing that bolts up to most Chevy V-8s. It is only 21¾ inches long and is one of the shortest but most robust automatics available. I know this, because we ran one in the Thacker and Shine roadster regularly to almost 200 mph. It weighs only 120 pounds and used a mechanical cable kick-down

Mick Jenkins of Mick's Paint was going with this TH400 in his big-block Chevy-powered Deuce, but it's a bulky casting that has been superseded by the 4L80E.

Here is the completed aluminum tunnel made by Pauly Rivera at Mick's Paint for Bob Garibay's blown Deuce roadster with a TH400 transmission.

mechanism that is attached to the throttle linkage. The aftermarket produces a ton of parts, including shift improver kits, torque converters, etc. The stock gearing is 2.52:1, 1.52:1, and 1:1.

The TH400 was introduced in 1964 in Buick and Cadillac cars, and the following year it appeared in Chevys and Oldsmobiles. It is a little longer than the TH350 at 24.37 inches and weighs in slightly heavier at 135 pounds. The gearing is 2.48:1, 1.48:1, and 1:1. The TH400 uses an electrical slide switch kick-down mechanism that is controlled by the throttle linkage. Interestingly, a variable pitch stator was available in the 1965–1967 Buicks, Cadillacs, and Oldsmobiles that could essentially vary the characteristics of the torque converter.

In 1990, GM changed the designation of its transmissions, and the TH400 became the 3L80 (3-speed, longitudinally positioned, 8,000 pounds GVW). An overdrive version called the 4L80-E is an electronically controlled 4-speed. Like the TH350, the TH400 bolts up to most Chevy engines.

From a rodder's perspective, the TH400 is a great but large transmission that fits 1932-and-later cars better than it does a Model A.

Rear Axles

Many rod builders will go for the early Ford banjo rear end because they are traditional, fairly plentiful, and robust. As with all things, you need to know what you're getting before you jump in and spend money because not all rear ends are made the same.

Go for the 1939–1948 axles with hydraulic brakes. However, juice brakes can be adapted to early axles, so the answers get no easier. The good news is that many Ford parts are interchangeable, so parts can be mixed and matched, but to do that, you need a good pile of parts to pick from. Remember also that the later Fords had a longer wheelbase than early Fords, so you will therefore have to shorten the torque tube, unless of course you're converting to an open drive. The axles got wider from 57 inches (drum to drum) for the Model A to 61 inches for the 1942–1948 models, and the springs were all over the place.

Here's my advice: unless you really know your early Fords, stick with the 1939–1941 rear that has

HOW TO BUILD AFFORDABLE HOT RODS

CHAPTER 6

juice brakes and bolt-on radius rods. In fact, for most traditional applications, the early Ford is the ideal choice. They're plentiful, you can interchange parts, and they are tough enough for most applications.

There is also the option of a Columbia 2-speed. Introduced in 1934, the Columbia 2-speed axle, when in overdrive, dropped engine revolutions by a whopping 30 percent and cut the revs at 60 mph from a roaring 2,840 rpm to a much more sedate 2,061 rpm in a car with a 3.78:1 ratio. They're out there and have historical cachet, but they are probably not the hot rodder's first choice for the simple solution.

Quick-Change Axles

Many builders want to go with the traditional appearance of a quick-change axle. I wonder why because the noise from those whining gears on a long journey is enough to drive you deaf, and how often has anybody (other than a serious racer) ever changed a gear? That said, despite the cost, people love them.

It's very difficult to trace the origins of the quick-change, but in speaking with Kevin Presidio of Cyclone Racing Equipment, we learned that there were some quick-changes made before World War II for the booming oval-track market by Ted Halibrand and also Cook's Machine Works that made products under the Cyclone brand. However, a shortage of materials meant that this was little more than a cottage industry at the time. It wasn't until after the war that things really got moving when racing quick-changes were more easily created from Spicer differentials manufactured for 3/4-ton trucks. Racers soon latched onto the assembly and adapted it to their needs. One racer was Pat Warren of Downey Machine Shop in Downey, California, who offered quick-changes and a center section to fit Ford rear ends in the April 1948 issue of *Hot Rod*. Sower's Engineering in Burbank, California, also offered quick-changes in the May 1948 issue of *Hot Rod*. Warren apparently only made a handful of rear ends, as other companies such as Halibrand Engineering quickly took the lead. Ted Halibrand started his company in Culver City, California, in 1947, and his first product was a racing wheel for Indy. He went on to pioneer the pin-drive system and quickly followed the wheel with a quick-change center section designed around the popular Ford rear axle assembly that utilized the axle housings, axles, ring and pinions, differentials, and brakes readily available to the racer. The quick-change, as its name suggests, allowed racers to make quick gear changes to their difficult-to-change, frequently breaking Ford rear ends.

For a while, Halibrand had it all his own way. He was on the USAC tech committee, after all. Eventually, Jim Frankland of Tampa, Florida, got into the quick-change business, and for many years both companies dominated the industry. Unfortunately, Halibrand changed hands several times and subsequently lost focus and allowed competitors to enter the market. There are now several companies that make quick-changes, including Coleman Racing Products, Diversified Machine (racing applications), Dutchman Axles, Frankland Racing, Hot Rod Works' Rodsville, Howe Racing Enterprises, PEM Racing, Speedway Engineering, Speedway Motors, Tiger Racing, and Winters Racing. Halibrand is now part of Holley, and at the time of writing, there were no plans to reintroduce the quick-change.

You can find plenty of used axles on the market, but beware because they can be costly to refurbish. The problem with buying a quick-change that has not already been adapted for hot rod use is that, as Mike Williams found, there's an awful lot of fabrication needed to fit the axle under the car.

Something else to watch for when buying a used quick-change axle assembly setup for a rod is that the brackets are welded on correctly. Jay Kennedy recently pulled one from Chuck de Heras's Ardun-powered Deuce roadster only to find that the ladder bar brackets were incorrectly mounted: one pointed up, while the other pointed down. Greg Hirota went to a lot of trouble to remove those wrongly welded brackets and replace them with new ones. It was not a cheap operation.

Ford 8-Inch and 9-Inch

The other main choice on the hot rodder's menu is the ubiquitous Ford 8- or 9-inch. Incidentally, the number refers to the nominal outside diameter of the ring gear. The 8-inch was introduced in 1962 and found its way under the performance cars of the day: Fairlanes, Mustangs, Falcons etc. The easy way to recognize an 8-inch from a 9-inch is to try a socket on the case nuts. If it goes on all the nuts, it's an 8-inch. If it will not go on the bottom two nuts and you need a wrench, it's a 9-inch. The 8-inch was only available with 28-tooth axle shafts, and most pundits say to avoid it because it's not as strong as its big 9-inch brother. That's true to some extent, but according to Joe Kennedy, an 8-inch

Mike Williams chose the early Ford-style Winters with tapered steel axle housing bells, just like the early Ford. However, there's a lot of work to do to mount the radius rods, spring mounts, shocks, Panhard bar, brakes, torque bar, etc.

Mike Williams's axle is painted and ready to install. The wishbone brackets were welded to the axle ends, and there are no spring mounts because Mike's truck will have coilover shocks.

is fine for most lightweight hot rod applications. In fact, there was one in James Jard's 1936 3-window when it arrived. It had never shown any signs of weakness, so it left with the same 8-inch. If you can't afford the 9-inch, go with the 8. After all, what's an inch between friends?

The 9-inch was introduced for the 1957 model year under the Fairlane and F-100 pickup. It looks much the same as the 8-inch being made from a series of stampings. The third member is cast iron, supports all of the gears and bearings, and is installed from the front to allow for relatively easy gear ratio changes. Interestingly, in the world of axles, these are known as banjo style, but in the traditional hot rod world, the word *banjo* refers to an early Ford axle. The 9-inch was superseded in 1986 by the 8.8-inch, which is a totally different animal.

The good news is that because of its inherent strength and versatility, there is a strong axle aftermarket. You can find everything from complete axles (from companies such as Currie Enterprises, Mark Williams Enterprises, Moser Engineering, and Strange Engineering) to brake hardware from drums to discs.

Columbia 2-Speed

Back in the day and when folks were restoring their early Fords, the Columbia 2-speed overdrive rear end was the hot ticket. Made by the Columbia Axle Co. of Cleveland, Ohio, it first appeared on the 1932 Auburn, and Ford offered it as an option on the 1934 Model 40. In 1937, the factory offered it as an option for V-12-powered Lincoln Zephyrs, and in 1939, it was offered on Ford and Mercury models.

Vacuum operated, the axle offered improved acceleration through a low gear ratio. Shifting to the higher ratio via a dash-mounted cable created an overdrive situation whereby engine revs dropped by 30 percent. For example, revs dropped from 2,713 to 1,940 rpm at 55 mph. You can see the benefits: it got off the line better and provided improved fuel economy. It actually worked in all three forward gears. What wasn't to like?

According to John, the owner of Columbia Two Speed Parts in Cottonwood, Arizona, the axles are tough, but like all early Ford parts, they are now 80 or more years old. Many are worn, and many may have been poorly repaired in the past. He recommends that you take them apart before you make a purchase to look for telltale signs of wear or breakage. He said you can do that at a swap meet or garage sale and sellers won't mind, but I'm not so sure.

CHAPTER 6

Here is a Columbia 2-speed overdrive axle spotted at Walden Speed Shop that has been modified for ladder bars and an anti-sway bar.

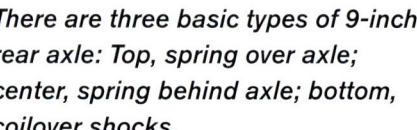
There are three basic types of 9-inch rear axle: Top, spring over axle; center, spring behind axle; bottom, coilover shocks.

Additional Information

Buying or building an axle is a bit like replacing a water heater in your house. It's a lot of work, expensive, nobody sees it, and nobody cares, but it has to be done. What most people don't realize is that there is a lot of planning, measuring, and work that goes into an axle. It has to have the right flange-to-flange width to clear the body and the right drum-to-drum width for the tires to look right and fit under the fenders. Then there is all the bracketry to consider. Ideally, the ladder bar brackets and spring hangers should be welded on before the flanges. The brackets can be split and welded on in two halves if your axle already has flanges. And remember, if you're using early Ford axle bells, they are tapered. There's cost involved with that. I checked Currie's website and the labor rate at the time of writing was $144 an hour for welding on brackets.

A quick way to identify the approximate year of an early Ford V-8 rear end is by the radius rods. The 1932–1936 radius rod mounts are a permanent part of the rear axle housing. The 1937–1940 radius rods are bolted to the axle housing/backing plates, are very long, and extend almost the full length of the torque tube. The 1942–1948 radius rods are short, attach to the housing/backing plates, and attach midway up the torque tube. Another quick identifier is the brakes: those from 1932–1936 are rod operated, those from 1937–1938 are cable operated, and those from 1939–1948 are hydraulic.

Generally, axle ratios are stamped into the banjo housing below the pinion bearing where there should be three numbers. Divide the first number into the second number to get the ratio. The 1936-and-later center section banjo (complete with the 1936-and-later ring gear) will work on any 1936–1948 axle/axle tube combination. However, there are differences in the number of spines on the pinion and in the driveshafts. As a general rule, if you are trying to upgrade the rear end (for example, of a 1933–1934 Model 40), stay away from anything earlier than 1935.

This is a typical 9-inch Ford set up in the traditional way with ladder bars, shocks, and a Deuce spring mounted on spring hangers welded to the axle.

CHAPTER 7

WHEELS AND TIRES

One of the great things about building a hot rod is that you have a huge array of wheels and tires from which to choose. There's everything from stock Ford wheels all the way to five-spoke mags, kidney beans, 12-spoke spindle mounts, or whatever takes your fancy. They can all look right on the right vehicle, and even Moon discs are correct on the right car, such as Jim Jard's tribute to Fred Allen's *Devil Deuce* coupe. Your pile of old magazines, photographs, and the internet will help you make the right, informed decision. A website I recommend is roadster.com/wheels/. It contains a wealth of information about vintage American racing wheels, such as American Racing, Cragar, Halibrand, etc.

If you're an amateur builder, you're unlikely to have a stash of wheels and tires to mock up and choose from like professional builders. Nevertheless, there are things you can do that will help you make the right choice. You can borrow some wheels and tires (or even just some tires of the right size) to use in your mock-up, or you can make some representative wheel and tire discs out of wood. That's what Rick Lefever did when he and his son Rayce started the build of Rayce's Model A coupe. Rick did not yet have the wheels for this project, so he cut some sheets of plywood into wheels so that he could see where they fall, calculate the backspacing, etc. It's easy to do, costs very little, and gives you a good and adjustable place to start.

Although they are important, wheel and tire combinations are not just about overall diameter. They're about width, backspacing, and scrub radius. Scrub radius refers to the intersection of a line drawn down through the center of the kingpin (axis) to the ground and a line drawn vertically down through the center of the tire. Ideally, for a car with a beam axle, the two lines should intersect on the ground at the point of contact. If the lines intersect below ground, you have positive scrub radius. If the lines intersect above ground level, you have negative scrub radius. The term is derived from the fact that if the two lines do not intersect on the ground, the tire will scrub, and more effort is needed to turn the wheel.

You can say that it doesn't matter in a hot rod, but if you set up your

When Chapouris first built this 1926 T for his father in the late 1970s, it sported steelies and radial tires. It could have looked just as good with a road-racing combination.

HOW TO BUILD AFFORDABLE HOT RODS 117

CHAPTER 7

In the 1990s, Chapouris installed a different set of steel rims shod with bias-ply BFGoodrich wide whites: 5.90 x 15s in front and 7.50 x 15s in back. It looked good in Muroc dust.

steering and suspension geometry correctly, your rod will be easier and more fun to drive. It's that simple. Deep dish, reverse rims are where you will probably encounter excessive negative scrub radius. You'll just have to look at the wheels you want to use, measure them, see where it falls, and be prepared to make some compromises if your car handles badly.

Wheel balance is something that a lot of rodders do not think about, but wheel and tire balance is critical to a good ride. Today's problem is that shops that understand early cars and how they need to be set up are disappearing. Be aware that tires (even new tires and especially bias-ply tires) are rarely round or in balance. The balance is fairly easily corrected once the tires are mounted on the rims, but the out-of-roundness is more of a problem because finding a tire shop that can shave your tires round is getting harder.

I know of only one tire specialist in the Los Angeles region that still offers tire shaving, and that is Nate Jones Tire Co. in Signal Hill, California. Finding a shop to do this in your region might prove to be difficult. A tire shaver is a machine that shaves the tire on the car as the tire rotates. After shaving, the wheels and tires can be balanced. You might think that it doesn't matter, but I've driven rods with unshaved tires and another with shaved-and-balanced tires, and the difference is measurable.

You could opt for old tires, and that's fine, as long as you remember that rubber hardens over time. While those pie-crust drag slicks might look cool, they might ride like Fred Flintstone's *Rockmobile*, and worse, they might begin to unravel while you're are on a road trip and dump you in the middle of nowhere. That's bad enough when you have an easily replaceable tire and even worse when you have an oddball vintage tire.

When selecting tires, be thoughtful as to what you will do with your ride. Is it just for around town? Will you take it on long road trips? Will you race it, hill climb it, or what? Of course, you can have different tires for different occasions, but as you build the car, look down the road for what you might need.

One thing to remember is that wheels can be widened or narrowed. This is not a process that is readily available in small towns and not something we recommend you try at home. One company that will alter aluminum or steel rims is Weldcraft Wheels in Livonia, Michigan. Its website is very informative and provides plenty of advice. Other companies that offer this service include Rim-Spec Wheel Repair and Rim Repair in Grand Prairie, Texas; and Gary's Custom in Panama City, Florida. Costs vary across the country, and you will have to pay shipping both ways, so add that to the cost of packaging and the work. It is a fairly expensive process if you can't get it done locally.

There are no hard-and-fast rules about wheel and tire combinations, but when the car looks right, it will look right even with different wheel and tire combinations. When Pete Chapouris originally built *Sirod* for his dad, it had steelies and radials. Years later, in the 1990s, Pete swapped the radials for bias-ply BFGoodrich wide whites. The car took on a new look and looked even better. We talked about the fact that the car could easily look as good with other wheel styles, such as kidney beans or early Ford wires.

Backspacing

Backspacing is defined as the distance from the hub mounting flange to the inside lip of the wheel. It's easy to measure with a straightedge and a tape measure.

WHEELS AND TIRES

To measure the backspacing of your wheels, lay a straightedge across the back face of the wheel and measure down to the hub-mounting flange.

If you want that traditional look in a high-performance tire, check out some of the lesser-known brands, such as Blockley, Stahl Sport Radial, or the Dunlop shown here on Lucky Burton's lakes coupe.

1 Lay the wheel face down on the ground so the backside of the wheel is face-up.

2 Lay a straightedge diagonally across the outermost lip of the wheel.

3 Measure the distance from where the straightedge contacts the outermost lip to the hub mounting flange of the wheel.

Balancing

Some people don't bother balancing their wheels and tires, but it's really important to do this because the wheels might be 100 years old. Tires of indeterminate age are rarely in balance, and even new tires need balancing. Consequently, if you want a shake-free ride, get them balanced.

Bias-Ply versus Radial Tires

The most basic difference between a bias-ply (or cross-ply) tire and a radial tire is the construction method. A bias-ply tire has the belts of construction material crisscrossing at 30 to 45 degrees to the centerline of the tire. A radial tire has the construction belts running at right angles to the tire centerline. You might think it won't make a huge difference, but the ride characteristics are night and day. About the only practical benefit of bias-ply tires is that due to their construction, they tend to roll straight. The most important thing is that they look right. Bias-ply tires feature a narrow tread profile with sharp shoulders that often have that desirable pie-crust look. A radial tire has a softer, rounder look and tends to squash down at the bottom compared to a bias-ply tire.

In 2013, Coker Tire introduced its Classic American style that has the narrow tread profile and aspect ratio of a vintage-style bias-ply tire with the internal construction of a radial. Coker says it's the best of both worlds, and it possibly is. Made in the US, the American Classic bias-look-radial is only available in 13-, 14-, and 15-inch sizes, so while there are lots of options for OEM and custom fitments for cars built in the 1940s through the 1960s, they are probably not an option for rods that typically require a 16- or 18-inch tire. That's a shame because it's a good idea.

Incidentally, if you're looking for some interesting, high-performance bias-ply tires, check out Blockley Tyre Company and Dunlop Tires. Blockley has a wide range of vintage-style tires in sizes 16- through 21-inch diameter.

Bolt Pattern or Circle

Simply put, the bolt pattern or bolt circle is the number of lug nut holes and their spacing. Most early Fords have five lugs on a 5½-inch circle. However, in 1936, Ford shifted to what is known as the wide-five pattern that had five lugs on a 10¼-inch circle. When sourcing vintage wheels, be careful not to confuse the American wide five with the English wide fives that were fitted to Anglias, Populars, and Prefects that were 5x8. Those English wheels are out there

HOW TO BUILD AFFORDABLE HOT RODS

CHAPTER 7

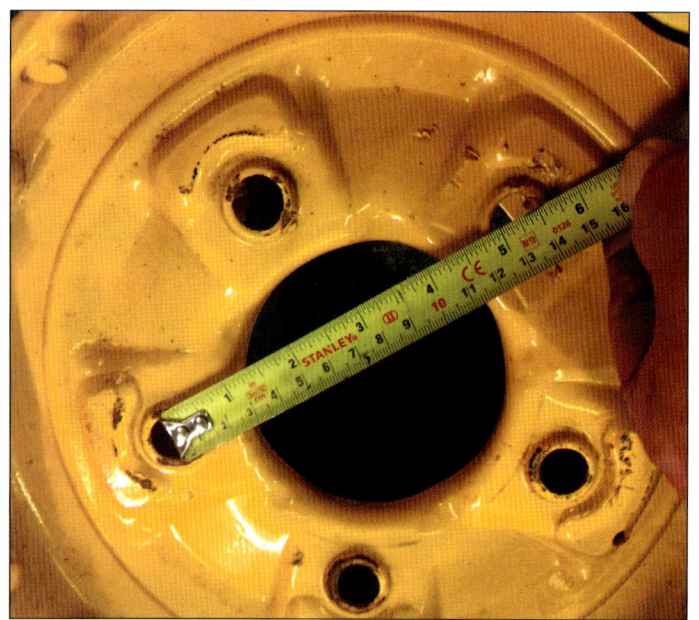

The bolt pattern, or bolt circle, refers to the number of lug holes and their spacing. In the case of most early Fords, the pattern is 5x5½. However, in 1936, Ford changed to a wide five with 5x10¼-inch bolt circle.

Originally, chrome-reverse rims were made by splitting the rim from the bolt flange, reversing the rim, and welding or riveting them back together.

because many of those cars were (and still are) rodded or raced. Bolt circle templates are available from a number of companies, and you can even print your own by visiting info.mpbrakes.com.

Chrome Reverse Rims

Reverse rims came out of racing when competitors looked for a wider-than-stock track. To reverse the rims, the rivets that connect the mounting flange to the rim are drilled out. Then, the rim is reversed and pushed out as far as it will go before the flange is reattached. Rodders saw this and adapted the concept to their rides. Both Norm Grabowski and "TV" Tommy Ivo had reverse rims on their T-buckets in 1957, but both had painted rims with baby moon hubcaps. It didn't take rodders long to realize that if they split the rims, they could widen them like the racers and chrome them, and so the chrome reverse rim was born.

But why reverse the rim and not just move the flange back? Well, the rim had a different profile on the back compared to the front, and when chromed, it looked superior and reflected well. Chrome reverse rims were soon all the rage, and you'll remember them from the Deuce coupe and the '55 Chevy featured in *American Graffiti*. In 1962, Spiegel Sales advertised a set of four for $69.50 exchange.

If you want some today, Stockton Wheel Service Inc. offers its Milner Special in a variety of rim sizes from 14x5 through 17x9 and bolt patterns 5x4 through 6x5.5. They are fully polished around the lug hole, and Stockton carries a selection of caps and trim rings to compliment the rims.

Dow 7

Dow 7 is a chemical conversion coating used to protect magnesium products (such as wheels and superchargers) that polish up well but oxidize before your very eyes. Dow 7 can be used on components that have dissimilar materials, such as inserts. The finish causes no appreciable dimensional change and results in

It's not so popular now, but Dow 7 was the finish for magnesium wheels when they were popular. Finding platers that will apply Dow 7 is no longer easy. (Photo Courtesy Dave Rocha)

flat, gold-like, brassy, or dark brown finish depending upon the alloy.

Dow 7 is not particularly durable and needs to be reapplied occasionally. It's not easy to find a plating company that will apply Dow 7 due to environmental regulation changes in the plating industry.

Ford Welded Wires

In 1926, Ford introduced *welded* spoke wheels that replaced the nipple-type spokes that required specialized manual assembly and regular adjustment. Welded spoke wheels were cheaper and easier to produce and didn't need adjustment. In 1927, Ford made the welded spoke wheel standard until 1936 when it switched to the wide-five stamped steel wheels.

If you use anything other than stock Ford brake drums or the later 1940–1948 hydraulic brake drums with 1928–1935 Ford wires, you will need wire wheel support plates. Sold by companies such as Mac's Antique Auto Parts, these steel supports look like wheel spacers except the raised lip around the central hole prevents the center of the wire wheel from collapsing when you tighten the lug nuts.

Between 1936 and 1939, Ford switched from a regular 5x5½ bolt circle to this 5x10¼ wide-five bolt pattern. It was popular on early race cars.

Ford Wide Five

In 1936, Ford made the change from a regular bolt pattern to what is commonly known as the wide-five bolt pattern. It switched from the standard 5x5½ of the 1935 Ford to the 5x10¼ bolt circle. In 1940, Ford reverted to the 5x5½ bolt pattern. When searching for wheels for your project, the wide fives are easily spotted. Wide fives also came in 18x3.62 for high clearance needs. It's interesting to note that English Fords, Anglias, Populars, Prefects, etc., all had their own 5x8 wide five, while VW and Porsche had a metric 5x205-mm wide five.

Year(s)/Type	Tire Size	Bolt Pattern
1928–1929	21x3	5x5½
1930–1931	19x3	5x5½
1932	18x3¼	5x5½
1933–1934	17x3¼	5x5½
1935	16x4	5x5½
1936	16x4	5x10¼
1937	16x4	5x10¼
1938	16x4	5x10¼
1939	16x4	5x10¼
V-8-60	16x3½	5x10¼
1940–1948	16x4	5x5½
Milk truck	18x3⅝	5x5½

On the left is an original Ford welded straight 32-spoke wheel. An aftermarket Kelsey-Hayes or MotorWheel Corp. bent spoke, 40-spoke wheel is on the right.

Kelsey-Hayes Wheel Co. and Motor Wheel Corporation

Formed in 1927, the Kelsey-Hayes Wheel Co. was an original equipment wheel supplier to Ford and other car manufacturers. By 1929 it made 10,000 wire wheels a day. Similarly, Motor Wheel Corporation controlled more than 30 percent of the entire US wheel business by 1934. Both companies produced aftermarket wheels for Ford vehicles that are easily

HOW TO BUILD AFFORDABLE HOT RODS

Vintage Kelsey-Hayes bent-spoke wheels were very popular in the resto-rod eras but are not so popular these days. Some 16s had a 4½-inch rim that might give you better tire choice.

These 18x3⅝ milk-truck wheels made by Kelsey-Hayes were popular with the lakes racers because they shared a 5x5½ bolt circle with Ford passenger cars. Here they are fitted with shaved tires.

identified by their bent-spoke design that was usually 40 spokes compared to Ford's 32 spokes. Some wheels have welded spokes as the Ford wheels did, but some had adjustable spokes. Both brands usually have identifying marks on the mounting flange.

There were some 19-inch wheels available for the Model A Ford, but these aftermarket wheels are typically available in 16-, 17-, and 18-inch diameters. Most have a 4-inch rim width, but some of the 16-inch wheels were available with 4½-inch-wide rims.

Milk Truck Wheels

Also known as Divco wheels because they were fitted to Divco commercial vehicles and Ford trucks that required high ground clearance, these 18x3⅝ steel wheels had a 5x5½ bolt pattern and were made by Kelsey-Hayes. Some people don't like them, but they were popular with lakes racers as they offered an easy way to get some tall gearing and run 18-inch racing tires.

The Kennedy brothers built this tribute to Fred Allen's Devil Deuce *for Jim Jard and installed a set of snap-on moon discs. They never look dated.*

Moon Discs

Wheel discs were around before Dean Moon, but Moon made them cool. They are on almost every land speed race car because they actually work. I've tested them in a wind tunnel. They were popular on street cars in the 1950s just before mag wheels became readily available. They are made of spun aluminum and fixed with Dzus buttons, screws, or clip-ons to add period correctness to certain cars.

Rayce Lefever's Model A coupe on his dad Rick's frame fixture with a mock-up engine and mock-up wheels are used to calculate the axle width flange-to-flange measurement.

Positive or negative offset is the distance from the rim of the wheel to the back surface of the mounting flange.

Mock-Ups

Rick Lefever is a very talented fabricator and does nothing by half measures. When he and his son Rayce began the build of Rayce's Model A coupe, they set the coupe body up on a frame fixture complete with a mock-up engine. At the time, Rick didn't have the intended wheels and tires, so he cut some mock-up wheels out of wood. In this instance, Rick is shown using the mock-ups to figure out the axle width.

Offset

Offset is defined as the distance from the hub mounting flange to the centerline of the wheel. Zero offset occurs when the flange is exactly in line with the centerline of the wheel. Positive offset puts the mounting flange toward the outside of the wheel, while negative offset puts the mounting flange toward the back of the wheel.

It doesn't really matter what offset you have as long as your wheels meet the other geometrical requirements, which are that your camber and caster need to be correct and the wheel can't have too much positive or negative offset to affect handling.

Measuring offset is the fairly simple process of laying a straightedge across the back of your rim, (preferably with the tire removed) and measuring down to the centerline of the wheel that often will not be the back surface of the mounting flange. It's a simple matter of measuring the rim width, dividing it by two, and calculating the offset using the first measurement.

Rollers (Mock-Up Wheels)

If you only plan to build one or two cars rollers, it might not make sense to have a set of rollers, but in a busy shop situation, it might be beneficial to have a pair that you can use to push projects around. Guniwheel offers a steel roller that costs more

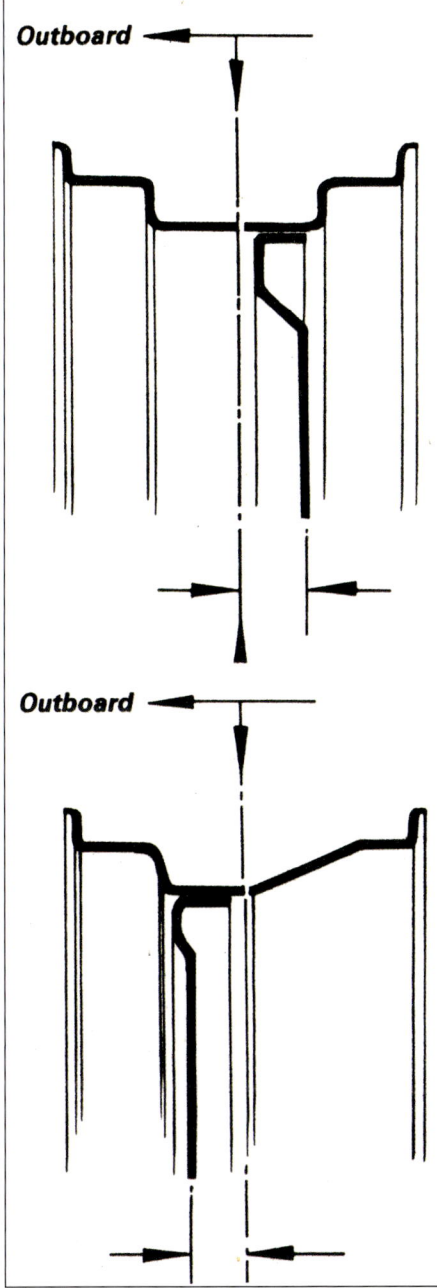

Wheel offset is the difference between the wheel mounting flange and the wheel center line. Positive offset is shown at the top.

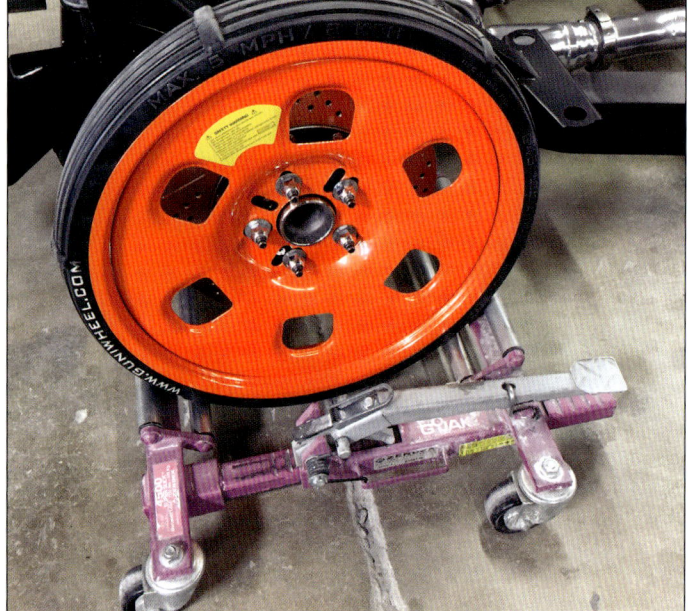

They are possibly too expensive for the homebuilder, but these mock-up wheels from Guniwheel might be the answer for a busy shop.

Rim width is measured across the inside of the well of the rim and not from edge to edge. This is a 4-inch-wide rim.

than $200 each, but a universal bolt pattern is available and will accommodate most 4- and 5-lug circles with a recommended maximum load of 1,290 pounds per wheel.

Rim Diameter and Width

Some people wrongly measure rim width using its outer edges. A rim should be measured across the well where the tire bead sits. The measurement will be approximately 1 inch less than the measurement from edge to edge. Ford rim diameters fell from 21 inches in 1928 to 16 inches in 1935. Meanwhile, rim widths increased from 3½ inches in 1928 to 4 inches in 1935. The exception was the V-8-60 models that had a 3½-inch rim width.

Scrub Radius

Scrub radius refers to the intersection of an imaginary line drawn down through the center of the kingpin (axis) to the ground and a line drawn vertically down through the center of the tire. A car with a beam axle should ideally have the two lines intersect just below the ground for a little positive scrub radius.

Spindle Mounts

Spindle-mount wheels from American Racing and Halibrand were a direct development of drag racing, where there was a desire for lightweight front wheels that didn't need front brakes. Initially, they were only available in magnesium for racing purposes. However, aluminum versions became available, as they became popular on hot rods, such as Model Ts.

The wheels were originally designed to fit British Ford Anglia spindles because that is what most drag racers used. As the wheels found more use on the street, the need for brakes increased. The wheels were designed with a meatier back flange so that a brake hat or disc could be bolted on. Some wheels converted to have brakes were suspect, so beware when you buy used wheels.

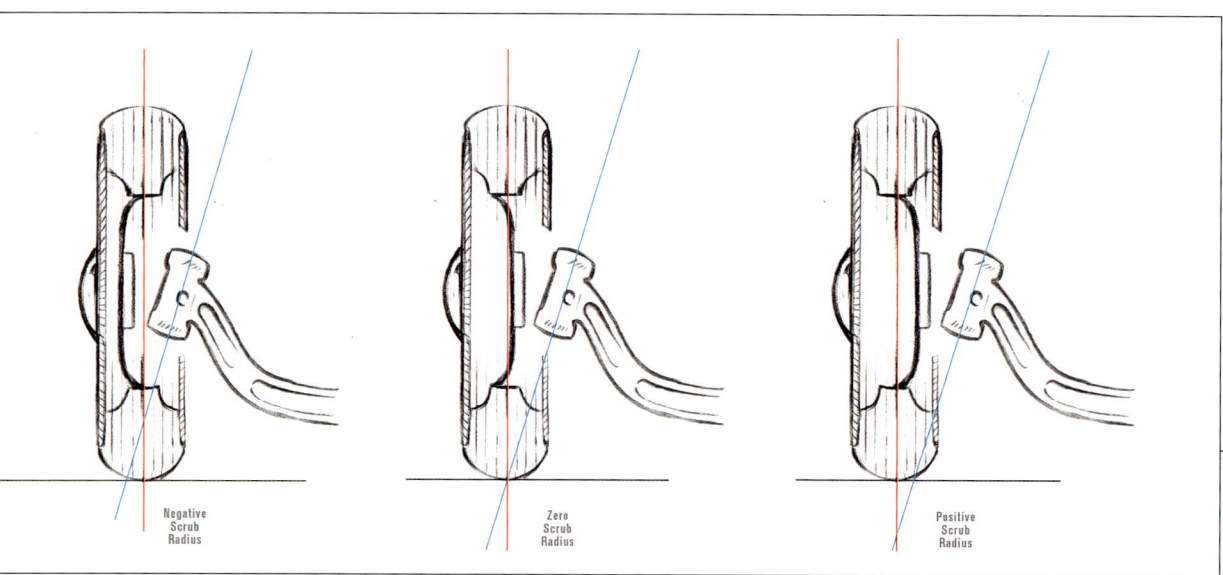

Ideally, you want a little positive scrub radius. You can live with a little more than a little, but a lot of either is not recommended. (Art Courtesy Alex M. Design)

These cast-aluminum, Sprint-style spindle mounts fitted to Bob Garibay's Deuce roadster were made by Halibrand, and they are fitted with disc brakes.

This Model A on Deuce rails was built by Kris Elmer of Salt City Speed Shop. It has great stance and a little bit of stagger with 5x16 fronts and 7.50x16 rears.

The wheels were also designed to fit heavier, early Ford-style spindles.

For a rod application, we suggest aluminum rather than magnesium wheels designed specifically for a brake application.

Stagger and Stance

In the hot rod vernacular, stagger refers to the difference between the size of the front and rear wheel and tire combo, not the difference in tire circumference between the left- and right-side tires as it does in sprint car parlance. Although it wasn't that way in the early days, most hot rods have different sized tires on the front compared to the back. This difference probably stems from the correlation between hot rods and drag cars that evolved to have a lot of front-to-rear stagger. For example, think Honda 50 wires up front and 12-inch slicks in back.

A dramatic difference in front-to-rear wheel and tire size probably doesn't matter too much on a rod, but if you are leaning toward seriously racing your rod, you want to eliminate that and go for a wheel and tire combo that is more compatible with your intentions. For example, when Jim Busby built his wicked road racing Deuce, he ran Dunlop Racing tires that were 5.50 M-15s up front and 650 M-15 CR65s in back. Not only did that coupe look tough but it hauled ass as well.

Stance (how your car sits) is somewhat in the eye of the beholder. Tastes and trends change over time. Those East Coast cars of the 1960s tended to be channeled pan draggers that West Coast rodders derided, but in reality, it doesn't really matter what style you go for. It's all acceptable in today's world. With that being said, if you care about the opinions of others, then you are going to have to consider the unwritten rules of rod building.

To be honest, those rules were rewritten or abandoned completely with the advent of rat rods, where all convention went out the window. Like all fashion, that trend has mostly disappeared, and people are building traditional rods in the traditional way with traditional styling: small tires in front, bigger tires in back, and a slight forward rake. For styling's sake, do not make that grille vertical when you rake the car.

Tire Shaving

Tire shaving is something that you don't hear much about these days, and it's increasingly difficult to find any tire shops that do it. Yet, with many rodders opting for bias-ply tires, it's more essential than ever. Few bias-ply tires are perfectly round or well-balanced, and if you want your traditional rod to ride as well as it can, it pays for you to shave and balance them.

This tire shop was on Colorado Boulevard in Pasadena, California, but sadly it's no longer there. Nevertheless, this is where we used to take SO-CAL roadsters to get the bias-ply tires shaved and balanced. It made all the difference in their handling.

CHAPTER 8

Body

It might be that a body chooses you rather than you choose a body. I'm saying that the right body might come along at the right price, but it may not be exactly the one you were looking for. You just have to go for it when it feels right. However, be sure not to make one of the two big mistakes that I see time and again.

(continued on page 128)

Bodies, such as the rear quarter of this 1936 5-window, are not worth salvaging and can really only be used for patching or repairs.

You can purchase something like this closed-cab pickup body, but look at the rust and consider the time and expense of repairing it. Besides, buying just a body leaves you with an awfully long shopping list of other parts needed to build a car.

BODY

A lot of old cars, especially Fords such as this 5-window, are going to have some signs of previous and possibly poor repair. You can leave it, or you can dig deeper.

If you dig deeper, it might look like this under that skim of body filler. Then, it will be decision time as to whether you ignore it or dive in further.

This original 1927 T roadster body was spotted at H&H Antique in California. The 1927s are hard to find, and not all parts are available, so you may have no choice other than to take the plunge.

Something like this complete 1928–1929 Model A Sport Coupe, found by Troy Ladd of Hollywood Hot Rods, in excellent condition is preferable. This car was part of a stash of cars found in Pasadena, California.

HOW TO BUILD AFFORDABLE HOT RODS

Instead of repairing a rusty old hulk at a great expense, you could purchase a brand-new 1932 pickup body from United Pacific Industries. It's not original, but at this stage of the game, who cares?

Brand-new 1928–1929 Model A roadster bodies (such as this example from Brookville with Deuce dash insert) are a great, rust-free place to start if you're short on skill.

The bodies for Dan Clare's T Modifieds were fabricated (mostly by Dan) from scrap metal. The blue banger is from an old box van, and the metal for the body for the red V-8 is from an old horsebox. Adrian Smith at Buckland Automotive wheeled up the cowl.

New versus Restored

First, don't bite off more than you can chew. That is, do not buy a body that is way beyond your capabilities just because it's the right 3-window or whatever. If you're not experienced with body work, trying to repair something beyond your expertise is going to discourage you and cause you to give up or go to a professional.

The second thing not to do is buy a body that needs way more work than it's worth. I've seen many people purchase a body for tens of thousands of dollars and take it to a body shop, where they then spend tens of thousands of dollars more to have someone repair it.

I'm not trying to put down the professionals. Talented metal bashers are worth their weight in gold, but it can cost you dearly if the body man says something like, "You'd be better off buying a brand-new body or, at least, an original body in better shape." A good metal shaper can cost as much as $100 per hour or more, and the hours add up very quickly when the work is painstakingly slow. A week's work can easily cost you $4,000–$5,000, and a rough body can take weeks of work.

You'd be far better off buying a new body for about $25,000. "But it's not original," I hear people say. No, but it's half the price and it's brand new. Get over it. You also probably have to pay for a new body in one hit, whereas you can pay the body man as you go, but the new body will invariably be cheaper in the long run.

About 10 or 20 years ago, it mattered that you had a rod with an original body, but it doesn't matter much these days. Market forces have adjusted prices, and while steel is real, originality has become somewhat irrelevant.

If you have found a car and/or body with some historical provenance, it may well be worth the cost of restoration. What is interesting and affects the market is that as the population ages, more vehicles are coming on to the market, and in many cases the prices are falling. I strongly suggest that you buy a complete car rather than just a body because it will probably include numerous parts that you don't yet know that you will need.

A bit of advice is not to sell anything. You never know what might come in handy as you complete your build. I've made the mistake of selling off what I thought were unwanted parts as I made changes or needed money, only to find later that I needed those parts.

Notwithstanding the purchase of a new body that needs no work, let's assume that you've acquired a body that is in fairly good shape but needs a bit of work. Thankfully, there are numerous sources, such as Brookville Roadster and United Pacific Industries, that supply parts and patch panels for many early Fords and other brands to build a complete body.

Before you hack into your body (especially if you are going to chop the roof), it's essential that you secure the integrity of the body by cross-bracing it with steel tube, a strap, or a mixture thereof to hold the body in shape.

Top Chopping

Unless you're building an open car, it's likely you're going to chop the top. This is not an easy task for the inexperienced, especially if you are chopping anything other than a Model A or similar style with a more-or-less vertical top. However, it can be done if you take it easy and don't just crash into it without a lot of thought and prep.

In the case of Dick Wade's 1932 3-window, the decision was made to lean the posts back and not stretch the roof as is often done when a top like this is chopped. Every builder will have his or her own method of chopping a top, and there is really no right or wrong way as long as the finished result looks good and is symmetrical. That said, I have seen guys (such as Bobby Walden) chop the doors before the top. Bobby forms wooden templates and cuts the doors first to make them exact mirror images. He then cuts the top because the doors are exactly the same. It makes sense when he explains it.

Before you embark on a roof chop, fabricate a structure inside the body that holds it all together once the roof is cut off. The structure can be made of steel tube or whatever you have on hand as long as it retains the integrity of the body dimensions.

Some people take the top-chopping opportunity to remove one of the three hinges to supposedly

An early car, such as Rayce Lefever's 1930 Model A coupe, has an almost-vertical turret and is therefore fairly straightforward to chop.

CHAPTER 8

Hammer Welding

In the past an inexperienced or lazy body man might have installed a patch panel by just lapping it over the existing bodywork, but many think that's not correct. The correct way is to cut the existing sheet metal to exactly fit the patch panel. This is exacting, time-consuming work and not particularly easy if you are inexperienced.

You'll then need access to a tungsten inert gas (TIG) welder. A metal inert gas (MIG) welder will suffice if it's all you have, but the finish and control are not ideal for this kind of delicate work. Of course, you can also use gas welding, but the heat will cause distortion of the sheet metal unless you are experienced.

When the patch is correctly fitted and securely clamped into position, weld it in place with a small tack weld every inch or two. Be careful not to overheat and distort the sheet metal. When the patch is fully tacked into place, go back and weld between the tacks. As you get each inch or two stitch welded, use a hammer and dolly to dress the weld and relieve the internal stress and alleviate shrinkage.

Hammering reduces the amount of metal to grind down before painting. This is a skilled operation, and if you've never done it before, I recommend practicing on scrap metal before you tackle your car and the patch panels. When you are practicing, use the same-gauge sheet metal as the final job so that you will have experience with the same material. When the patch panel is fully welded into the body, grind the weld down for priming and paint. ■

This Deuce roadster at the Kennedy brothers' shop had some rusted-out inner fender wells. You can see the well on the left has been repaired, while the right side is removed for repair.

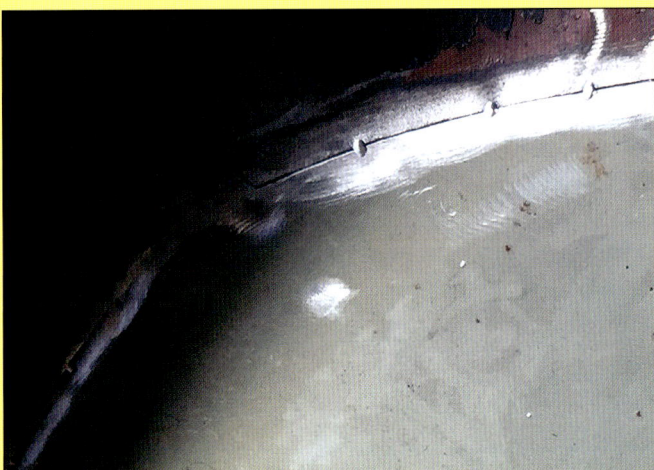

The patch panel, the lower gray area, and the original wheel well have been carefully cut for an exact fit. This is time-consuming but critical work.

Using a TIG welder, which offers a cleaner and more controllable weld, Jay welds between his tack welds. Notice that he only does a single 1- to 2-inch stretch at a time.

Jay uses a body-shaping hammer and a dolly to hammer the weld. This helps relieve stress in the metal and reduce the shrinkage caused by heat.

BODY

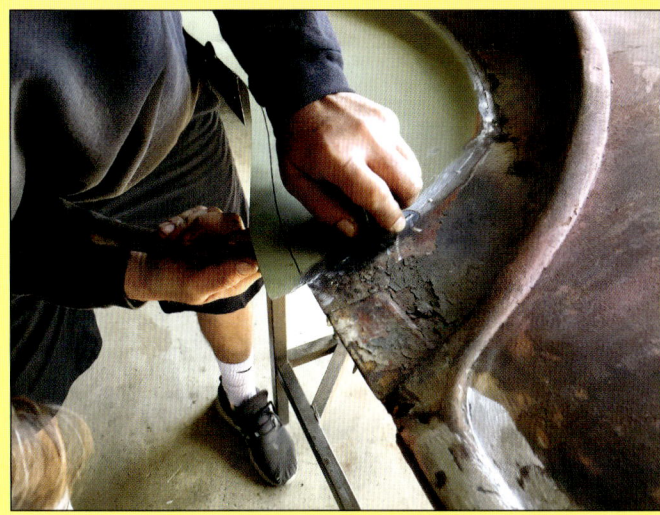

Jay reverses the hammer and dolly and repeats the process of hammering the weld from the underside this time.

Jay has trimmed the patch panel and the inner fender well to perfectly align so that the necessary weld will be minimum.

This close-up shows where Jay has just begun the hammering process to flatten out the weld. It will take minimal grinding to ready the surface for paint.

Finished and shot with some red oxide primer, you cannot see the repair to the right-side inner fender.

This is the other inner fender, but it shows how the finished patch panel will look once it is welded into place.

HOW TO BUILD AFFORDABLE HOT RODS

CHAPTER 8

A 1936 coupe, such as this one owned by James Jard, has a much more conical- and round-shaped top that is obviously more difficult to chop than a Model A.

make it easier to re-hang the doors, but the smart people who I know retain all three hinges as those old doors tend to be heavy, especially the 3-window doors.

Old photos of people chopping tops back in the day show them using hacksaws and all sorts of saws. These days, most people will use a cut-off wheel. I have heard that the material in the cut-off wheel can contaminate the metal that's being cut, but we're talking old cars, and I don't really think it matters.

Once all the cuts have been made, clamps can be used to hold the pieces together while they are welded together. MIG welding is preferable, but TIG will work if that is all you have. It will just mean the possibility of more distortion and a bit more cleanup work at the end.

When everything is welded, hammered, and ground smooth, a little bit of body filler should be all you need to smooth out the edges. Don't forget to protect the exposed bare metal and body filler with sealer because the body filler is porous.

Chopping Dick Wade's 1932 3-Window

Here's the starting point before Dick Wade's 1932 3-window got the chop. This car had been in storage for a number of years before Dick had the Kennedy brothers started the project.

This is out of sequence, but this shot shows the inner bracing structure built by the Kennedy brothers to hold Dick's Deuce body together while Jay chopped the top. In this case, the roof was not stretched. Instead, the posts were leaned back.

BODY

The back half of the roof has already been chopped and semi-finished. Look carefully and you can see the stitching around the driver-side drip rail.

The passenger's side of the roof has the panel stitched into position, and you can see how Jay sectioned the roof and where the panels were welded.

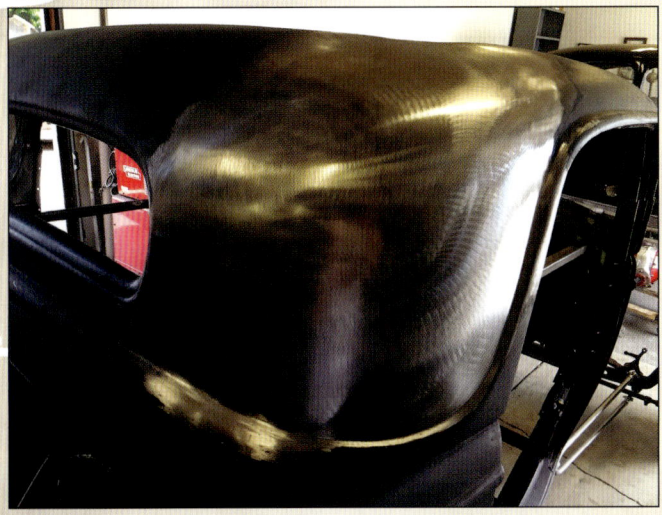

The passenger's side is now completely welded, hammered, and ground down. It is ready for priming. You can hardly see the joint!

Since the Deuce 3-window has a tapered top, the front windshield posts no longer align once the rear section of the roof has been chopped.

A saw cut about 8 inches long was made into the roof where the A-pillar turns. The windshield top and posts were then pulled forward to align with the lower posts that had been cut at the cowl.

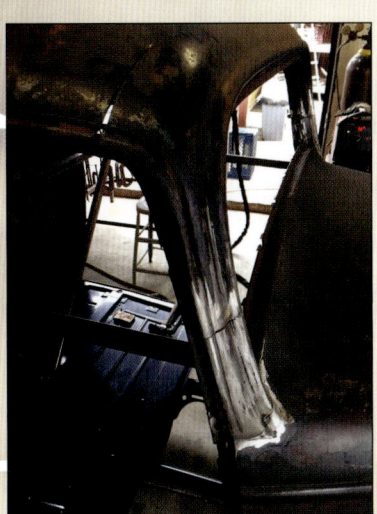

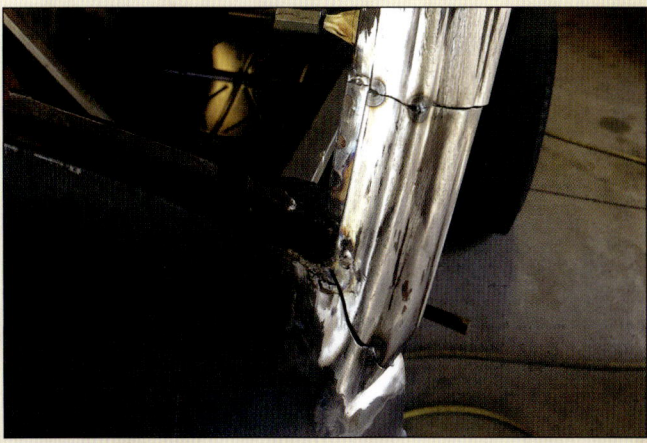

The top and bottom of the windshield posts were pulled into alignment and tacked into place with a metal inert gas (MIG) welder.

HOW TO BUILD AFFORDABLE HOT RODS

CHAPTER 8

A small wedge of steel was cut and shaped to fit the V in the roof. It was tacked into place with a MIG welder before it was hammer welded and ground.

With the windshield frame in place, you can barely tell the coupe has been chopped unless you park it next to an unchopped car.

Joe used a little body filler to smooth out the modifications, but in all honestly not much filler is required if the work is done properly.

In the before photo, the frame is on jack stands, and in the after photo, it's on wheels. A few inches make all the difference, and you can see how lowering the lid made Dick's Deuce much tougher.

134   HOW TO BUILD AFFORDABLE HOT RODS

There are many ways to make the cut, and Tom Busch's 1932 3-window came to the Kennedy brothers' shop already chopped. Unfortunately, the roof had not been stretched to match the chop and was therefore under some tension. Jay had to re-cut the top and relieve the stress. Luckily, it was repaired at the same time as they chopped Dick Wade's coupe to show a side-by-side comparison.

Tom Busch's Deuce 3-window had been chopped without leaning back the posts. The roof was not stretched to match the top and therefore was under some tension. Jay's task was to relieve the tension.

Jay made a cut two-thirds of the way back, and the roof sprung apart almost 1 inch. He then folded up some sheet metal to fill the gap.

Here you can see where Jay folded up a strip of sheet metal to follow the profile of the roof and welded it into place.

Notice how Jay cut the door just above the uppermost hinge to help retain the original door alignment and integrity. He always retains the three hinges where possible.

Jay uses a body hammer to shape his folded insert to fit the complicated profile of the door. This process takes patience unless you have a spare door frame from which to cut.

You can see the difference in the two chops with Dick Wade's coupe (foreground) with the leaned back posts and Tom Busch's coupe (background) with the regular posts.

CHAPTER 8

Assembling a 1934 Roadster

As luck would have it, a customer arrived at the Kennedy's shop with parts of a 1934 Model 40 Ford including a frame, a floor pan, and bits of a roadster body including the rear quarters, doors, and cowl. The rear quarters were in bad shape, but the doors and cowl looked salvageable.

As the quarters were not usable, the customer sourced some new quarters and other replacement panels from Steve's Auto Restorations. While these parts were still in stock at the time of writing, they were in limited supply and the rear quarters were listed at $1,095 each.

After tidying up the original frame and floor pan, Jay installed the reproduction oak door posts with aftermarket cast-brass L-shaped brackets that bolt to the frame through the floor pan. The replacement wood in this case was oak, while Ford originally used birch and maple. According to the Kennedy brothers, the best wood kits come from Brad Brown at Brad's Woodshop in Friday Harbor, Washington.

Next, Jay installed the driver-side rear quarter. It looks easy in these step-by-step photographs, but there was a lot of pushing, pulling, and swearing involved to getting it correct.

With the quarter panel in place, Jay installed the lower rear panel that runs across the body and joins the quarters, the passenger-side quarter, and the upper rear cowl section, all of which were brand-new parts. Photos make it look simple, but there was a lot of work involved as nothing is quite factory except the factory parts. Everything must be adjusted to fit. For example, the shape of the factory lower rear cowl structure was quite different from the repo upper rear cowl structure, and the two parts had to be coerced together.

As the original wood was quite rotten, a repro wood kit was supplied by the owner, but these parts were also not quite to factory specs and had to be manipulated to fit. Quite a lot of work was necessary in the front cowl section where the new wood had to be adjusted to work with the factory brackets. Eventually, Jay was able to pull it all together to form a fairly reasonable roadster given the condition of the parts delivered.

The frame and floor pan went into the shop, and Jay installed the reproduction door post, wood, and brackets that hold them to the frame.

These oak reproduction door posts were installed using cast-brass, L-shaped brackets that bolt to the frame through the floor pan. None of the repro parts were quite to original specs.

BODY

The customer supplied these original rear quarter panels that looked rough but were possibly repairable. It turned out that they were not.

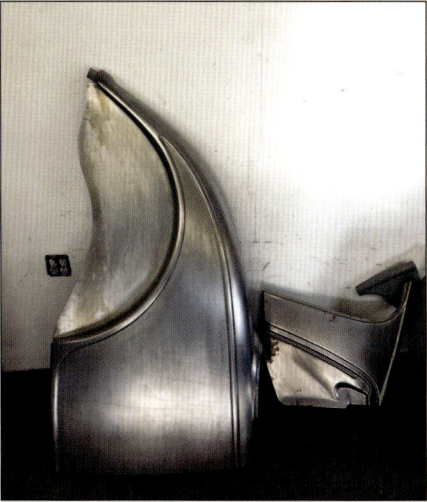
These brand-new rear quarter panels were sourced from Steve's Auto Restorations. They were still available at the time of this writing but were in limited supply.

The driver-side rear quarter was installed first along with the panel that goes across the back. The panel was also from Steve's Auto Restorations.

The upper-rear cowl section was new from Steve's Auto Restorations, but the lower section (here painted red oxide) was original 1934 Ford.

The customer supplied a pair of original doors with the other body panels. They were in usable condition but nowhere near perfect condition.

The original door wood was in poor condition, but it was there and offered a good starting place. Original factory wood was birch or maple.

HOW TO BUILD AFFORDABLE HOT RODS

CHAPTER 8

Unfortunately, the profile of the stock doors and the reproduction rear quarter panels did not quite jive, and some remedial work was necessary.

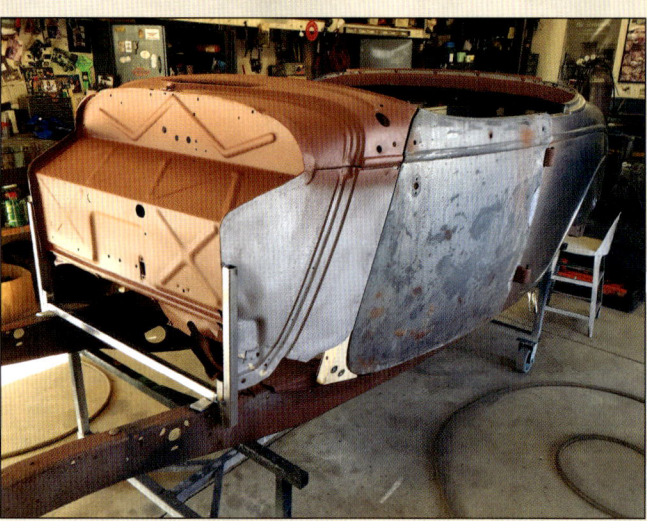

The stock cowl was installed and aligned with the original doors, but the lower quarter panels were rusted away at the bottom on both sides.

Jay achieved a nice door gap, but the lower cowl quarter panels were rusted away. Both needed a patch panel.

The wood runs up the door post and across the underside of the cowl. It also required some adjustment to make the factory brackets fit correctly.

CHAPTER 9

ELECTRICAL AND WIRING

With Help from Steve Sbelgio, Eclipse Engineering

Until 1956, all Ford vehicles were 6-volt with a positive ground. Ford then changed to 12 volt with a negative ground, which means that your very first electrical decision is to decide whether to change to 12 volts or stick with 6. The answer is an unequivocal yes; change to 12 volts. You can stick with 6 volts, but 12 will give you better starting, lighting, and charging. It just makes good, practical sense.

It's almost impossible to tell you how to wire your rod because they are all different and use different components. However, the basics are the same, and we have provided some simple diagrams toward the end of the chapter to guide you.

Ballast Resistor

If you are using a regular distributor with conventional points, you will need a ballast resistor, or use an ignition coil with an internal resistor, to allow the ignition system to operate at a lower voltage until the engine starts. It then functions to regulate the voltage going to the ignition system to avoid additional wear on the system.

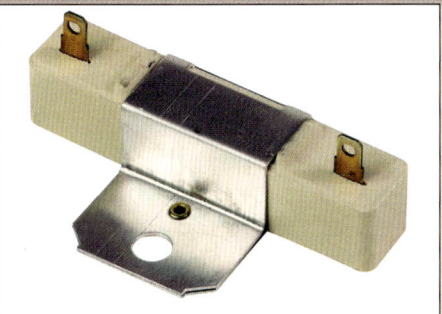

This is a traditional-looking MSD ballast resistor available from Holley, but you can purchase one from any good auto parts store.

Batteries

If you make the upgrade to a 12-volt system, you will need a good 12-volt battery. However, if you endure with a 6-volt system, there are 12-volt batteries that drop to around 8 volts for normal running. These batteries were popular a few years ago and might still be available.

I prefer to use a name brand such as Odyssey or Optima if you are going for a glass mat–type battery. If you choose a conventional-style battery, I recommend Delco or Interstate. Both types are widely available with a good warranty. If you don't run your car

I recommend that you always buy the best battery that you can afford. NAPA has a good reputation in the conventional type and Optima and Odyssey in the glass-mat type.

often, I suggest using a battery tender. I don't personally recommend battery disconnects because they can be a big source of power feed problems and are not necessary when a car is wired correctly. They can be used as a very poor security system but are often easily found and defeated.

Charging System

While a 6-volt starter will work with a 12-volt system, your charging

HOW TO BUILD AFFORDABLE HOT RODS

system must be entirely 12 volt. The starter motor does not necessarily have to be changed or modified. You can leave it as is and do nothing.

With that being said, some builders (including the Kennedy brothers) feel that it's better to upgrade the components to 12 volt. Incidentally, switching polarity on the car does not reverse the direction the starter motor turns.

While you can run 12 volts through a 6-volt starter, it's preferable to convert your charging system (especially the generator) to 12 volts.

Coil

An ignition coil is an induction coil in the ignition system that transforms the battery's low voltage to the high voltage needed to create an electric spark in the spark plugs to ignite the fuel. An internal resistor is preferred because it eliminates the need for an external ballast resistor.

Fuses

Just as we have suggested with all ignition and wiring components, use the best you can get or afford because they will give you reliability, which translates to less down time and time on the side of the road. Fuses are equally important because cheap fuses can melt rather than work properly and cause a fire that could possibly destroy your ride.

Cheap fuses, such as the one shown, are false economy. This fuse melted and didn't do its job to act as a fuse. It could have easily caused a fire and burned down the car. That would have been a costly mistake.

Alternator versus Generator

An AC alternator and a DC generator basically do the same thing: convert mechanical energy. In this case, it's belt-driven into electrical

Traditional-looking round ignition coils in black or chrome are available from PerTronix. Holley also manufactures coils under the Accel, Mallory, MSD, and Street Fire brands.

Kev's Rod & Custom in La Habra, California, can supply these small-scale alternators (right) that look just like an old-style generator. He also has mounting brackets and hardware available.

energy. In the former, electricity is produced when a magnetic field spins inside the stator (windings of wire). In a generator, on the other hand, the armature or windings of wire spin inside a fixed magnetic field to generate electricity. Generators are generally large and have a solid body, whereas an alternator can be very compact and typically has a ventilated body. Alternators generate a higher output than generators and produce voltage when needed, while generators produce voltage at all times.

Which one should you use: an alternator or a generator? It's entirely up to you depending on the style and look you're trying to achieve and the space you have available. Mike Abssy of Schrader's Speed & Style in Azusa, California, chose to mount his alternator off the rear end and drive it off the driveshaft. It's a good idea except the alternator won't produce power when the vehicle is not moving. This

ELECTRICAL AND WIRING

concept works great on a race car that is operated mostly at speed when its charging needs are needed, but I'm not sure it's practical for a street car.

Distributors

A distributor is what it says it is. It distributes high-voltage current from the ignition coil to the spark plugs in the correct firing order and for the correct amount of time. It's the heart of your engine and pumps blood down the veins to the plugs as you need it. A good distributor is essential, as is a heart, and the distributor needs a good set of points, a good condenser, and a good cap unless you have electronics. Economizing here will only cause you grief.

Holley/MSD offer a small range of replacement distributor caps, such as this black Rynite example, for popular Chevy, Chrysler, and Ford MSD distributors. This cap also fits original GM points distributors. Most caps have an optional wire retainer.

even stock 8-cylinder Delco caps, although they are nearly $300.

Fuel Tank Sender

A lot of traditional rod builders will use nothing more than a stick as a fuel gauge. Jim Jacobs has a piece of cardboard tucked in his door trim on which he writes down his mileage. That might be too much for some, so I suggest a Stewart Warner fuel level sender, as it will likely be most compatible with traditional rod instruments.

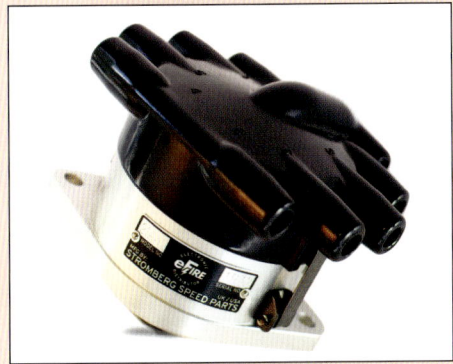
Stromberg Speed Parts has now developed these authentic-looking 2- or 3-bolt e-Fire distributors for flathead Ford V-8s. Timing is adjusted on the side just like the original.

Distributor Cap

You want the best cap you can acquire. Opt for a phenolic cap rather than a plastic cap. A cheap plastic cap will possibly crossfire and cause ignition problems. Whenever possible, get a good OEM cap.

If you're really stuck, Kip Motor Company in Dallas, Texas, can cast you a new phenolic resin cap. They

Ground

We made the decision earlier to go with a 12-volt negative ground, and a ground is nothing more than a connection to the body or other metal surface of the vehicle. The body is connected to the negative terminal of the battery. A good ground is essential in any vehicle, and a little grease on the ground and the negative terminal will help prevent corroding and loss of ground.

It's recommended that you ground the engine to the frame as well as the fuel sender. You can't have too many good grounds.

Good grounds are imperative to a good running car. You need a good ground for the battery to the frame (shown) and the engine. It's also good to ground other components.

Stewart Warner has a large range of fuel level senders, such as this unit, suitable for tanks 6 to 12 inches deep, such as a Deuce tank. However, if you have a different fabricated tank, you will need a different unit.

HOW TO BUILD AFFORDABLE HOT RODS

CHAPTER 9

Horn

It's always a good idea to install a good, loud horn. Just as a 6-volt starter will work in a 12-volt system, so will a 6-volt horn. Like a starter, they are only powered for a short period, and the extra juice will not hurt them. It'll be loud, but it'll be okay.

Traditional instruments can be whatever you want, and there are many on the market. I tend to gravitate toward the name brands, such as Stewart Warner, because they are traditional and work well with other like-minded components, such as tank senders.

Many rodders might decry a horn, but in my experience, they come in handy and are easy to tuck out of sight under the frame. Because they are rarely used, you can use a 6-volt horn in a 12-volt system.

Instruments

Traditional hot rods can run the gamut on the instrument front and go from next to nothing to a full complement in the style of Doane Spencer. Everything is right and nothing is wrong. I tend to prefer traditional brands, such as Stewart Warner, because it has the right stuff to work well with other components, such as tank fuel level senders. However, that is not to say you can't mix things up and try a different approach.

Something to consider with a traditional rod is that you really do not need many electrically operated gauges. The speedometer and tachometer can be mechanical, as can the oil pressure. The only electrical gauges that you need are water temperature, fuel, and volts, and you might choose not to worry about them.

Kill Switch

A battery kill or disconnect switch is a simple security device usually hidden out of sight (such as under the seat squab) that disconnects the power from the battery to the ignition switch. A determined thief is going to find it easily, but it may give you peace of mind.

Kill switches can be purchased for less than $10 and offer a simple measure of security that can be mounted in the front of the seat pan.

Lights

Lights are like instruments and can pretty much be anything the builder wants to use. I always go for the name brands (such as Sylvania and Wagner) and avoid the cheap brands that tend to be lower quality. This industry has addressed the lighting issue, and you can buy

There's a wide range of front and rear lighting available. I always try to go for good quality brands, such as Sylvania and Wagner, with a quality sealed-beam lens, some of which have an integral turn signal.

ELECTRICAL AND WIRING

headlights with built-in turn signals that don't detract from the traditional look. Otherwise, you can go for the Guide-style 682-C light that has a top-mounted parking light and is available with a 7-inch sealed beam and built-in indicator.

Points

There are pros and cons to using points instead of a modern electric ignition. They do wear, need adjustment, and will eventually need to be replaced. However, if you're troubleshooting a fault on the side of the road, they are fairly easy to troubleshoot compared to an electronic ignition that can only be looked at. Whatever your choice, I highly recommend that you carry a spare ignition, condenser, and even an electronic module (if that's what you're using) because if it goes out on the highway, where are you going to find another one?

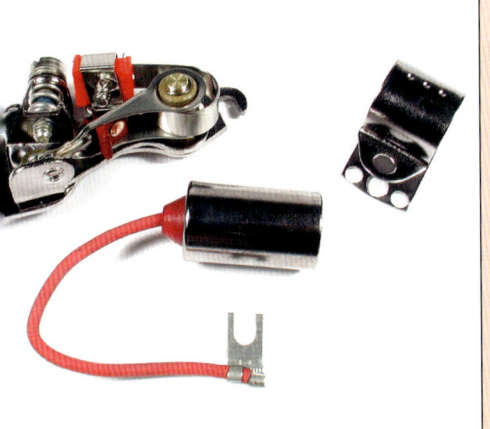

Holley makes heavy-duty points kits complete with a condenser for the small-block Chevy under its Accel brand. They have extra thick contact arms to prevent high-RPM flexing. Condensers contain Mylar foil windings to help prevent points pitting.

Magneto

I'm not a proponent of using a magneto in a street application; they're just not designed for that. They tend to be costly, and if you buy a used one, it will invariably need rebuilding. Joe Hunt Magnetos makes a high-performance distributor that looks like a magneto if that's the look you want.

This distributor from Joe Hunt Magnetos looks like a magneto, but it's actually a distributor that incorporates a specially built, high-output coil, electronic pickup, and advance mechanism.

Plug Wires

If you want that correct old-time look, PerTronix Performance Products has a black 7-mm wire (modern wires are usually 8 mm) that uses the same core as its 8 mm wires but has a 7-mm silicone outer jacket. The wires feature two current paths: a spiral-wound stainless steel alloy primary and a carbon-impregnated fiberglass core. These wires are available in a 100-foot spool (as tailored sets) or as a universal kit for a unique configuration.

If you want a vintage-looking, cloth-covered wire, take a look at those available from Bob Drake Reproductions, Inc. They're designed

The Veazie Brothers offer these vintage-looking, cloth-covered wires in a variety of authentic colors, such as red/black or yellow/black. They're designed specifically for Ford V-8 engines, but they could possibly be adapted to other engines.

specifically for Ford V-8 engines, but they probably can be adapted to other engines if that is the look you desire.

Starters

The good news is that 6-volt starters will work with a 12-volt-system starter motor. The starter motor does not have to be changed or touched. Just leave it as is and do nothing. Switching polarity on the car does not reverse the direction the starter motor runs.

Starters only operate for short periods of time, and they will therefore tolerate and survive the short burst of power. In fact, rather than the slow turn, they tend to work like they should have in the first place. Of course, they are bulky, and you might need to get them rebuilt, but you know the stock starter will fit your engine depending on your transmission choice. That said, a brand-new, lightweight starter from a company such as Powermaster might be a better answer.

CHAPTER 9

While they might not look authentic, a modern starter, such as this unit from Powermaster, might be a better solution. You can make them almost disappear with the removal of the decals and a coat of satin black paint.

Switches

As with all other electrical components, I prefer to use good quality name brands whenever possible. When it comes to switches, I prefer those made by the Cole Hersee Company, which was acquired by Littlefuse in 2010. They have an extensive website that includes everything from manual battery disconnect switches and push-pull switches to rotary switches and even foot-operated headlamp dimmers and hydraulic and mechanical brake light switches. Littlefuse is a manufacturer, so you will have to find a local distributor.

Personally, I like the range of switches from SO-CAL Speed Shop, most of which are Cole Hersee switches available with a wide range of custom knobs, such as a keyless, pull-operated ignition switch to a floor-mounted dimmer.

Incidentally, if you want an indicator switch that clamps to the steering column, they are available from a number of sources, including LimeWorks Hot Rod Parts and United Pacific Industries.

Wiring

I'm very particular about wiring. I've been doing this a long time, learned a lot, and have made some informed decisions. Most people know nothing about electrical systems and should stay out of it. However, there are many tools that can help the amateur wire his or her own car with little or no experience.

My favorite wiring kit for a simple, traditional-style hot rod is American Autowire's Highway 15 kit that is available in basic form for about $400 and as the Nostalgia kit for about $1,400. That might seem like a lot, but the kit takes all the guesswork out of the task, includes all you need to get the job done, and uses the latest cross-link technology.

Cross-link wire is manufactured using a chemically cross-linked polyethylene insulation to make it more durable and resistant to heat than the standard GPT automotive wire. It is also resistant to moisture, grease, oil, gasoline, most acids, and solvents, and it emits fewer toxins when burnt than conventional wire. You might not think that's important, but you wouldn't believe how many fire-damaged vehicles I have dealt with.

The American Autowire Highway 15 Nostalgia kit was developed

Column-mounted turn-signal switches, such as this aluminum-bodied assembly, are available from companies such as CW Moss, LimeWorks Hot Rod Parts, and United Pacific Industries.

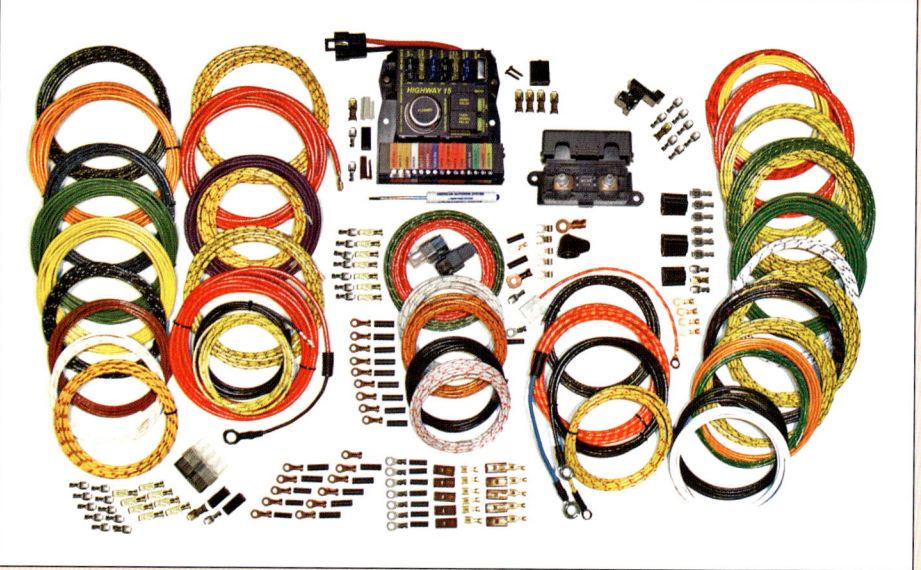

The American Autowire Highway 15 Nostalgia kit is quite expensive but highly recommended and comes with everything you need and more, including a 175-amp Mega Fuse system. It has a traditional, high gloss, braid, and lacquer finish.

ELECTRICAL AND WIRING

to handle the most demanding power requirements and accessories. It has the most flexibility in fuse box placement and is offered in a trunk-mounted kit that provides additional wire lengths and the freedom to customize your vehicle however you like. Each wiring kit comes complete with easy-to-understand instructions to guide you through every step. The steps are divided into individually labeled bags that contain everything you need to complete the step to keep you organized and get you on the road faster.

The beauty of the Nostalgia kit is that it is available in traditional, high gloss, braid, and lacquer finishes. Included in the Nostalgia kit is a new dash-mounted ignition switch, headlight switch with an auto-reset circuit breaker, and floor dimmer switch, all with mating connectors and terminals.

Rewiring a 1936 Ford

Everyone has a different approach to building a rod. Even when it comes to wiring, there are different ways to bite the elephant. For example, Joe Kennedy prefers to have his 6-volt starters and generators reconfigured to 12 volt by M & L Parts in Pomona, California.

We dropped in on Phil Sigmon at M & L, who said, "When you give a 6-volt starter 12 volts, it doubles the speed, and that can cause damage to the pinion gear of the starter Bendix, or the ring gear, or both. That is not something you want to happen on the road."

If you do change from 6 to 12 volts, Joe is of the opinion to also change up the battery ground cable and all the bulbs. Also, change the 6-volt gauges, such as the fuel sender, etc., because volt drops are hit or miss; sometimes they work and sometimes they don't. Therefore, it is better to have the gauges converted to 12 volt.

As this chapter came together, Joe took on the task of rewiring a 1936 that had been converted to 12 volts but not to his taste. He had to rip out the entire wiring and convert the starter and generator to 12 volts. Other components, such as bulbs and instruments, were also upgraded to help make this 1936 all the better for this simple upgrade.

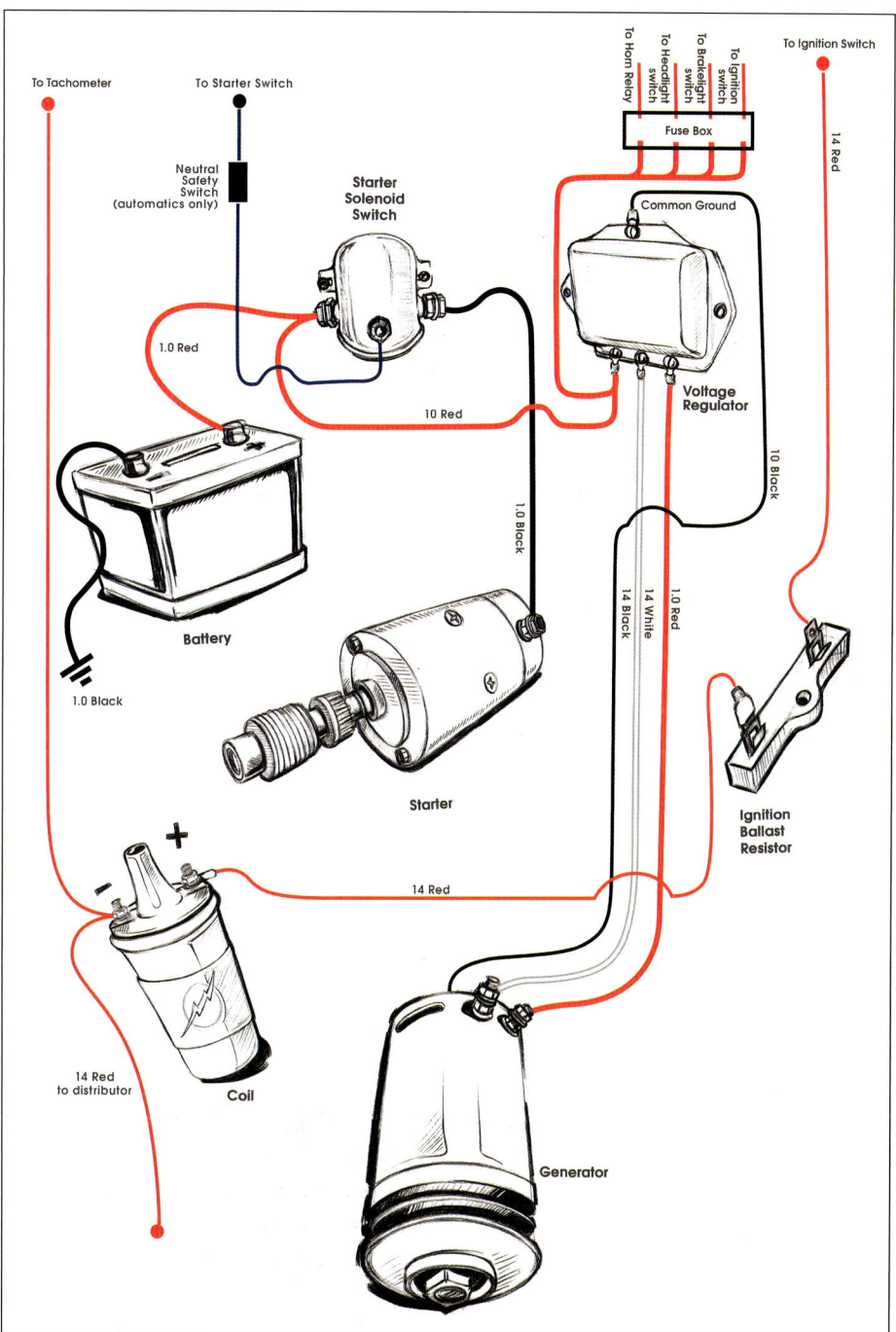

CHAPTER 9

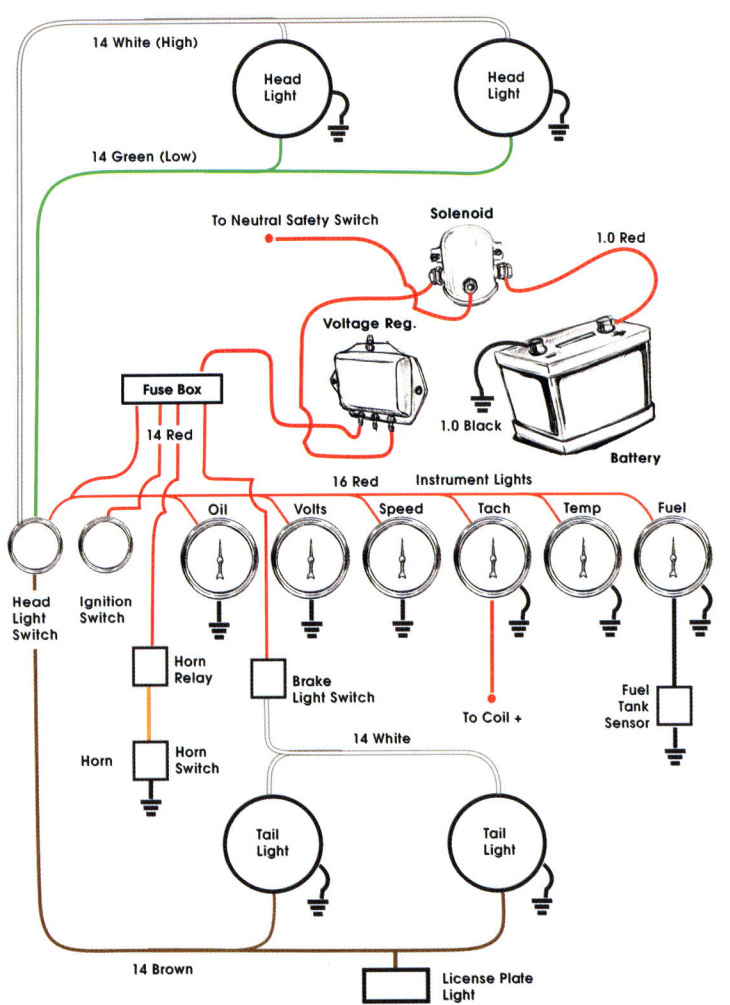

There was a small mess of wiring behind the dash, and unfortunately none of the original instruments worked.

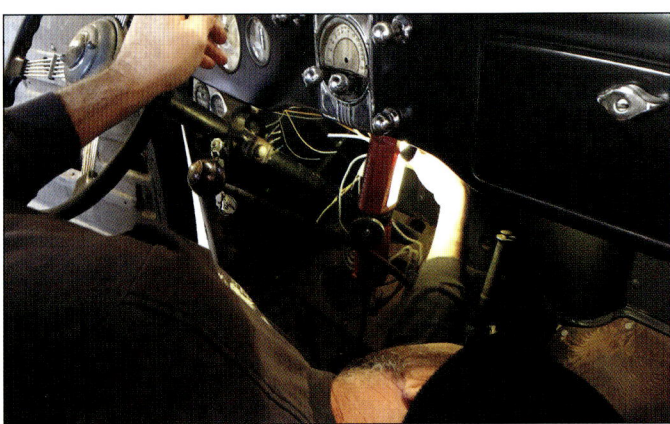

Joe began the task of rewiring the 1936 by removing all of the original wiring with the intention of starting over.

Under the hood was a nice, Stromberg 97-equipped flattie that was converted to 12 volts. However, the starter and generator were both 6 volt.

This is a view of the backside of the dash that shows the stock speedometer (upper left) and the two mechanical accessory instruments (lower right).

146   HOW TO BUILD AFFORDABLE HOT RODS

ELECTRICAL AND WIRING

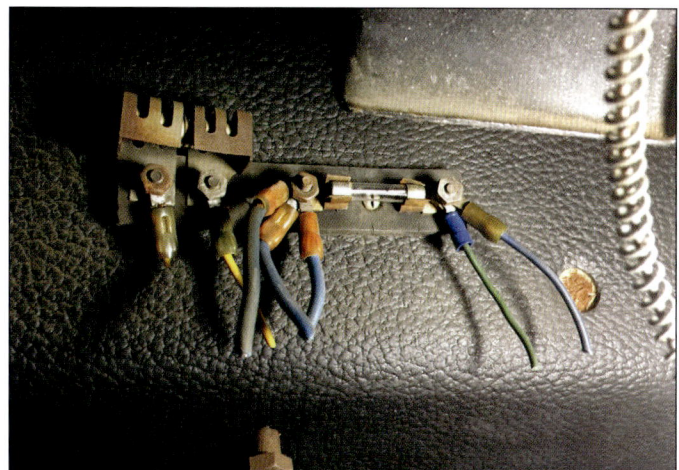

Under the dash, there is a Ford fuse block (right) for the lighting and a resistor (left) for the ignition.

New/old taillight buckets were rattle-canned black to match the patina on the stands and installed with new 12-volt bulbs.

According to Joe, flatheads like a little fuel pressure to help them start, so he ran an electric pump in the line to assist the mechanical pump. It has a good ground to the frame.

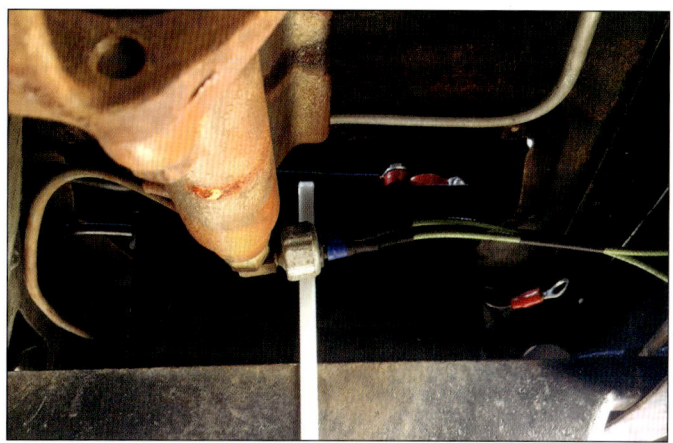

Joe wired in an existing but previously unused brake-light switch that was mounted behind the existing brake master cylinder.

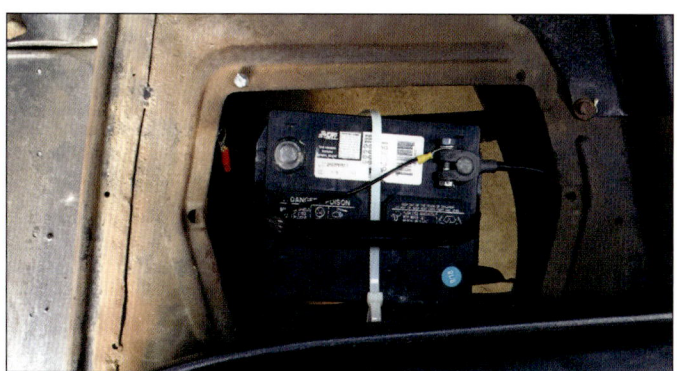

The terminals were cleaned and a good new ground strap was installed to replace the corroded wire mesh strap. The heavy-duty tie strap was retained per the owner's instructions.

The stock Ford 6-volt generator was converted to 12 volts by Phil Sigmon at M&L Parts. An NOS 12-volt regulator was also used. The voltage regulator and generator must be polarized together so that the charging system works properly.

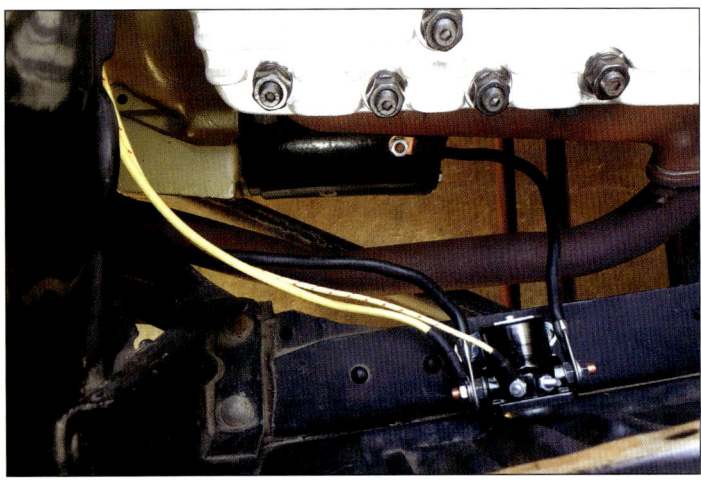

It's imperative that the correct-size cable (6 or 12 volt) is run from the starter solenoid to the battery. This stock 6-volt starter was converted to 12 volts by M&L Parts.

Joe pulls wires from the frame-mounted solenoid to go to the voltage regulator and ignition switch.

Joe used the original 1936 Ford column-mounted ignition switch and installed a starter push-button in an existing hole in the dash and a toggle switch for the fuel pump underneath. The original floor-mounted starter switch was deleted.

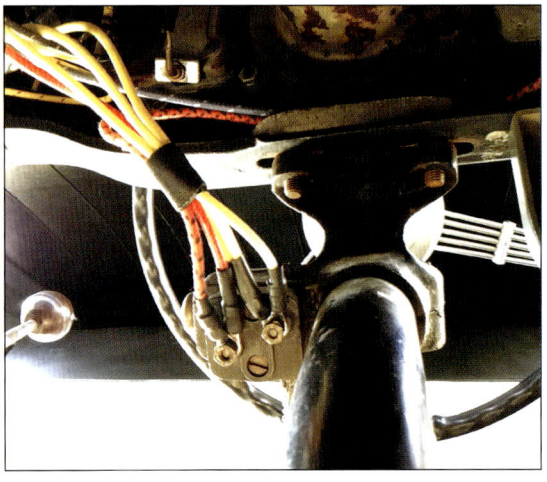

The view from the underside of the dash clearly shows the wiring to the stock Ford ignition on/off switch.

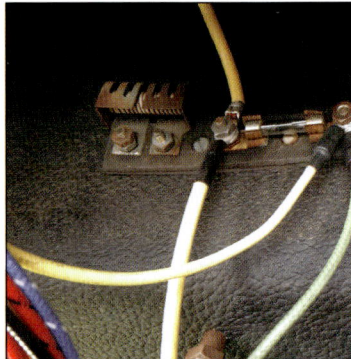

The original Ford fuse block (right) for the lighting was retained, but the ignition resistor was not used, as Joe used a 12-volt coil with an internal ballast resistor.

Joe affixes the wire to the back of the generator. Some generators have a lug for a ground, but Joe grounds to the voltage regulator (as Ford did).

A new 12-volt coil with an internal resistor and a new 12-volt voltage regulator were neatly mounted to the firewall. All wires for the dash go through one original hole in the firewall.

CHAPTER 10

DETAILS

By Troy Ladd, Hollywood Hot Rods

They say that the devil's in the details (and he may well be), but details can make your rod. Some clever trick you incorporated (that maybe nobody else has thought of or done as well) might make your ride all the richer. Even if you're not very crafty or talented with metal, you can sometimes find a way to add a feature that perhaps has been lifted from some other genre and modified to fit your purpose. For example, instruments, seats, switches, or tanks out of an airplane can be implemented into your rod. Yes, that's been done before, but there's always another way to skin the cat.

Here, we'll take a look at some neat details that can make your rod stand out from the crowd. In most cases, these details were created by professionals, but that is not to say that you can't create something similar at home if you have the time and patience. Just dive in. You might surprise yourself, and none of these details have to be costly; they're just the result of thinking a little bit off-center.

Watching Matt Bryant work on frames was a revelation. He forms bits of metal to make them organic and cast in appearance. Here, Matt works on a frame at Walden Speed Shop.

This engine mount that uses a flathead-style biscuit mount was fabricated by Ellis Simmons of Iron Hill Hot Rods. Note the sunken leaf-spring mount.

HOW TO BUILD AFFORDABLE HOT RODS

Check out Matt's engine mount that he created for Walden Speed Shop. It looks as if it were cast, but it was actually fabricated from pieces of steel.

This steering shaft firewall support was also fabricated by Matt. What is intriguing about this work is that it only takes time, not money, because you can't go out and buy it.

A neat front shock mount was made by Matt Bryant for Walden Speed Shop by using pieces of steel welded together to look like a casting.

A combination of paint, polish, and chrome by Hollywood Hot Rods make the quick-change on Pat Gauntt's coupe a work of art from the springs on the exhaust to the spring clips on the torque arm.

Pat Gauntt's coupe, built by Hollywood Hot Rods, has numerous inspirational details from the X-form radiator stays to the louvered floor pan.

Up close, you can see the hood support, although it's not in use here. Nevertheless, the craftsmanship is superb and something you could aspire to do.

This grille, a variation on the Deuce grille, was designed and built at Hollywood Hot Rods. It's perhaps beyond the average builder but is inspirational nonetheless.

DETAILS

Boling Brothers' Lincoln front brakes were neatly detailed by Ellis Simmons of Iron Hill Hot Rods with stainless mesh inserts in the vents.

There are many details to inspect on this Hollywood Hot Rods build from the Track Master Products side-steering box to the swinging pedal assembly.

An overflow tank is a must for some rods, but they can be a nuisance and obtrusive. Mick Jenkins's answer was to recess it into the firewall of his Deuce roadster.

This hand-formed, polished steel fan shroud created by Rick Lefever for Carl Akins's Deuce 3-window is beyond the capabilities of most builders, but it is inspiring.

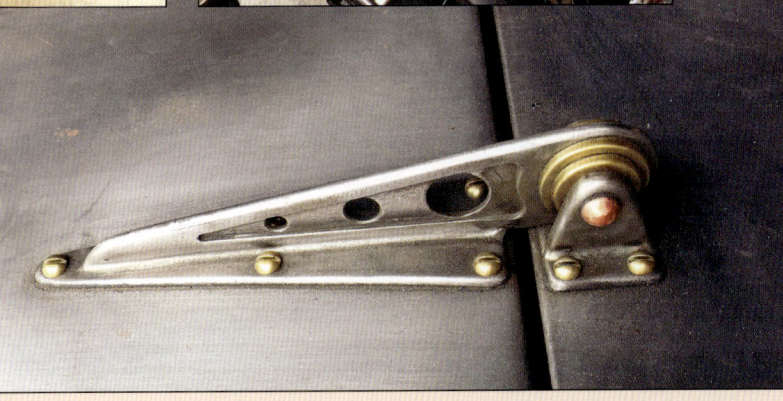

There's nothing on this decklid hinge at Hollywood Hot Rods that the homebuilder can't replicate if putting his or her mind to it.

HOW TO BUILD AFFORDABLE HOT RODS

Sunken racing-style gas caps (such as this Monza-type on Billy F Gibbons's Whiskey Runner) are popular, but remember to put a drain in the recess.

This gas filler, fabricated at Hollywood Hot Rods, looks complicated and expensive, but it's just stacked sheets of brass and a filler cap detailed with aligned brass screws.

Dan Clare likes to troll the swap meets for things such as this fuel tank of unknown origin. It's probably from an old tractor. Note the handmade brass straps, cap, etc.

Now this is a different tank. It was found at an aircraft surplus store and installed in Scott Robertson's pickup by Aaron Broughton's Foothill Fabrication. Check out the milled bed frame.

This is a typical aircraft oxygen tank from a World War II bomber. They came in various sizes and can still be found in aircraft surplus stores such as G&J Aircraft.

Even inner fender wells at Hollywood Hot Rods get the detail treatment. In this case, the work replicates Hollywood's crown logo.

Not everything has to be concours quality. Dan Clare makes everything, including his tach drive and exhaust header, look like it was made in an 18th-century foundry.

There are some interesting details on this engine compartment from Hollywood Hot Rods. Notice the combined coil and fuel-filter mount on the firewall.

In some cases, shops have to use new engines (such as this 5.0 Ford Coyote in Devin Jiminez's 1940 Ford), but they can be disguised to look old with the addition of adapters for vintage valve covers.

The finished makeover of Devin Jiminez's 5.0L Ford Coyote by Hollywood Hot Rods effectively disguises the origins of the species to make this new engine look old.

Rather than expensive chrome, look at other finishes, such as these gold iridited bolts on this flathead Ford V-8 in Michael Sinacola's truck that was rebuilt at Jimmy Shine's Speed Shop.

Black is not the only color you can use. Bennie Cervantes of Long Beach, California, used gray to accent the small-block in his 1930 coupe. Check out those wrapped headers.

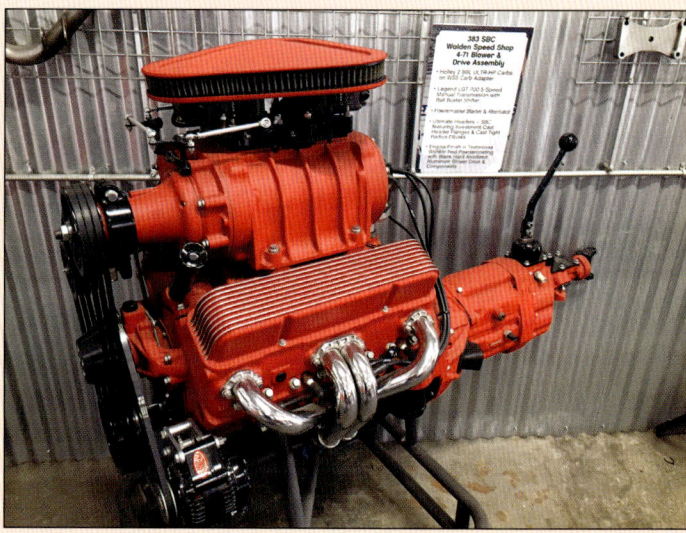

Dare to be different. This is Bobby Walden's take on the Walden-blown small-block Chevy engine assembly treated with Ferrari-style wrinkle red paint.

There are many good details on this 1931 roadster, *The Grudge* from Hollywood Hot Rods, particularly the 4-into-2 slash-cut pipes.

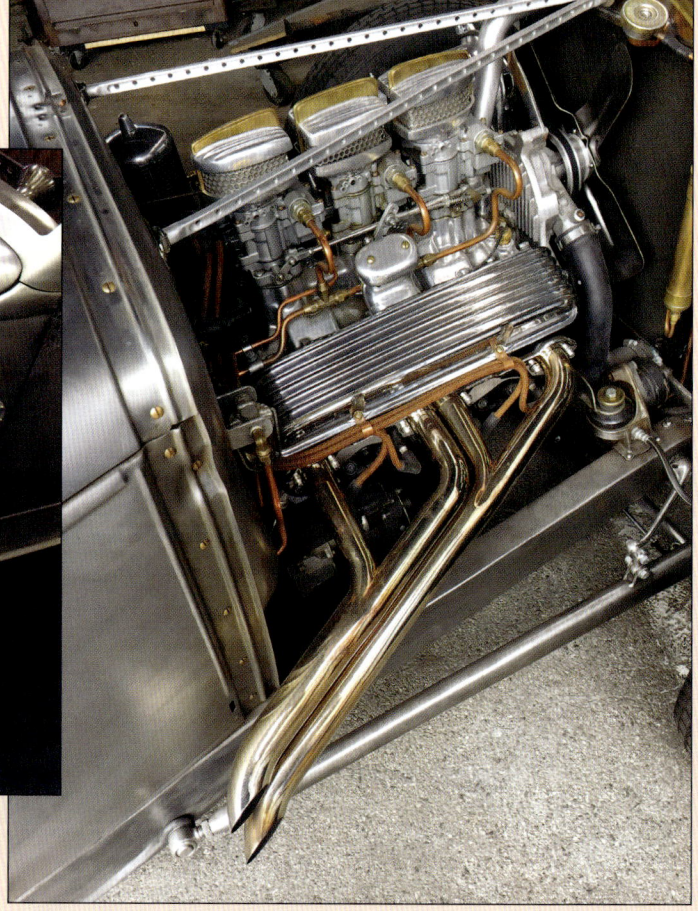

The other side of the engine in *The Grudge* shows even more neat detail from the carburetor plumbing to the choice of ignition wires and their brass retainers.

DETAILS

Though it's not finished, there's a lot of nice detailing on the Cadillac in Pat Gauntt's Hollywood Hot Rods–built coupe from the Strombergs down to the parallel leaf springs.

Everyone has a different take on exhaust pipes, but we liked the approach at Kev's Rod & Custom to a three-barreled shotgun header for a flattie. It's beauttifully formed.

CHAPTER 10

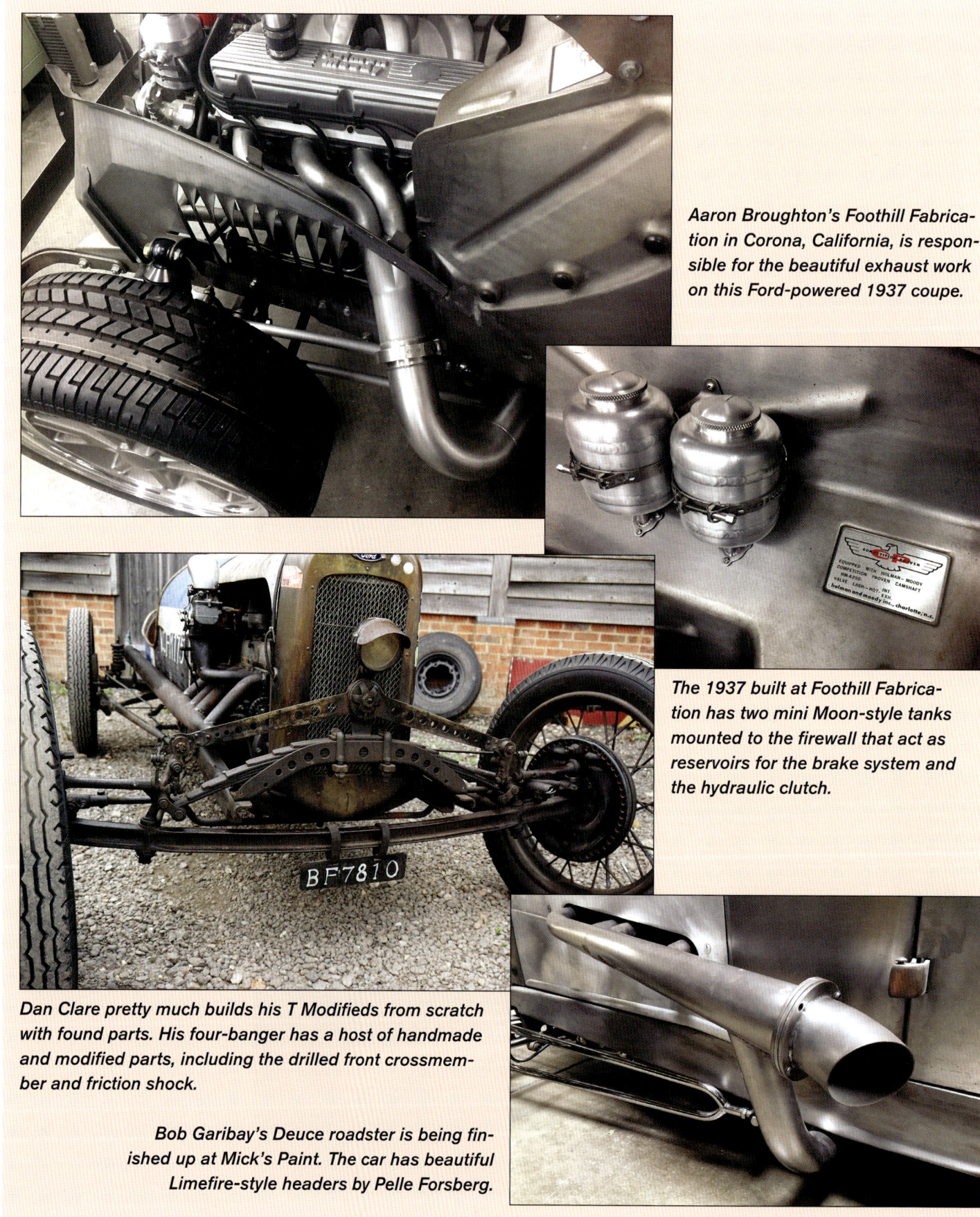

Aaron Broughton's Foothill Fabrication in Corona, California, is responsible for the beautiful exhaust work on this Ford-powered 1937 coupe.

The 1937 built at Foothill Fabrication has two mini Moon-style tanks mounted to the firewall that act as reservoirs for the brake system and the hydraulic clutch.

Dan Clare pretty much builds his T Modifieds from scratch with found parts. His four-banger has a host of handmade and modified parts, including the drilled front crossmember and friction shock.

Bob Garibay's Deuce roadster is being finished up at Mick's Paint. The car has beautiful Limefire-style headers by Pelle Forsberg.

156   HOW TO BUILD AFFORDABLE HOT RODS

CHAPTER 11

INTERIOR

One of the great things about building a budget rod is that you don't have to spend money on a fancy interior unless you care to. It can be whatever you want from a pair of bare metal buckets to an old bench seat with a Mexican blanket. In today's world, anything goes. Of course, a good or interesting upholstery job can actually enhance your ride, provide a comfortable environment, and not cost the earth.

For example, take the interior of Suzanne Williams' 1934 Tudor. It's very traditional with wide pleats, but when you lean in and look up, check out that amazing headliner with lightning bolts emanating from the dome light. It's traditional and wild all at once.

Of course, you can't get any more traditional than the Dewar Coupe that Troy Ladd of Hollywood Hot Rods recently acquired. This time-warp 1932 3-window has an entirely original white pleated interior complete with a pleated top and white-painted running boards. The car was parked in 1961. Consequently, the interior by Greg Schifano (with a double-stitched headliner, dragon tail details on the seat sides, and a trunk upholstered to show standards) was obviously done earlier. It's authentic, and incidentally, Schifano patented a machine for pleating upholstery.

Pleats, or *tuck 'n' roll*, as it was often called, shouts traditional, but

It's hard to fault this stunning headliner in Suzanne Williams's 1934 Tudor with lightning bolts emanating from the dome light. Suzanne did the design, and Willy Sopher of Orange, California, handled the stitch work.

The Dewar Coupe was put away in 1961 and wasn't touched until 2019 when Troy Ladd of Hollywood Hot Rods acquired it. The circa-1960 interior was upholstered to show standards by Greg Schifano, who worked out of Arcadia, California, from 1954 to 1965.

HOW TO BUILD AFFORDABLE HOT RODS

CHAPTER 11

the current trend in traditional hot rods is bomber seats or a variation on that theme with minimal upholstery.

It's interesting how creative rodders can be when they are trying to save a few bucks. I've seen everything from school dining chairs to seats out of a Ford Tri-Motor airplane in Jim Stroupe's 1927 T. They don't look comfortable, but they sure look good and are rare—being that they only built 199 Tri-Motor planes.

Thankfully, early Ford interiors are simple. From the seat pan forward, the floors are wood and are easily constructed at home from a sheet of marine plywood and a jigsaw. First, you'll want to think the process through. You might need to fabricate a steel frame to support the toe board. You can use 1/2-inch square steel tubing or even angle iron for this. You only really need to do this if you have moved the engine back for some reason. Sticking with stock early-Ford parts in their stock locations typically means that you don't move the toe board. Incidentally, Bob Walden has produced some stamped-steel toe-board risers.

You'll probably need to cut a hole in the floorboard to access the master cylinder and make a small, easily removable, sheet metal cover for the hole. Do likewise for the battery if it is located under the floor. All of this is fairly easy using cardboard for your template. You'll also likely have to make a cutout for the pedals. Again, cardboard is the obvious template medium.

Depending on your choice of transmission, you will probably need to make a transmission cover. Maybe not if you have a compact 4-speed, such as a Muncie, but if you're running any kind of automatic, you will need to fabricate a cover. This can be done in aluminum (or steel if you have the skills), or it can be out of fiberglass if that is easier for you to work at home.

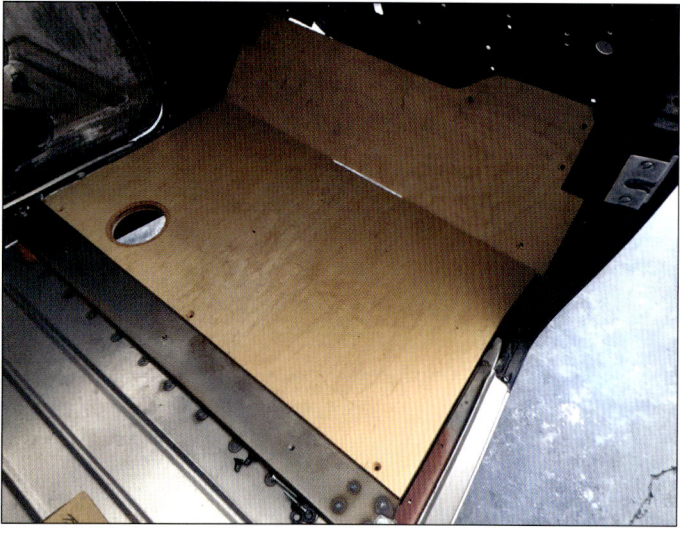

A typical floorboard installation in a Deuce shows the floorboard and toe board that have yet to be cut out for the transmission. If the engine is set back, you'll probably have to move the toe board back a similar amount, which will reduce leg room.

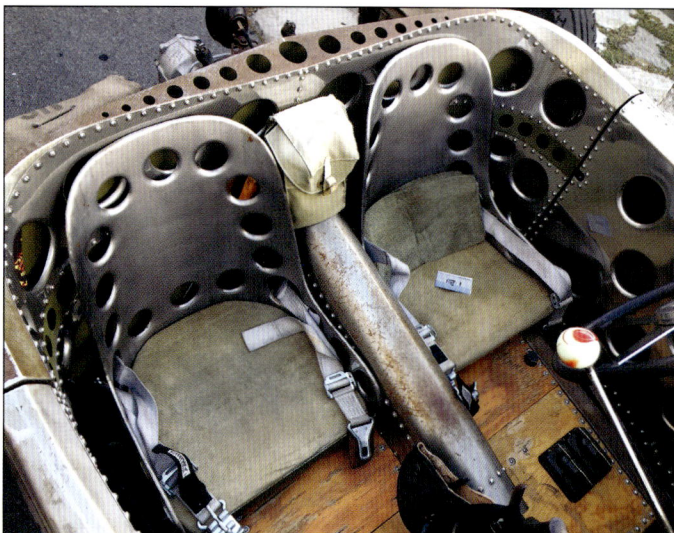

No access plate is needed here, as the dual master cylinders poke up through the distressed wooden floorboards, and that's okay. There's nothing wrong with a hot rod that looks mechanical.

Rods with large transmissions need some kind of transmission cover, and here Pauly Rivera works on an aluminum transmission cover for Bob Garibay's Deuce roadster at Mick's Paint. Talented folks can make one from steel in two or three days, or you can use fiberglass.

INTERIOR

A steel or aluminum cover can be quite complicated, difficult to make, and time consuming if you do not have the necessary metalworking skills and tools. Believe it or not, a nice transmission cover can take one, two, or three days to make even in a professional shop. They're not as simple as they look. It might take 24 hours, which might cost $2,000 or more, depending upon the prevailing labor rate in your area.

Seats

Most early Fords had some kind of a seat frame riser that you can choose to use or not. If you don't have one but need one, you can buy them new from United Pacific Industries, along with a seat frame set. You can buy universal riser brackets that are adjustable in height and length from Trique Manufacturing. From that point on, you can do as you please and build any kind of seat that you want.

Rods tended to stick with stock seats for almost 40 years until Pete Chapouris changed the game by pushing the seat back and under the rear cowl. He did this on the 1926 T roadster he built for his dad, who was over 6 feet tall. Pete Sr. needed more legroom in the cramped car, so Pete ingeniously tucked the seat under the cowl.

The Glide seat is fully adjustable fore and aft 7 inches. The seat base flips up for storage, and the back folds down to access another storage area.

Pete Chapouris built this 1926 T track roadster for his dad in the late 1970s. Both were over 6 feet tall, and Pete had a clever idea to push the seat back under the rear cowl to increase legroom. Clever, eh?

Pete Chapouris used his old trick of pushing the Glide seat back under the rear cowl to increase legroom in a string of SO-CAL roadsters.

Another reason for moving the seat back is because SO-CAL and other builders move the engine back two or three inches to accommodate electric fans and shrouds, air-conditioning equipment, etc. This backward move necessitated moving the toe board back a similar amount, which is something to be aware of.

Pete did the same at SO-CAL Speed Shop when he built Deuce roadsters. He took the Glide Engineering seat and shoved it under the rear cowl to give the Deuce more legroom. The seat was adjustable fore and aft a full 7 inches. Meanwhile, the cushion flips up and forward to reveal storage space for on-the-road items, and the reclining back flips forward to allow access to another storage area behind the seat where the battery is located. It was all very well thought out.

Not a lot of people know this, but there is a huge source of very inexpensive and historically correct seating right under our noses (well, asses) in those fiberglass bucket seats fitted in so many race cars, kit cars, buggies, and the like from the 1960s. It's a little-known fact that those early

This roadster owner used Chapouris's trick of sliding the seat under the rear cowl to give himself more legroom. Rather than typical upholstery, he placed a Mexican blanket over the seat foam. It works and didn't cost a whole lot.

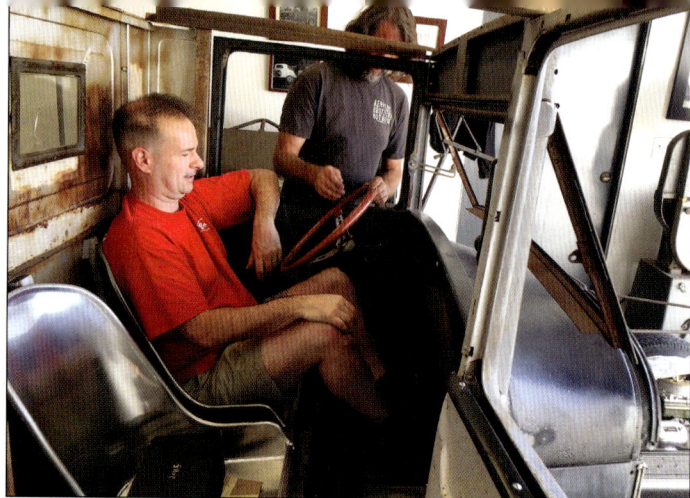

Mike Williams and Jay Kennedy check out the seating position in Mike's Model A truck, which is a tight space. Mike opted for Speedway aluminum buckets, so it was important at this stage to see where the steering wheel sat. Padding will push it up a bit.

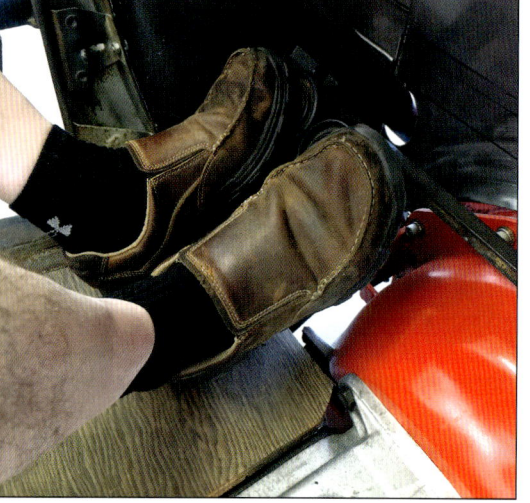

Mike is 6 feet tall, the Model A truck cab is tight, and Mike is going with a manual transmission, so it was important at this stage to make sure the pedals are accessible and comfortable. He could have worn pants!

This original surplus bomber seat in an old SO-CAL roadster has been stripped of its military paint and polished. Real seats from military or aircraft surplus stores are probably getting too expensive now, but there are numerous replicas viable.

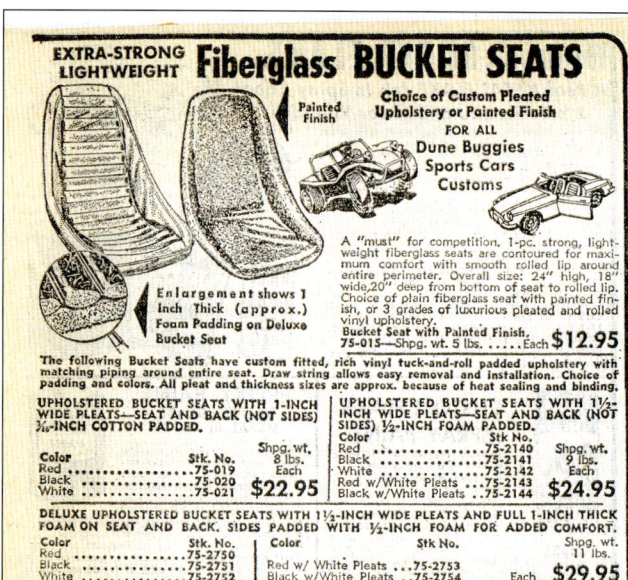

These fiberglass or plastic bucket seats were popular in the 1960s from Honest Charley, J.C. Whitney, etc. You can find them at yard sales and swap meets.

Jim Stroupe found a pair of rare seats out of a Ford Tri-Motor airplane and installed them in his V-8-60-powered 1927 T. They may not be the most comfortable seats around, but they are perhaps the coolest.

INTERIOR

It's bare bones, and maybe the padding is in the wrong place, but this seat looks very appropriate in this Model A roadster application.

Bare aluminum buckets in the style of old airplane bomber seats are very popular. While they do give good lateral support, they are not at all comfortable, so some kind of padding or upholstery will be necessary.

I found this pair of interesting seats at the Kennedy brothers' shop. They are aluminum, tubular-framed seats from a helicopter and are perfect for a rod.

The funkiest seats I found were these cast-aluminum items at Aaron Broughton's Foothill Fabrication. They are stripped-down furniture pieces in Scott Robinson's 1934 cab on 1932 rails.

The latest project from talented builder Lee Pratt is this neatly upholstered 1932 5-window with reproduction early Porsche 356 seats.

fiberglass bucket seats that were sold by the Honest Charley Speed Shop and many other speed shops were actually splashed from school seats designed by Charles and Ray Eames. They are easy to find, well contoured, and you can still buy slip-on upholstery covers for them, along with the seats from Empi and Jaz Products.

He wasn't the first, because they were fitted to many postwar race cars, but we have to thank Jimmy Shine of Shine Speed Shop for reintroducing us to the aircraft bomber seat in *Bare Nekid*, his 1934 pickup. The build started in 1997, and the seats came from California Airframe Parts in Oakland, California. Bomber seats became ubiquitous and inevitably passé, but, if nothing else, they gave rodders a new perspective on what a hot rod interior could be, and we've

CHAPTER 11

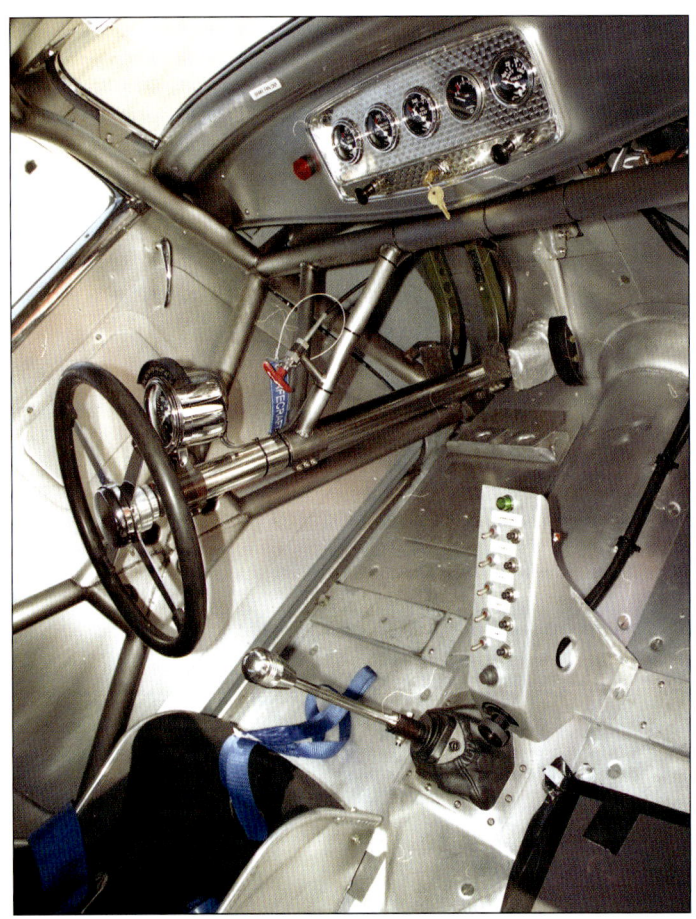

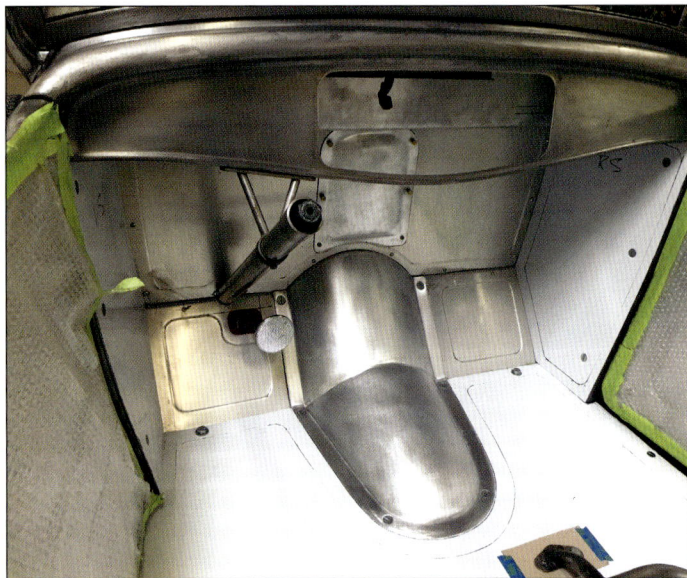

This is not yet complete, but you can see where this aluminum, race car–inspired interior by Pauly Rivera at Mick's Paint for Bob Garibay is heading. This is something you could do at home for the cost of the aluminum.

If you're going to go for the race car look, then look no further than the interior of Jim Busby's road racing 3-window. It's all business except perhaps for the Auburn dash.

always developed upon that theme.

There is a truly complex science that goes into creating an automobile seat. The important point is known as the H-point, or hip-point, and is the pivot point between the torso and the legs. Most rodders know nothing about the H-point, but it boils down to being in a comfortable driving position.

It is very important to sit in the car and establish a comfortable seating position during the mock-up stage and to get a feel for where everything falls: where the pedals are and where they can be operated comfortably, where the steering column sits, and the size and position of the steering wheel.

Finally, there's the position of the shifter to consider. Believe me, I've ridden in some very uncomfortable rods where all of the controls are not quite in the right position, and it makes driving any kind of distance tiring, so use the mock-up stage wisely and get it as right as you can. It's so much harder to go back later to try to fix things.

I'm intrigued by seats, so I'm always on the lookout for something unusual that can be adapted for automotive use. Old sports cars, especially the British ones, that are small and compact offer endless possibilities. However, the prices are rising, so look in unexpected places for inspiration. Early Japanese sports cars offer similar solutions, but prices are rising.

You're going be spending a lot of time sitting in your car, and you might as well make it as inviting and as comfortable as possible even if you are on a budget.

Volvo invented the three-point harness in 1959, and it has become the automotive standard. If you're installing safety belts, consider the three-point system. (Photo Courtesy Tony Adsley)

INTERIOR

If you're planning on some serious driving, like Craig Watts with his Autocross 1934 coupe, you might want to look at something like this 5-point harness from Crow Enterprises.

Josh Shaw Vintage Racing makes a very authentic 17-inch, 4-spoke, Bell-style wheel in a variety of finishes with the right-feel rubber in optional colors.

Seat Belts

When you have decided upon a seat style, ask yourself or your customer if seat belts are on the agenda. In many cases, the answer is no. However, if the answer is yes, decide whether it's a lap belt or a 3- or 4-point harness. Make sure that if you install seat belts, you install good anchors and that you try the seat belts during the mock-up stage for comfort.

Something else to consider is the safety aspect of a lap belt compared to a multi-point harness. If you're going to have belts, at least have belts that will help in an accident.

Steering Wheels

Steering wheels can be as simple as an original early Ford item, track roadster, 3- or 4-spoke Bell-style wheel, or banjo. They can also be as wild as you care to make them. It's good to consider practicality and comfort over looks and a desire to be different.

Large diameter, 17-inch wheels will give you more leverage, but they will possibly decrease legroom. I see guys cut chunks out of their steering wheel in an effort to emulate race cars, but it makes no sense on the road. In an emergency, you might go to grab that part of the wheel that is missing and get yourself into a tight spot.

Dan Clare used an original but inexpensive Ford Model T wheel in this build of his Modified. Note how he wrapped the four-spoker with electrical tape for better grip.

HOW TO BUILD AFFORDABLE HOT RODS

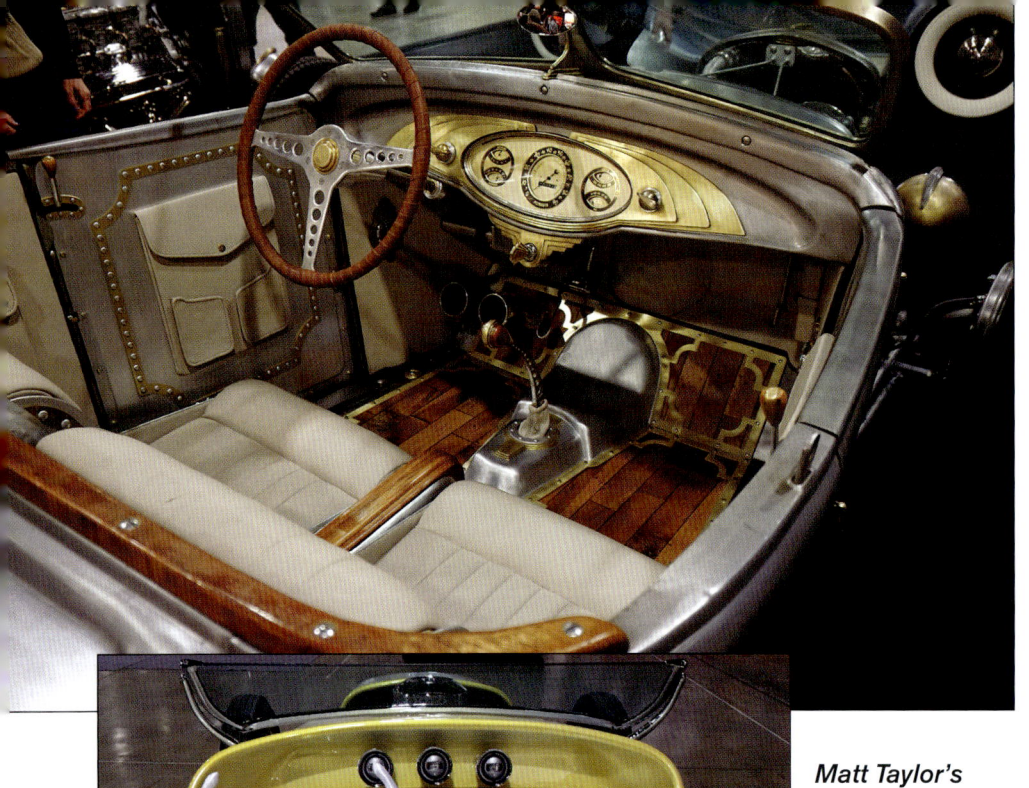

This amazing interior by Hollywood Hot Rods for Mike Juergens is inspirational. It can be replicated given patience, talent, and a couple sheets of brass. The stitching is by Julio Auto Upholstery.

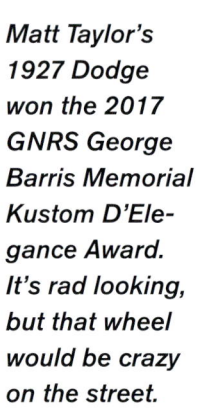

Matt Taylor's 1927 Dodge won the 2017 GNRS George Barris Memorial Kustom D'Elegance Award. It's rad looking, but that wheel would be crazy on the street.

Of course, there's always the metal-flake wheel from Mooneyes that is so iconic and seen here in one of Billy F Gibbons's rides.

Traditional banjo steering wheels can be made more interesting when combined with a translucent plastic rim.

INTERIOR

This stunning Art Deco–inspired interior was built entirely at Hollywood Hot Rods and features a handcrafted, leather-wrapped, three-spoke wheel with stepped brass accoutrements.

Quick-release steering wheels, such as this four-spoke Bell-style in Bob Garibay's Deuce roadster at Mick's Paint, are good for racing applications and when there's limited cabin space.

If you're doing any kind of racing (or even if you're not), consider a quick-release steering wheel that can easily be detached by pulling up the release ring or pushing in a release button. Another reason for a quick-release wheel is for a car with a tight cockpit, such as that of a Model A.

Instruments

Dashes and your choice of instruments and their placement is another area where you can express creativity without spending a fortune. If you're trying to save money, you can run minimal instrumentation, and what you do run you can source at swap meets or on the internet. You don't even have to use automotive instru-

You don't need the full complement of instruments. If cost is an issue, just go with the essentials, such as this four-gauge cluster seen at Walden Speed Shop.

HOW TO BUILD AFFORDABLE HOT RODS

CHAPTER 11

I like the simplicity of this old-meets-new dash in Jules Marcogliese's Deuce roadster. The 1950 Ford speedometer somehow works with the aircraft switches and the modern tachometer.

You can see how a full set of instruments is being mocked up in a Doane Spencer–style, engine-turned insert for a 1932 roadster. A mock-up to see how it's going to look is important.

ments if you don't want to. Instruments sourced from aircraft surplus stores and industrial applications can be cheaper than automotive instruments. As always, it's a matter of looking outside the box and being creative with your choices and applications.

Pedals

Pedals are something that many builders don't give much thought to until it's time to work on them. In most cases, if you are building an early Ford-based rod, you have to look no further than what Ford supplied. Ford's simple but nicely formed pedals were made from forged steel and, like other original Ford parts, they are malleable and can be heated, bent, and welded to reconfigure to your exact needs. In many ways, they are the most cost-effective way to go, but

There's not a whole lot you can do to make an early Ford pedal better other than plate them, perhaps drill them, and add unique pedal pads that are easy to make.

166　HOW TO BUILD AFFORDABLE HOT RODS

INTERIOR

Aftermarket pedal assemblies can be softened and made to look like castings by filing down the sharp edges, tumbling or blasting them, and drilling a few holes for looks.

you might have other requirements that dictate using aftermarket pedals and assemblies.

The issue I have with many aftermarket pedals is that they are cut from a sheet of flat steel and have square edges as opposed to the Ford's rounded edges. They're just not as organic. Of course, you can grind the edges round at no cost other than your time, but that's a lot of work. You can also drill them full of holes (as you can with the Ford pedals) to make them lighter and racier looking.

There is no reason your pedal assembly cannot be as detailed as you want to make it.

Ellis Simmons of Iron Hill Hot Rods of Newark, Delaware, made this pedal assembly by using handformed pedals with handmade wire-mesh pads and Wilwood master cylinders.

CHAPTER 12

PAINT

By Mick Jenkins, Mick's Paint

My very first top chop and paint job was back in 1980 on my friend Keith Atkinson's Ford Pop. We were both pleased and excited when it was featured in the April 1981 issue of Britain's *Custom Car* magazine. Little did I know, it was the start of something much bigger that exploded when I moved to the US in 1995 and opened Mick's Paint. It definitely hasn't been an easy journey dealing with the regulations and the cost of doing business in California, but I have the privilege of working with and for some of the best rod and custom builders in the nation, not the least of whom is Pete Chapouris, who gave me the opportunity to be shop manager at SO-CAL in 2000.

The SO-CAL experience was invaluable. It taught me so much and introduced me to many customers who became friends. Unfortunately, that situation came to an end and I re-opened Mick's Paint in the same building in what was the SO-CAL complex in Pomona, California. Meanwhile, I had the privilege of painting many red and white cars, including most of the GM Bonneville fleet, as well as a host of hot rods.

In 2018, I collaborated on a book

Mick's first roof chop and paint job was on Keith Atkinson's Ford Pop Orange Appeal, *which was built in the early 1980s in England. It's still around but has since been repainted.*

for CarTech with my friend and author Tony Thacker titled *How to Paint Muscle Cars & Show Cars Like A Pro*, which deals specifically with painting American muscle cars to show quality, and the principles of executing a good paint job are exactly the same for a hot rod. You might find that a rod can have a lot more components to paint than the typical muscle car. Conversely, it might have a lot fewer.

In 1996, Tony and I laid out all the components of Bruce Llewellyn's

168   HOW TO BUILD AFFORDABLE HOT RODS

PAINT

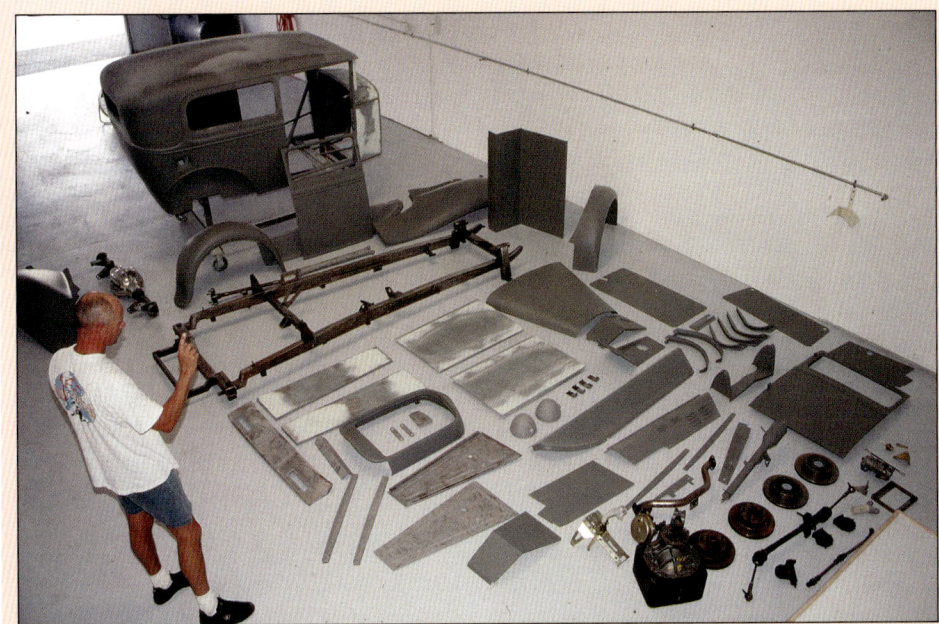

A young Mick Jenkins tallies up the 74 components of Bruce Llewellyn's Model A Tudor, plus engine and transmission that all needed to be prepped, primed, painted, cleared, and polished.

full-fendered Model A Tudor that needed to be painted red. There were a staggering 74 parts that had to be completely cleaned, prepped, sealed, primed, and painted (this was single stage), not forgetting all the sanding between coats, etc. It was a huge job that never gets any easier if you want to do a good job.

Just look at Pat Gauntt's 3-window coupe that we recently painted for Troy Ladd's Hollywood Hot Rods. That was a very complicated car with dozens of parts, including wire-spoke wheels that had to be completely disassembled and painted. And people wonder why a paint job costs so much. Take into consideration the time, which is typically 400 hours or more to paint a roadster, and materials. A gallon of paint in Los Angeles now costs in excess of $1,000, so you can see easily how it adds up. Materials alone can cost $3,500 for a top-level job.

Over the past 30 years, I've painted dozens of rods, three of which have won the coveted America's Most Beautiful Roadster (AMBR) Award at the annual Grand National Roadster Show (GNRS). The first win came in 2000 with Chuck Svatos's *0032* designed by Chip Foose. It was a solid black car handbuilt by Marcel's that was originally the yellow *Boydster II*. It was built at Hot Rods by Boyd and reworked by Foose with a lot of help from my friend and fellow Brit John West.

The second winner was Bill Lindig's *Indy Speedster* in 2012. Jackie Howerton originally started the

In 2007, Mick built himself a 1934 roadster powered by a 396-ci Chevy big-block. For his personal rides, he prefers black, but it does take an inordinate amount of work.

Mick's current project is this electronic, stack-injected big-block Chevy-powered Brookville Deuce roadster on a SO-CAL chassis. Work seems to get in the way of completion.

CHAPTER 12

Before you even start, it's always a good idea to figure out exactly how the project is to be finished. Here, Mick consults with builder Troy Ladd of Hollywood Hot Rods on the various finishes for Pat Gauntt's 1932 3-window.

and then we sand the surface with a dual-action (DA) sander. After the surfaces are sanded, they are prepped with Turco Alumiprep 33 (aka Bonderite C-IC33), an acid-based cleaner. It's important to note that the Alumiprep needs to be neutralized after the application with water or a chemical cleaner. It's important to read and follow the instructions.

After the surface is thoroughly cleaned, it's sanded, cleaned, and degreased again before PPG DP90LV epoxy primer sealer is applied. Typically, we use black, but you can use white DP48LV or gray DP50LV. From that point on, the steps are the same as for a paint job on steel.

Bare Metal

My first rule is to absolutely not use WD-40 on your car if you have even the most remote intention of painting it. WD-40 or other similar preservatives soak into the metal and contaminate it. If you try to apply paint later, the WD-40 will give you problems. The only real way to eliminate WD-40 and similar products is to

roadster that featured a handcrafted aluminum body, but it was finished at SO-CAL under Chapouris's watchful eye. The aluminum body was quite complicated because of the polished aluminum scallop and the roundels on the door commonly known as meatballs.

You don't have to spend tens of thousands of dollars on a paint job, especially on a traditional budget rod that might not have any paint at all, but I have found that most rodders at some point in their build career want a finished, painted car. It's hard for me as a professional painter with a reputation to maintain to dumb down the instructions. I just can't do that, so I'm going to tell you how I do it.

Aluminum

You might think that it's unimportant to talk about painting aluminum, but many rods have aluminum hoods, decklids, and sometimes other panels, and aluminum needs to be treated a little differently from steel. Initially, we strip the aluminum, typically with a chemical stripper,

The late Bill Lindig's Indy *was originally going to be fully painted until the decision was made to polish the nose, part of the hood, and the meatballs. The paint had to be stripped and the aluminum metal finished and then polished, eventually with 1,500 grit. Those areas were masked so that the rest of the car could be painted.*

A bare metal finish can be cool, especially in the regions where it doesn't rain much. However, don't ever protect it with WD40 because it contaminates the metal.

acid-dip the panels. It's the only sure way to clean them. As a hard and fast rule, we don't even allow WD-40 into our building. If you insist on running bare steel but want to prevent it from corroding, wipe it down with Gibbs Brand Lubricant. It contains no silicone and is a water-repellent corrosion inhibitor.

Primer

Some people like to run their cars in primer (be it gray, black, or whatever), but remember that some primers, especially polyester primers, are porous and will absorb moisture and can consequently mess up a good paint job. In the UK, where it can get damp, I painted Pete Fowler's 1930 sedan delivery. In my naivety, I wet-sanded the primer. Later, the car was left in a typically English damp garage, and the paint just bubbled up where the moisture in the primer caused oxidation. When it dried out, the bubbles receded but there was nothing to do other than strip the car and repaint it. Put that one down to experience.

Red Oxide

Red oxide is another choice for some rodders, but you have to be careful to choose the right, non-porous red oxide. Most plain red oxide primers require a top coat. However, I recommend PPG DP40 acrylic enamel, which is a non-porous, self-etching primer.

Gary Lorenzini's coupe was the first car flamed by Hot Rods by Boyd, then it was black, and Gary finally settled on a particular tint of red oxide that was sealed and protected with flat clear.

Some primers absorb moisture, and if they are allowed to do so, it can come back to haunt your paint job later.

CHAPTER 12

The Painting Process

There really are no shortcuts to a good paint job. When people ask me where they can save some time and money, I respond by saying, "Do you mind if I use cheap paint?" They usually respond with an emphatic, "No." I then ask if they mind if it's a bit wavy through the side. Typically, they do mind. Finally, I ask, "Are you okay with some orange peel then?" Invariably they reply, "No." "So, you don't really want a cheap paint job then; you just don't want to pay for a good paint job."

All joking aside, the only way to get a cheap paint job is to cut corners, and I'm not prepared to do that, as it's my reputation on the line. Just look at Chuck Svatos's *0032* that I painted in 1999. It won the America's Most Beautiful Roadster Award in 2000. It was displayed again at the 2020 Grand National Roadster Show, and it still looks as good as new.

Do it right once, and you won't have any comebacks or have to do it again.

Mick's Paint used a couple of engine stands attached to tubes that replace the Deuce spreader bars to enable us to rotate the frame during the prep and paint stages.

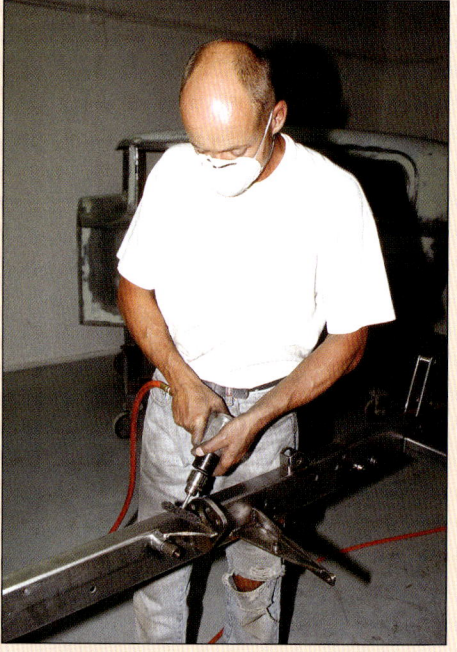

Begin by following the manufacturer's instructions on how to clean and get every part that will be painted ready for metal prep. At Mick's we prefer to use PPG DX579 for steel surfaces.

The first step in the actual painting process begins with the body being sealed for protection with black PPG DP90LV. You can also use white DP48LV or gray DP50LV.

After applying the sealer, everything to be painted is block-sanded using 150-grit to highlight any areas that require attention and to ensure good adhesion for the primer.

172　　HOW TO BUILD AFFORDABLE HOT RODS

PAINT

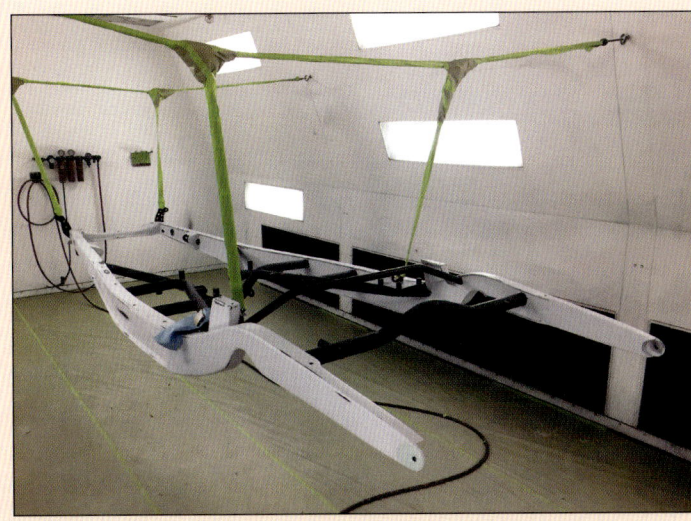

A frame is a very tricky thing to paint while ensuring even coverage. At Mick's, we sometimes like to suspend the frame so that we can reach all of the out-of-the-way places.

Before the primer is applied, the surfaces to be painted are cleaned with a tack cloth before they are given two coats of black PCL High Performance Hi-Fill Polyester Primer Surfacer No. 903.

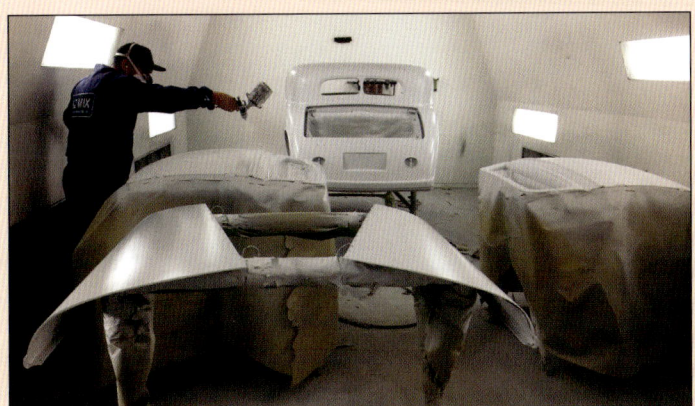

After the second coat of black primer surfacer, four coats of gray PCL High Performance Hi-Fill Polyester Primer Surfacer No. 901 are applied. Give it a 15-minute flash-off between each coat.

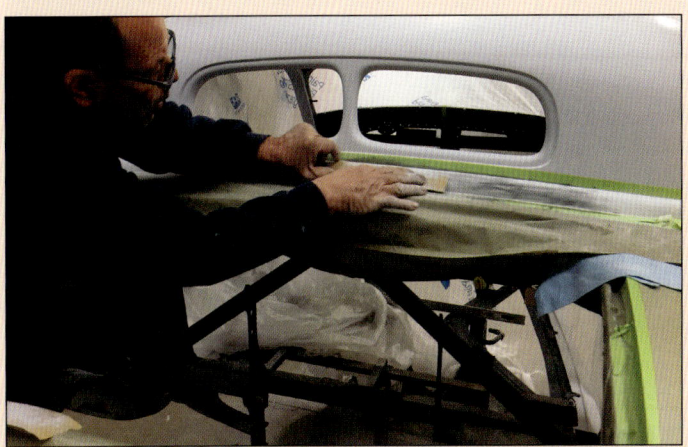

After the primer is allowed to dry for as long as possible—a month is good—all the surfaces are block-sanded with 150 grit and working through to 500 grit.

At Mick's Paint, Paco sands Carl Akins's Deuce chassis and is careful to define the smile that runs along the bottom edge of the rails; it's the defining feature.

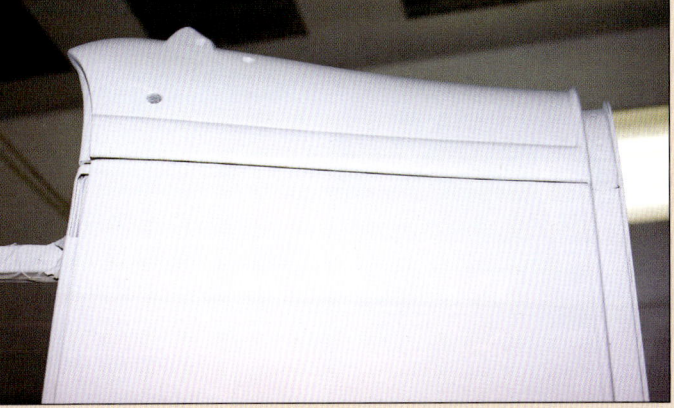

All early Fords have several exposed seams, such as this one, where the Deuce cowl top meets the lower quarters. If you just paint over the crack, the paint will, well, crack.

CHAPTER 12

After careful masking, two light coats of DP sealer (color is dependent upon the final topcoat color) are applied before the surface is lightly sanded (de-nibbed) with 800 or 1,000 grit.

Carl Akins's Deuce frame was suspended and painted by Juan. Note that he wears full protection from the chemicals.

On Carl Akins's frame, you can see the consistency and quality of finish you can get if you take your time, follow the instructions, don't cut corners, and be patient.

After the color has been applied, the surface is given six coats of clear coat and allowed to sit for as long as possible, a week at minimum. Pat Gauntt's Deuce 3-window, built at Troy Ladd's Hollywood Hot Rods, is clear-coated and ready for color sanding prior to buffing.

One way to paint the bottom of your rod is to flip it onto its firewall, assuming it has not been painted. In this instance, we were shooting DP90.

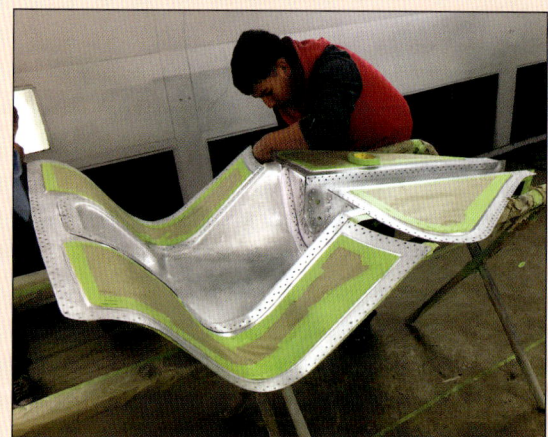

Prepping and painting the aluminum floor panels for Pat Gauntt's coupe was a huge task because they were partly brushed aluminum, partly painted, and full of rivets.

HOW TO BUILD AFFORDABLE HOT RODS

Source Guide

Antique Ford Parts
9103 Garvey Ave.
Rosemead, CA 91770
626-288-2121

American Speed Company
14575 Jib St.
Plymouth, MI 48170
734-451-1141
americanspeedcompany.com
Email: sales@americanspeedcompany.com

Baileigh Industrial
920-684-4990
baileigh.com
Email: sales@baileigh.com

Bendtsen's Speed Gems
806H S. Division St.
Waunakee, WI 53597
763-767-4480
transmissionadapters.com
Email: sales@transmissionadapters.com
Specialty: transmissions

Best Way Stamping
14943 Desman Rd.
La Mirada, CA 90638
714-994-1995

Blockley Tyre Company
Unit 91 Northwick Business Park
Blockley, Moreton-in-Marsh GL56 9RF
United Kingdom
+44 1386 701717
blockleytyre.com
Email: info@blockleytyre.com
Specialty: vintage tires

Boling Brothers
128 W. Apia St.
Lindsay, CA 93247
559-562-5840
BolingBrothers.com
Email: BolingBrothers@gmail.com
Specialty: brake components, brake conversion kits, frames, and parts

Brad's Woodshop
1661 San Juan Dr.
Friday Harbor, WA 98250
360-317-5723
Email: bradswoodshop@hotmail.com
Specialty: replacement wood kits

Brookville Roadster
718 Albert Rd.
Brookville, OH 45309
937-833-4605
brookvilleroadster.com
Email: customerservice@brookvilleroadster.com
or Kenny@brookvilleroadster.com

Buckland Automotive Engineering
Unit 5 High Barns Farm
Roxton, Bedford MK44 3ET
United Kingdom
07768-058060
bucklandautomotive.com
Email: Adrian@bucklandautomotive.com

Centerville Auto Repair
12865 Pine Cone Cir.
Grass Valley, CA 95945
530-272-1564
centervilleautorepair.com
Email: nailhead_russ@yahoo.com
Specialty: vintage auto repair, transmission adapters

Cole Hersee/Littelfuse
8755 West Higgins Rd. Suite 500
Chicago, IL 60631
773-628-1000
littelfuse.com
Specialty: switches

Columbia Two Speed Parts
P.O. Box 1587
Cottonwood, AZ 86326
951-719-4077
columbiatwospeedparts.com
Email: columbiatwospeed@gmail.com
Specialty: Columbia two-speed axles and parts.

Cyclone Racing Equipment/Cook's Machine Works
4845 Telegraph Rd.
Los Angeles, CA 90022
626-329-2815
Specialty: Cadillac cylinder heads and quick-changes

Dearborn Deuce
1204 Main St. #339
Branford, CT 06405
860-669-3232
dearborndeuce32.com

Dutchman Motorsports
1250 E. Piper Ct.
Meridian, ID 83642
503-257-6604
dutchmanaxles.com
Specialty: rear axles, including Ford V-8 style quick change

Early Ford Store of CA
108 W. Bonita Ave.
San Dimas, CA 91773
909-305-1955
earlyfordstore.com
Email: Earlyfordstore@verizon.net
Specialty: early Ford parts

Eclipse Engineering
12353 Whittier Blvd. #B
Whittier, CA 90602
562-696-1209
Email: sbelgio7056@gmail.com
Specialty: electrical engineering

Flat-o Products
2195 Commercial N.E.
Salem, OR 97303
503-364-2934
Flat-o.com
Email: info@flat-o.com
Specialty: transmissions

Foothill Fabrication
1441 Pomona Rd. #13
Corona, CA 92882
951-278-4800
Specialty: hot rod fabrication and parts

Holley Performance Products
1801 Russellville Rd.
Bowling Green, KY 42101
270-782-2900
Tech line: 1-866-464-6553
holley.com
Specialty: performance products

Hot Rod Works
3719 Lake Ave.
Caldwell, ID 83605
208-455-7971
hotrodworks.com
Email: sales@hotrodworks.com
Specialty: hot rod parts, including quick-change parts and open drive conversions

Hollywood Hot Rods
2617 N. San Fernando Blvd.
Burbank, CA 91504
818-842-6900
hollywoodhotrods.com
Email: info@hollywoodhotrods.com
Specialty: hot rod building

Joe Hunt Magnetos
11333 Sunco Dr. Suite #100
Rancho Cordova, CA 95472
916-635-5387
huntmagnetos.com
Email: huntmagnetos@huntmagnetos.com
Specialty: distributors, magnetos, and ignition components

Kugel Komponents
451 Park Industrial Dr.
La Habra, CA 90631
562-691-7006
kugelkomponents.com

Nate Jones Tire/Cowboy Tire
1896 Redondo Ave.
Signal Hill, CA 90755
562-597-3369
natejonestire.com
Specialty: tire balancing, shaving, and truing

Kennedy Boyz Bomb Factory
1000 East End
Pomona, CA 91766
626-506-5320

Kev's Rod & Custom
651 E. Lambert Rd. Suite E
La Habra, CA 90631
714-686-8982
Email: kevsrodandcustom@gmail.com
Specialty: hot rod fabrication and components, including alternator/generator

Kilmer, Wagner & Wise Paper Company
12751 Monarch St.
Garden Grove, CA 92841
714-892-3380
800-729-2311
kwwpaper.com
Specialty: boxes and paper supplies

Gear Vendors
1717 North Magnolia Ave.
El Cajon, CA 92020
800-999-9555
gearvendors.com
Email: info@gearvendors.com
Specialty: overdrive units

KIP Motor Co.
2127 Crown Rd.
Dallas, TX 75229
888-243-0440
Email: sales@kipmotor.com
Specialty: vintage distributor caps

Lincoln Electric
22801 St. Clair Ave.
Euclid, OH 44117
216-481-8100
Specialty: Welding equipment

Legend Gear & Transmission, Inc.
820 Cochran St.
Statesville, NC 28677
LegendGT.com
Email: sales@LegendGT.com
Specialty: transmissions and rear axle assemblies

Lucas Oil
302 North Sheridan St.
Corona, CA 92880
800-342-2512
lucasoil.com
Specialty: oil and chemicals

SOURCE GUIDE

McMaster-Carr
9630 Norwalk Blvd.
Santa Fe Springs, CA 90670-2932
562-692-5911
mcmaster.com
Email: la.sales@mcmaster.com or le.ventas@mcmaster.com
Specialty: tools and equipment

Mac's Auto Parts
6150 Donner Rd.
Lockport, NY 14094
716-210-1340
800-828-1051
macsautoparts.com
Email: customerservice@macsauto.com

Miller Electric Manufacturing
1635 W. Spencer St.
P.O. Box 1079
Appleton, WI 54912-1079
920-734-9821
millerwelds.com
Specialty: welding equipment

Millworks Hot Rods & Supply Co.
200 Pleasant Street Unit B
Tewksbury, MA 01876
800-678-2647
millworkshotrod.com
Specialty: traditional hot rod parts and services

Mitchell Overdrive Manufacturing
1157 Parker St.
Colusa, CA 95932
800-859-2088
mitchelloverdrives.com
Email: mitchmanfc@frontiernet.net
Specialty: synchro kits for Model As and overdrive units

M&L Parts
4093 E. Mission Blvd.
Pomona, CA 91766
909-622-3590
Specialty: 12-volt conversions for generators and starter motors

P-Ayr Products
1098 Windy Hill Rd.
Kyle, TX 78640
512-295-2683
mockupmotors.com
Specialty: lightweight plastic mock-up motors

PerTronix Performance Products
440 E. Arrow Hwy
San Dimas, CA 91773
909-599-5955
pertronix.com
Specialty: ignition components

Quality Restorations
San Diego, CA
858-271-7374
qualityrestorations.com
Email: dennis@qualityrestorations.com
Specialty: steering wheel restoration

Rod End Supply
1128 S. Payne
P.O. Box 2080
Olathe, KS 66051
800-284-2902
rodendsupply.com
Specialty: rod ends and suspension components

Ross Racing Engines
1763 N Main St.
Niles, OH 44446
330-544-4466

SEMA
1575 S. Valley Vista Dr.
Diamond Bar, CA 91766
909-978-6721
sema.org
Email: san@sema.org

Josh Shaw Vintage Racing
Waterford, MI
513-257-5121
shawsvintage.com

Shine Speed Shop
867 N. Commerce St.
Orange, CA 92867
714-288-1125
shinespeedshop.com
Email: info@jimmyshine.com
Specialty: hot rod builds, parts, and louvering

Silver Sport Transmissions
2250 Stock Creek Blvd.
Rockford, TN 37853
865-609-8187
shiftsst.com
Specialty: Tremec transmissions

SO-CAL Speed Shop
1357 E. Grand Ave.
Pomona, CA 91766
909-469-6171
est1946.com
Email: sales@so-calspeedshop.com

Steve's Auto Restorations & Real Steel
4440 SE 174th Ave.
Portland, OR 97236
503-665-2222
stevesautorestorations.com
Email: parts@realsteel.com
Specialty: steel 1934 Roadster bodies and chassis packages

Stewart Warner
1090 N. Charlotte St.
Lancaster, PA 17603
800-676-1837
stewartwarner.com
Specialty: instruments and related electrical components

Stockton Wheel Co.
648 W. Fremont St.
Stockton, CA 95203
800-395-9433
stocktonwheel.com
Specialty: vintage-style wheels and wheel accessories

Strong Hand Tools
8750 Pioneer Blvd.
Santa Fe Springs, CA 90670
800-989-5244
stronghandtools.com
Email: sales@stronghandtools.com
Specialty: tools and Adjust-O Magnetic squares

Stromberg Carburetor
Unit 6, Seven Acres Business Park
Newbourne Rd.
Waldringfield, Suffolk IP12 4PS
England
01473-811700 (local)
011-44-1473-811700 (from U.S.A.)
stromberg-97.com
Email: sales@stromberg-97.com or tech@stromber-97.com
Specialty: Stromberg carburetors and ignitions

Tremec
46643 Ryan Court
Novi, MI 48377
800-401.9866
Tremec.com
Email: customer.service@tremec.com
Specialty: high-performance transmissions

United Pacific Industries
3788 E. Conant St.
Long Beach, CA 90808
888-986-6088
upauto.com
Email: antique@upauto.com
Specialty: restoration parts and bodies

VanPelt Sales
1081 State Route 28 Bypass Suite 258
Milford, OH 45150-2090
513-724-9486
vanpeltsales.com
Email: sales@vanpeltsales.com
Specialty: vintage Ford parts

Veazie Brothers Fabrication
8424 Comet St.
Rancho Cucamonga, CA 91730
909-342-0627
Specialty: hot rod fabrication and parts

Walden Speed Shop
1040 Price St.
Pomona, CA 91767
909-623-3747
waldenspeedshop.com
Email: waldenspeed@yahoo.com
Specialty: bodies, chassis, and metal fabrication

Weldcraft Wheels
11881 Belden Ct.
Livonia, MI 48150
734-779-1303
weldcraftwheels.com
Email: James@weldcraftwheels.com
Specialty: wheel widening, narrowing, and repair

WeldingSupply
1161 McCabe Ave.
Elk Grove, IL 60007
847-290-1070
weldingsupply.com
Email: shipping@weldingsupply.com
Specialty: welding equipment

Wescott's Auto
19701 SE Hwy 212
Damascus, OR 97089
800-523-6279
wescottsauto.com
Email: info@wescottauto.com
Specialty: fiberglass bodies and components

Wheel Fit
251-377-6724
thewheelfit.com
Specialty: wheel offset measuring device

Wilcap Co.
P.O. Box 763
Pismo Beach, CA 93448
805-481-7639
Wilcap.com
Email: pmcguire@wilcap.com
Specialty: transmission adapters

Wilwood Engineering
4700 Calle Bolero
Camarillo, CA 93012
805-388-1188
willwood.com
Email: customerreply@wilwood.com
Specialty: brake systems and components